# Forgotten Forests

# FORGOTTEN FORESTS

Twelve Thousand Years of
British and Irish Woodlands

Jonathan Mullard

WILLIAM
COLLINS

William Collins
An imprint of HarperCollins*Publishers*
1 London Bridge Street
London SE1 9GF

WilliamCollinsBooks.com

HarperCollins*Publishers*
Macken House
39/40 Mayor Street Upper
Dublin 1
D01 C9W8
Ireland

First published in Great Britain in 2025 by William Collins

1

Copyright © Jonathan Mullard 2025

Images © individual copyright holders, see Image Credits

The quotation from John Muir on page v is excerpted from *John of the Mountains: The Unpublished Journals of John Muir*, edited by Linnie Marsh Wolfe, John Muir Papers, Holt-Atherton Special Collections and Archives, University of the Pacific Library. ©1984 Muir-Hanna Trust.

Waldo Williams's poem 'Yr hen allt' is published in *The Peacemakers* (Y Lolfa, 2023). The extract on page 242 is included by permission of the publisher.

The quotation from Leonard Clark on page 253 is included by permission of the Literary Executor of Leonard Clark.

Jonathan Mullard asserts the moral right to be identified as the author of this work in accordance with the Copyright, Designs and Patents Act 1988

A catalogue record for this book is available from the British Library

ISBN 978-0-00-856104-8

All rights reserved. No part of this publication may be reproduced, stored in a retrieval system, or transmitted, in any form or by any means, electronic, mechanical, photocopying, recording or otherwise, without the prior permission of the publishers.

Without limiting the author's and publisher's exclusive rights, any unauthorised use of this publication to train generative artificial intelligence (AI) technologies is expressly prohibited. HarperCollins also exercise their rights under Article 4(3) of the Digital Single Market Directive 2019/790 and expressly reserve this publication from the text and data mining exception.

This book is sold subject to the condition that it shall not, by way of trade or otherwise, be lent, re-sold, hired out or otherwise circulated without the publisher's prior consent in any form of binding or cover other than that in which it is published and without a similar condition including this condition being imposed on the subsequent purchaser.

Typeset in Baskerville by Palimpsest Book Production Ltd, Falkirk, Stirlingshire

Printed and Bound in the UK using 100% Renewable Electricity
at CPI Group (UK) Ltd

This book contains FSC™ certified paper and other controlled sources
to ensure responsible forest management.

For more information visit: www.harpercollins.co.uk/green

*The clearest way into the Universe is through a forest wilderness.*

John Muir

# CONTENTS

| | | |
|---|---|---:|
| | Preface | 1 |
| 1 | After the Ice | 11 |
| 2 | Under the Waves | 44 |
| 3 | Axes and Agriculture | 60 |
| 4 | What the Romans Did for Forests | 92 |
| 5 | A Reliable Resource | 113 |
| 6 | Taming the Landscape | 139 |
| 7 | The Forest Economy | 164 |
| 8 | Death, Recovery and Dissolution | 179 |
| 9 | The Floating Forest | 195 |
| 10 | Industry and Animals | 219 |
| 11 | World Wars and Conifers | 242 |
| 12 | New Forests | 260 |
| | Acknowledgements | 291 |
| | Bibliography | 294 |
| | Illustration Credits | 315 |
| | Index | 317 |

# PREFACE

*It is not so much for its beauty that the forest makes a claim upon men's hearts, as for that subtle something, that quality of air, that emanation from old trees, that so wonderfully changes and renews a weary spirit.*
Robert Louis Stevenson

This book has its origins in one of my regular journeys in the Scottish Borders. On the left-hand side of the A68 as you approach the town of Jedburgh from the south there is a prominent oak tree, the Capon Tree. It is obviously very old, and there is a sign visible from the road giving its name. A survivor from the ancient Jed Forest, it is a renowned individual, one of the fifty trees included in the Tree Council's book *Great British Trees*, which was published in 2002. A painting of the Capon Tree by the Victorian landscape painter Arthur Perigal the Younger is displayed in Jedburgh Museum. There were also once 'capon trees' at Brampton in Cumbria and Alnwick in Northumberland. The name of these trees appears to have been derived from the Scots word *kep*, which means 'to meet' – the trees being places where the Border clans rallied for action in times of trouble. Another, less likely, suggestion for the name of the Jedburgh tree is that it is derived from the *capuche*, the hood worn by the monks who might have sheltered under its branches on their way to or from the nearby abbey.

Living in a border town, Jedburgh's families were continually involved in fighting the English, and the Jethart Callants had a reputation for outstanding bravery. For a long time, these were 'debatable' lands, neither England nor Scotland. Both Callants and Capon Tree are celebrated each July, when 'The Callant', a young person chosen to represent the town, leads a mounted cavalcade on a series of historic rides, the most important being to Redesdale in Northumberland to commemorate the last cross-border skirmish

*Victorian glass lantern slide of the Capon Tree near Jedburgh, one of the last remnants of the ancient Jed Forest, showing the tree before it was supported by timber props.*

on 7 July 1575. On Festival Day itself, the Callant visits Ferniehurst Castle and on the return home stops at the Capon Tree, taking a sprig of oak and wearing it in the lapel of their jacket.

Unfortunately, in 2022 one half of the tree, which was previously supported by timber props, collapsed to the side and landed on the ground. As the root is still intact the landowner, Lothian Estates, intends to leave the enormous bough in place to see if it survives. The Jethart Callant has planted a tree next to it, grown from one of its acorns, in order to provide continuity should the whole tree die.

Over the years I started to wonder what happened to the Jed Forest. Was it really felled to build wooden ships for the Royal Navy, as is often stated, and, if so, why did the Capon Tree survive? Despite another sign saying that the tree was 'the last survivor' of the old forest, I subsequently found out that it was not alone. Around 600 metres to the east, on the other side of the road, stand the mighty King of the Wood and the Crooked Family, while a similar distance to the west is the Oak Bush. These four ancient oaks are the sole remnants of a vanished ecosystem.

I have always loved woodlands and forests, but it was my grandfather, Tom Bachelor, who really taught me to appreciate trees. I spent many of my summer holidays in the 1960s with him, going out into the south Shropshire countryside during his work as an adviser for the Ministry of Agriculture, Fisheries and Food. Thinking about the loss of the Jed Forest reminded me that, as we travelled from farm to farm, my grandfather would often point out trees that were possible survivors from the Morfe Forest, which once stretched from Bridgnorth to the appropriately named Six Ashes and Claverley. Apart from the Jed and Morfe Forests, there were undoubtedly many other forests in Britain and Ireland that had been lost. But where were they and what were their stories? When did they first come into being? And who remembers them now? I decided to find out.

One of my most treasured possessions is a magnificent leaf-shaped flint dagger found by my grandfather as it lay shining in the sun on the freshly ploughed surface of a field near Catherton Common in Shropshire. Flint daggers were made, used and ritually deposited in the period 2250–2000 BCE, during the Early Bronze Age. They are thought to be copies of metal daggers, representing a period of transition from stone to bronze.

The traditional three-age system used to define the framework of European prehistory – Stone, Bronze and Iron – is based on durable materials, and takes no account of wood, or of the forests from which wood was acquired. Over forty years ago the archaeologist John Coles pointed out that, as a result, woodlands and forests were rarely considered by many of his colleagues. Times have changed, and the focus is now on how their presence affected people's experience of the landscape in which they lived. As another archaeologist, Gordon Noble, has stated, people in the Neolithic lived in timber buildings that creaked and moaned as the wood changed with the weather, they fitted their stone axes with wooden handles, and they cut and tended trees much as they tended their crops. They also created huge monuments out of giant tree trunks and, in some cases, their dead literally resided within the heart of these massive timbers. We need to add a 'Wood Age' to run in parallel alongside the other ages if we are to really understand Europe's past.

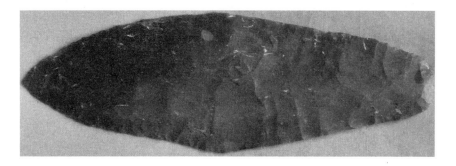

*The Catherton dagger, a 4,000-year-old flint found on the surface of a ploughed field in Shropshire by the author's grandfather. Dating to the Early Bronze Age, it represents the transition from stone to bronze.*

# Preface

Similarly, books on woodlands and woodland management – and indeed woodland ecologists themselves – occasionally display a cultural amnesia, forgetting that the trees that exist today are sometimes the remains of once-extensive forests. As the naturalist William Condry wrote in the 1970s, 'Though you may not live near any famous old forest it is possible, especially in Lowland Britain, that any small oakwoods you know could be fragments of one of the lesser-known forests.' Today, with the current emphasis on rewilding, which encourages people to see the bigger picture, there are new approaches developing. The title of this book, *Forgotten Forests*, is intended therefore to cover a lot of ground.

While some forests, such as the Forest of Bodfari, which once lay in the Vale of Clwyd between Rhuddlan and Ruthin in north Wales, the English forest of Duffield Frith, north of Derby, and the Great Forest of Aughty in Ireland, can truly be said to be forgotten by most people, the same obviously cannot be said of such well-known English forests as Sherwood Forest, the New Forest, or indeed Epping Forest. In Scotland, Abernethy Forest on Speyside is often described as a typical forest of Scots pine. What we know of the history of these areas can help us make sense of the many forests that have disappeared from the landscape, such as Birnham Wood, which was famously mentioned in Shakespeare's *Macbeth*. Its only remnant today is the 600-year-old Birnham Oak on the south bank of the River Tay, opposite the town of Dunkeld. The tree was almost certainly not standing at the time the real Macbeth ruled in the eleventh century. But it might have been there in 1589 when it is believed William Shakespeare was one of a troupe of English comic actors or 'strolling players' who visited Perth, Aberdeen and Birnam at the invitation of James VI of Scotland.

Several thousand years ago Britain and Ireland were mainly covered by forests, but they have been progressively fragmented, partly due to climatic changes but largely because of the activities of people. Marjan Shokouhi, a lecturer at the University of

Granada in Spain, has stated that 'the history of human civilisation is often synonymous with the history of deforestation', and Britain and Ireland are no exceptions to this rule. The loss of forests has been a dominant feature of Europe's landscape for millennia, with what we now know are negative consequences for carbon storage, as well as ecosystems and the wildlife they support.

Natural forests that have developed completely free from human interference probably no longer exist anywhere on Earth. It used to be thought that the best examples were to be found in North and South America, mainly in the forests of Canada and Alaska and the tropical forests of Amazonia, but researchers are beginning to realise that many of these forests have been 'gardened' by native peoples for millennia. In Europe there may be some unchanged habitats remaining in the Urals and the Carpathian Mountains, but they are very rare. The extensive forests in northern Russia, together with certain areas of Scandinavia, are probably all we have left of habitats that are more or less unaltered by people, and even these are no longer sacrosanct. The extensive Russian wildfires of 2019 burned through 13.1 million hectares, including 4.5 million hectares of Siberian taiga, the subarctic coniferous forest. As Annie Proulx wrote in her book *Fen, Bog and Swamp*, the conflagration was downplayed in Russia as naturally occurring forest fires, despite reports of arson, in order to hide illegal logging operations. The catastrophe is ongoing, with the total area of the fires still burning in May 2023 estimated at 5.2 million hectares. To date, around half of the Earth's forests have been cleared, and we continue to destroy the rainforest in places like the Congo basin that play important roles in regulating the atmosphere.

Given that the destruction of the forests started so long ago, it might be asked why we should be concerned about it now. The answer, surely, is that apart from an intrinsic interest in our natural and cultural heritage, an understanding of long-term changes in forest cover, especially those associated with human activities, is critical for our future survival. It now seems certain that the large-scale felling of forests started significantly to alter greenhouse gas emissions, and the global climate, thousands of years ago. As the pace of climate change accelerates, we now need to do everything we can to restore the habitat and offset the changes that are becoming more and more apparent. Only by understanding the process by which our forests were lost can we begin to plan for their renewal.

People have an instinctive affection for forests and the trees within them. When David Attenborough, who has probably experienced more habitats than anyone else on Earth, was asked in 2010, 'Where do you like to spend time – mountain, desert, ocean, forest or city?' he replied, 'Forest'. In 2019, to mark the Forestry Commission's centenary, people were questioned about how woods and forests made them feel. Many recalled experiencing a sense of freedom. Others reminisced about childhood memories. Almost everyone mentioned feeling relaxed and stress-free, as highlighted by Robert Louis Stevenson in the words quoted at the beginning of this preface. It is claimed that spending time in forests reduces the stress hormone cortisol, producing a calming effect. In addition, forests are said to boost the immune system as visitors breathe in the anti-microbial and insecticidal phytoncides that are emitted by the trees.

I have already used a number of terms to describe groups of trees. Since the various terms are often used somewhat vaguely, and indeed interchangeably, by different authors, it is useful to define them. Aljos Farjon's book on *Ancient Oaks in the English Landscape*, published by the Royal Botanic Gardens at Kew, includes a useful set of definitions, and I have followed a similar scheme in this book. In summary, there are three types of landscape in which trees are present, and where trees are usually the dominant growth form. A *forest* is a habitat dominated by trees, in which, in its optimal undisturbed state, the canopies of the trees are in contact. As described later, the term may also be used in the medieval sense of a royal hunting area. A *wood* is a forest that is or has been managed, either as coppice (with or without standard trees) or as a plantation. In contrast, *woodland* is a broader term, referring to a landscape that may contain anything from closed-canopy forest to pasture woodland, or even grassland with shrubs and single trees, or a mosaic of different landscapes.

To these labels must be added the *wild wood* of Kenneth Grahame's classic children's book, *The Wind in the Willows*. The term was later adopted and popularised by Oliver Rackham, a Cambridge academic and landscape historian, and is now taken to mean the natural forested landscape that developed across large areas of Britain and Ireland after the last glaciation.

In the early 1980s, I was lucky enough to work for Max Nicholson, a renowned environmentalist, on developing the first urban woodland strategy for the Ecological Parks Trust, now the Trust for Urban Ecology. We set up a community project in south London to conserve Dulwich Upper Wood in Crystal Palace, a fragment of the Great North Wood, a forest of oaks and hornbeams that once stretched from the River Thames into Kent. It is commemorated in the name for this area of London – Norwood. On one occasion, when we were filming in the wood with Channel 4 television, Max said that I should write a book on trees and woodlands. It has taken me over forty years, and there have been other books along the way, but I have finally achieved that goal. In the intervening decades there has been much new research, and the story of forests in Britain and Ireland is constantly being updated, with often surprising conclusions. In particular, innovative approaches in dendrochronology, the science of dating tree rings, have transformed our understanding in certain areas. While taking account of new information, however, I have done my best to avoid using too many technical terms.

We all have different concepts of time, which affects the way each generation sees the world, including the natural environment. In 1995 the fisheries expert Daniel Pauly received an email from the editor of the journal *Trends in Ecology and Evolution* urgently asking for help. A contributor had failed to deliver a one-page article and the editor needed something to fill the space. Pauly

# Preface

9

quickly wrote a piece based on what he was thinking about at the time. In what is now one of his most celebrated papers he described the concept of a 'shifting baseline syndrome' as a way of explaining our generational blindness to environmental destruction.

Basically, shifting baseline syndrome concerns the redefinition of what is normal by each generation, based upon the memories and experiences of their youth. Pauly stated that, as far as fisheries science was concerned, what was considered the normal size of fish stocks, the baseline, was being redefined with every passing generation. The result is that the ongoing depletion seems less significant than it really is, since for each individual it is measured over the course of just a single lifetime. Pauly is very clear that if you want to fight the loss of memory and knowledge about the past, you have to rely on information which is often viewed, wrongly, as anecdotal. We therefore need to abandon the idea that the past is a provider of anecdotes and the present is a provider of knowledge.

This book, incorporating both anecdotes and knowledge, aims to push our mental baseline of forests in Britain and Ireland back, to increase awareness of past losses and future opportunities. While generally chronological, *Forgotten Forests* will sometimes weave backwards and forwards through time to take the reader on a journey through the forest, landscape and human history of these islands. The story starts, around 12,000 years ago, with the retreat of the glaciers.

# CHAPTER 1

# *After the Ice*

*It is hard for us to picture the majesty and silence of those primeval woods, that stretched from Ireland far across northern Europe.*

Frank Mitchell

We often forget that in Britain and Ireland we spend our lives in landscapes that have, for the most part, been sculpted by the flow of ice. The power of frozen water moving across the land produced a wonderful variety of features as it eroded the ground beneath it. One of the most spectacular is Cwm Idwal, a valley high in the Glyderau mountains of Eryri (Snowdonia) that was one of Charles Darwin's favourite areas. Darwin had seen glaciers and icebergs in South America during his famous voyage on the *Beagle,* and on his return, when he made a second visit to Cwm Idwal in 1842, he realised that the smoothed rock surfaces and scattered boulders there were in fact ice-scarred rocks created by the last glaciers. As a result, he became a pioneer of the science of glaciology. Much later, in 1954, Cwm Idwal was designated as the first National Nature Reserve in Wales, as the effects of the glaciers are clearer here than almost anywhere else.

Glaciers also moulded and streamlined the Scottish Lowlands, producing dramatic 'crag-and-tail' features such as Edinburgh's

Castle Rock and the Royal Mile. In Ireland too the effects of ice can be clearly seen, and the landscape, especially in the north, is marked by over 20,000 drumlins, named from the Irish *droimnín*, or little hill, formed from the material deposited by the ice sheets. The elongated mounds, like the Royal Mile, indicate the direction of the glacier's flow.

Despite the fact that our planet is now rapidly warming, we are, perhaps surprisingly, still living in an ice age, since they are defined as periods when there is ice at both the North and South Poles. But it is probably too late now to save the summer sea ice in the Arctic. During the past three billion years there have been five or six major ice ages, the latest of which began 34 million years ago. Within an ice age there are colder 'glacial' periods and warmer 'interglacial' periods, and forests around the globe have contracted and expanded in time with these. The last glacial period began 33,000 years ago and ended about 12,000 years later, so the Earth is currently in an interglacial.

*Cwm Idwal, a spectacular ice-carved valley high in the Glyderau mountains of Eryri which inspired Charles Darwin to study the effects of glaciers on the landscape.*

*After the Ice* 13

For over 20,000 years though Britain and Ireland were covered by a vast sheet of ice. In Britain the frozen landscape stretched from the Scottish mountains to Yorkshire and the Welsh coast, with an offshoot extending down the North Sea coast as far as Norfolk. The traditional view was that Ireland was only partially covered by ice, but we now know that the whole of the island was affected. At its maximum extent the cold conditions extended far to the south, around the latitude of Lisbon, and in London the bones of a polar bear have been found in the gravels of the River Thames near Kew Gardens.

Few places in the world have experienced changes during the last few thousand years as drastic as those in the areas that were covered by the massive ice sheets. When the ice finally melted everything was dramatically transformed, with enormous volumes of water pouring across the landscape and debris deposited in piles called moraines. There was also a steep rise in sea levels as the water locked up in the ice was released, compensated to some extent by the land rising as the weight of the ice was removed. In Britain, a line drawn between Morecambe Bay in Lancashire and Berwick upon Tweed in Northumberland defines an important 'hinge line', the land to the south having subsided following the retreat of the ice and the land to the north rising, with the greatest change in levels being in the Scottish Highlands where the ice was heaviest.

Once the ice retreated the change was extremely rapid, and it has been suggested that northern Europe went from Arctic conditions to a warm climate within the space of 20–50 years, an extremely rapid transformation in relation to geological timescales. Over that short period, July temperatures in England apparently rose from around 8 °C to 17 °C. There are a number of theories about why the climate changed so quickly, but the sudden input of fresh cold water, as the ice started to melt, could have interfered with the circulation of the Atlantic Ocean that underpins the Gulf Stream, bringing warmer water to these islands once more.

The fact that northern Europe was one of the most heavily

glaciated regions in the world meant that it was one of the last areas to be recolonised by people. The thaw marked the beginning of the period archaeologists call the Mesolithic, the Middle Stone Age. Britain was still connected to Europe at this time, and it took around 4,000 years before it became an island, but it is still not exactly clear when Ireland separated from the continent. Finds of early human remains are rare owing to the destructive effects of the glaciers, but excavations by the archaeologist Martin Stables at Heaning Wood Bone Cave in Cumbria have pushed the timeline back. In January 2023 it was reported that a human bone and a bead made from a perforated periwinkle shell found here were 11,000 years old. This is one of the earliest dates we have for humans in Britain after the last glaciation, providing clear evidence of Mesolithic burials in the north of England and information on how people reoccupied the land as the ice retreated.

As soon as the climate began to warm, a great wave of trees spread north from 'ice-age refugia' in the Balkans, Italy, Spain and Portugal. The evidence suggests that many species survived the cold in the mountains of southern Europe and, possibly, parts of western Asia. Scattered trees may also have survived in moist locations, such as ravines, as they do today in China, Iran and parts of Turkey, Tajikistan, Uzbekistan and Kazakhstan. Some 3,000 years later, however, the temperature dropped again. The 1,200 years of very cold, dry weather which resulted are known as the Younger Dryas after a small member of the rose family, mountain avens (*Dryas octopetala*), as its leaves are abundant in sediments from this time. Growing in areas where snow melts early, it still occurs in the Scottish Highlands, Eryri, the North Pennines and, in Ireland, on the great limestone pavement of the Burren in County Clare and a few other sites. From this low point of extreme cold, the transition to milder conditions seems, once again, to have taken place very quickly, with an extremely sharp rise of about 7 °C producing average summer temperatures of 15.8 °C. It is likely that the permanent reoccupation of Britain by modern

*The Younger Dryas, a relatively cold period that occurred in Europe some 12,900–11,700 years ago, is named after the mountain avens (*Dryas octopetala*), since its leaves occur frequently in deposits from this time.*

humans followed the Younger Dryas, but the evidence for this is disputed by some archaeologists.

While the drop in temperature during the Younger Dryas created hostile conditions for the forests that had been spreading rapidly northward, as soon as temperatures increased again the wildwood started to expand once more. From this time onwards we can track the development of forests right up until the present day. While it is, at its heart, a story of fragmentation and loss it is also a story in which forests and people are intimately entwined, like the branches of an old and venerable tree – fact and folklore coming together in sometimes unexpected ways.

As the ice retreated and the trees returned, they brought with them ghosts of a earlier ecosystem, being adapted to cope with animals that no longer existed. Large herbivores were generally less abundant, having been decimated by humans. In the previous interglacial period, between 130,000 and 115,000 years ago, 'megafauna' such as straight-tusked elephants and narrow-nosed rhinoceroses roamed the landscape. Scimitar cats, lion-sized animals with large curved fangs, preyed on their young. Large numbers of grazing animals dominated the environment in this period, producing a greater mixture of semi-open vegetation and forest than existed in the forests that grew back after the last glaciation. The trees were the ones that we are familiar with today, including oak, beech, hornbeam and hazel, but the dynamics of the environment were very different. As a result, the landscape was dominated by closed forests, with relatively small open areas – but, as we will see, this assumption has been questioned by some researchers.

The extinction of the large herbivores has had impacts that we are only just starting to appreciate. The writer and activist George Monbiot, for example, has suggested that the reason most deciduous trees in Britain and Europe resprout from wherever the trunk is broken is that they evolved to survive the attentions of tree-smashing elephants. By breaking trees, elephants improve their food supply, as the shoots produced by a damaged tree are easier to reach and more nutritious than the older branches. Elephants could also explain why trees such as box, holly and yew are so resistant to breakage and have such strong roots. The ability of some trees to survive the removal of their bark might be another adaptation, as elephants often strip bark with their tusks. Finally, Monbiot suggests that blackthorn's long spines appear to be 'overengineered' to resist browsing by deer or cattle, but not perhaps by rhinoceros. Equally, Oliver Rackham proposed that the ability of trees to resprout from ground level, or a point higher up, is evidence of 'adaptions to recovering from the assaults of elephants and other giant herbivores. The extermination of the great tree-breaking beasts in Palaeolithic times may have been mankind's first and farthest-reaching influence on the world's forests.'

Scientists use a variety of methods to reconstruct the history of these ancient forests, but the most widely used is pollen analysis.

The technique was pioneered by Lennard von Post, a Swedish geologist who, in 1916, embarked on a study of the pollen that had been preserved in sediments in bogs and lakes. He produced diagrams showing how the pollen from different plants varied with depth and therefore time, allowing the presence, or absence, of species to be determined. Eryri has one of the most intensely studied pollen records in Britain, which can be traced back to when the first plants were colonising the newly exposed landscapes. These records show that, in the beginning, birch was the most important tree, together with juniper, but around 9,000 years ago the climate had become warm enough for hazel to start invading the birch forests, and for the next 1,000 years or so it was hazel that dominated the landscape.

*Hazel gloves, a parasite of glue crust fungus, on a hazel stem in Ballachuan hazelwood, Seil Island, Scotland.*

Today these ancient hazel forests have almost disappeared, but it is not hard to imagine what they would have looked like, as their remnants can still be found in a number of places, especially the western coasts of the Scottish Highlands and Ireland. Some of the best examples are to be found in Scotland at Ballachuan on Seil Island, Struidh Wood on the Isle of Eigg and Resipole Ravine on the Ardnamurchan peninsula. In Ireland the hazel woods of the Burren are well known to botanists. Probably because of the continuity, these woods are home to some of the richest collections of mosses, liverworts and lichens in the whole of Europe. They also support some fascinating and beautiful fungi, such as spring hazel cup and the curious hazel gloves, two fungi which, as their names suggest, are almost always found growing on old hazel trees. Hazel gloves has been described as 'a fungus that grows on a fungus', since it is actually a parasite of glue crust fungus, which it often covers entirely. Glue crust fungus is so called because it smothers the branches of its host tree, gluing them together and obtaining nutrients from the decaying wood underneath.

Many people have misunderstood the nature of hazel, mainly because of the way that it has been managed since the Middle Ages, especially in lowland England. Here 'coppice-with-standards' was a traditional method of obtaining the maximum amount of timber from managed woodlands. Hazel was the 'coppice', regularly cut every seven years or so as the highly valued 'underwood' product, and combined with 'standard' trees grown for larger sizes of timber. These traditions, preserved over many centuries, have affected the way many woodland managers regard hazel. In addition, the books on woodland ecology that have formed the basis for our understanding of the way trees behave mainly originated from Cambridge and Oxford universities, the authors incorrectly assuming that the local management techniques applied everywhere else. Following a visit to the Burren, Sir Arthur Tansley, a leading ecologist of the first half of the twentieth century, was one of the first people to challenge the accepted wisdom that

*After the Ice* 19

hazel was naturally an understorey shrub. Tansley, who publicised the term 'ecosystem' in 1935 after it was suggested to him by a fellow botanist, Roy Clapham, recognised that the vast hazel woodland here on the exposed limestone was a 'climax' community that would never become covered by taller tree species. Indeed, hazel rarely flowers, or produces nuts, while it is shaded by other trees.

The domination of hazel did not last forever though, and the pollen records from Eryri also show that, around 8,000 years ago, oak forest became the main habitat in the lowlands. Within 500 years it had also spread into upland areas, forming dense forests as high as Llyn Llydaw, a natural lake on the flanks of Yr Wyddfa (Snowdon) some 440 metres above sea level, in an area that is today almost devoid of vegetation. The two species of oak, pedunculate and sessile, cannot be distinguished by their pollen, so we do not know if they appeared simultaneously, or one after the other. At lower altitudes it is likely that sessile oak, probably mixed with some pedunculate oak, formed the basis of the first truly mixed deciduous forest to develop following the retreat of the ice, eventually including elm, small-leaved lime, ash and alder. Birch and hazel, on the other hand, declined as these other species came to dominate the more fertile soils.

Another study of fossil pollen, this time in Norfolk, has also highlighted the expansion of the ranges of several tree species in this period. Norfolk Wildlife Trust's Cranberry Rough nature reserve in Breckland hides a secret, for lying beneath the existing vegetation is a lost lake – Hockham Mere. Formed over 10,000 years ago, probably by the collapse of the underlying chalk bedrock, the mere is estimated to have covered some 81 hectares, with core samples suggesting it may have been up to nine metres deep. In the Tudor period there was still a large expanse of water here, but it was drained during the following two centuries and had dried up completely by the middle of the eighteenth century. Boreholes have revealed that the lowest layer of sediment is sand and silt, washed, or blown in, off bare land surfaces at the end of the last glaciation. Above this layer is a complete pollen record that has provided evidence of the changing vegetation here. Once again, as in Wales, a sparse birch forest grew up, then thick forests of oak, alder and elm appeared as the climate warmed.

Because Ireland was completely covered by the ice sheet, trees, along with other plants, had to migrate there from the south, and from radiocarbon dating it has been possible to estimate their actual arrival times. The data for birch and juniper, for instance, indicate that they spread throughout the island in the space of 500 years. Their relatively rapid recolonisation suggests that they had survived nearby, on a now drowned area of land. Once again hazel followed birch and juniper, and by 9,000 years ago it had covered a large part of the island. Scots pine arrived in the southwest and migrated

*The Kiltubbrid Shield (front and back), an Iron Age shield made from a large alder tree about a metre in diameter. Originally circular, it has shrunk and is now distorted. (© National Museum of Ireland)*

in a northerly direction, but appeared to move faster on the west and east coasts than through the midlands. It is a poor competitor on the richer soils and, as it had been preceded by hazel which thrives in such an environment, it would have encountered less competition on the coasts, where the soils are poorer and there is less shelter. Elm also migrated from the south and moved north, as did oak, which, like pine, migrated slightly faster along both coasts.

Alder appears later in the pollen record and, in the past, this has been regarded as evidence that it was the last tree to migrate into Ireland before the Irish Sea flooded. Recent studies have shown, however, that isolated populations of alder already existed alongside pine and oak until environmental conditions favoured its expansion. Many of these trees were very much larger than anything we are familiar with today. The Kiltubbrid Shield, an Iron Age shield made from alder which was discovered during the nineteenth century in County Leitrim, is a metre across, a diameter unlikely to be achieved by any alder trunk in Ireland today. The Irish historian Roderick O'Flaherty stated in 1685 that the Irish name for alder was *fearn*, because 'shields are made of it'. The word *sciath*, meaning shield, was used instead to describe a shallow oval wicker basket. The barrier presented by the Irish Sea is illustrated by lime and beech. Both were late immigrants to Britain, lime reaching the west coast of Wales around 7,000 years ago and beech arriving there 1,000 years ago. Neither species managed to make it across to Ireland on its own, but both were subsequently introduced by people, and thrived there.

In Scotland the iconic tree is, of course, the Scots pine, one of the three species of conifer that established themselves in Britain after the last glaciation (the others being juniper and yew). Interestingly, the current forests have their origins in two very different locations. It is thought, for example, that the pine forests of southwest Scotland, despite the barrier of the North Channel, owe their existence to trees invading from Ireland. But pine first appeared in the northwest of Scotland around 9,000 years ago, probably originating from isolated populations in an ice-free area to the west of the mainland, now lost beneath the waves. From there it spread across the Highlands as far south as the northern tip of Loch Lomond. East Glen Affric, around 25 kilometres west of Loch Ness, one of the largest areas of remaining native pine woodland in Scotland, has probably been continuously wooded ever since.

Whatever their origin, these pine forests reached their maximum extent during a warmer and drier period between 5,200 and 5,000 years ago when the species spread from its core area and colonised peat bogs in the north and west of Scotland. They are our version of the vast boreal forests that ring the northern hemisphere, north of the 50th parallel, but are not really appreciated as such. There are no boreal forests in the southern

*The Glen Strathfarrar pinewoods near Loch Ness provide a glimpse of the ancient forest and are an important area for rare lichens, despite being overgrazed by red deer.*

hemisphere, as the landmasses of South America, South Africa and Australasia are further from the pole. In Scandinavia and western Russia, the boreal forest is divided into 'light forest' communities, dominated by Scots pine, birch, rowan and aspen, and 'dark forest' communities dominated by Norway spruce with smaller proportions of other conifers.

Our native pinewoods are the western, oceanic, outliers of the light forest, although they tend to have more broadleaved species than the continental version. Some ecologists therefore regard them as a transitional type, calling them 'hemi-boreal', meaning half-boreal. The whole boreal forest is usually referred to as taiga, the 'land of the little sticks' in Russian, not just the northern fringe where it thins out near the tree line. Scots pine has the largest natural distribution of any conifer, ranging from Norway to Spain and from Scotland across Europe and Asia to Siberia and China. The pines in Scotland, which form this westernmost outpost of the taiga of post-glacial Europe, are estimated to have once covered 15,000 square kilometres, nearly 20 per cent of the land area. Today they are a sadly depleted habitat, having lost characteristic animals such as reindeer, brown bear, lynx, wolf and beaver – though the beaver is now slowly making a comeback thanks to various reintroductions.

Like Glen Affric, the nearby Glen Strathfarrar pines are a remnant of the ancient forest, but the area is suffering due to overgrazing by red deer. Probably as a result, the lower part of the glen, once a National Nature Reserve, was de-designated in 2006. The area was previously considered to be 'the last of the great unspoiled glens', but the building of the Monar Dam, the largest arch dam in Britain, across the River Farrar for a hydro-electric scheme sealed its fate. Despite this the glen contains one of the most significant pinewoods in Britain for lichens and, together with areas of birch, oak and alder, is currently known to support over 300 species, including 28 rarities. These include forked hair-lichen, Caledonian pannaria, witch's-hair lichen and button jelly

24 *Forgotten Forests*

lichen, a collection that is quite different from the communities found in Scandinavia.

Even as late as the end of the sixteenth century, large undisturbed fragments of these pine forests still existed. At this time there was dense and extensive tree cover along the south shore of Loch Maree, once known as Loch Ewe, which is situated in a remote part of Wester Ross in the northwest Highlands. As well as pine it contained birch, oak, ash, aspen, elm and holly and was described as one of the best forests in the west of Scotland. A description of the surviving wild wood here, probably by the great Scottish mapmaker Timothy Pont in the 1590s, conveys his excitement at seeing something that was, at that date, obviously exceptional, even if he quickly turns to a practical analysis of what use could be made of the timber:

*Upon this Lochew, do grow plentie of very fair firr, hollyn, oak, elme, ashe, birk and quaking asp, most high, even, thicke and great, all-longst this loch . . . [it] is compas'd bout with many fair and tall woods as any in the west of Scotland, in sum parts with hollyne, in sum places with fair and beautiful fyrrs of 60, 70, 80 foot of good and serviceable timmer for masts and raes, in other places ar great plentie of excellent great oakes, whair may be sawin out plants of 4 sum tymes 5 foot broad. All thir bounds is compas'd and hem'd in with many hills, but thois beautifull to look on, their skirts all adorned with wood even to the brink of the loch for the most part.*

Unfortunately, Pont never left a finished map of the area, and the great wood has now largely disappeared, but it was certainly an unusual survivor of the natural forest. Today the area forms part of Beinn Eighe and Loch Maree Islands, the UK's first National Nature Reserve, set up in 1951. The lower slopes of the mountain ridge still support fragments of the ancient forest, known as Coille na Glas-Leitire ('the Wood of the Grey Slope'), as do the sixty islands scattered across Loch Maree. The first reference to pine on

*Beinn Eighe and Loch Maree Islands National Nature Reserve in western Scotland contains fragments of the vast and ancient boreal forests that ring the northern hemisphere.*

the islands was in the first *Statistical Account of Scotland*, published in 21 volumes in 1794 by Sir John Sinclair, incidentally the first person to use the word 'statistics' in the English language. The largest island, Eilean Sùbhainn, is unusual because there is a small loch on it which in turn has an even smaller island on it. There was once an old pine on this miniature island, and over the years the 'island on a loch on an island on a loch' attracted a great deal of attention, with a Gaelic legend that it is the earthly seat of power of Queen Mab, Queen of the Fairies. The tree was also a traditional nesting site for ospreys, and the species has recently returned to breed in the vicinity.

Once widespread, Scots pine seems to have become extinct elsewhere in Britain around 4,500 years ago and about 1,550 years ago in Ireland. For some years though there have been discussions about whether some naturally occurring populations have survived outside the Highlands until the present day. One notable example of a potential native English pinewood is the Kielderhead Pines, located in a remote valley at the heart of Kielder Forest in Northumberland. Debate about the origins of this small population of apparently wild pines has been ongoing since the 1950s. Originally there were eight mature trees, but unfortunately two are now dead. The oldest tree germinated between 1844 and 1851, well before the earliest plantings for the modern forest in 1926. Further research is necessary, but the possibility that they are locally native has provided the basis for creating a Northumbrian version of the Scottish pine forests, using seeds and grafts from the remaining trees.

Deciduous trees such as oak, elm and alder only arrived in Scotland between 8,500 and 8,000 years ago. A mix of birch and hazel came to dominate the Outer Hebrides, the Northern Isles, and Caithness and Sutherland, while woodlands in the Highlands consisted mainly of pine and birch, and the coastal areas of the west and east were covered in birch, hazel and oak. The lowlands, and indeed much of the uplands, in southern Scotland were mainly covered with oak, elm and hazel. It has been suggested that, at this time, at least 60 per cent of Scotland was under some form of forest. Today one of the country's oldest and, arguably, richest forests lies hidden in the dramatic gorges of the Clyde valley, where rivers have gouged out deep ravines in the soft sandstone. These ancient woods of oak, ash, rowan and hazel now form part of the Clyde Valley Woodlands National Nature Reserve, surviving in the ravines there because the terrain was too steep to fell the trees.

Despite all the research into these early forests, some of the factors involved in their spread are still unclear. One puzzle is that the data indicate that trees were migrating faster than would be expected solely through the dispersal of their seeds by gravity and wind, with all the species investigated moving more than 3.7 kilometres per generation. Certainly, when the size and weight of hazel, oak and beech seeds are considered, other factors must be involved. Many of these are anecdotal, and further research is needed, but the involvement of animals, including humans, is almost certainly the answer.

A study published in 2021, for instance, identified one of the mechanisms by which the trees probably migrated. More than half the trees in two new oak woodlands in lowland England were found to be planted not by landowners, or environmental charities, but by jays, those large and colourful birds of the crow family. Former fields next to Monks Wood, a National Nature Reserve in Cambridgeshire, were rapidly turned into a forest with no need for plastic tree guards, watering or expensive management. At the time though, in the 1960s, there were virtually no deer in the area and the rabbit population was still low after myxomatosis. The second woodland was established when both deer and rabbit populations had increased, and as a consequence it has a much lower density of trees. In both cases, however, thrushes were found to have spread seeds of bramble, blackthorn and hawthorn, with the resulting scrub providing natural tree guards for the oaks that grew from acorns buried in the ground by jays. The acorns are usually

*The 'chattering acorn-gatherer', the jay, buries acorns for later retrieval. Those which are forgotten grow into trees.*

hidden in damp ground, to be retrieved when food is scarce. It has been estimated that a single jay can bury between 4,500 and 11,000 acorns a year and, incredibly, remember their location up to ten months later. One bird was even seen recovering an acorn after burrowing through over 30 centimetres of snow. Jays are not perfect, however, and some of the acorns they forget about become saplings by the spring. The scientific name of the jay, *Garrulus glandarius*, in fact means 'chattering acorn-gatherer'.

While acorns are regarded as the favourite food of jays, they will also eat beech and other seeds. Like the European jay, the North American blue jay's fondness for acorns is credited with helping the spread of oak trees after the last glaciation. As a result of studies on blue jays, the so-called 'dispersal distance' of American beech has been revised from several hundred metres to several kilometres. Indeed, many species in the Corvidae family, which includes jays, crows, rooks and magpies, have a mutual relationship with large-seeded plants such as beech and oak. There are reports of rooks burying walnuts and pine cones, as well as acorns. This behaviour appears to be particularly common in Scotland, and farmers in Aberdeenshire sometimes describe self-seeded trees there as 'craw-sown' – that is, rook-sown.

After just 24 years, the first field at Monks Wood contained 132 trees per hectare, 57 per cent of which were oaks. After 59 years, the second field resembled a mature forest, with 390 trees per hectare, of which 52 per cent were oaks. Alongside jays and other birds, grey and red squirrels and wood mice are probably the key distributors of acorns. They bury large numbers of acorns in the autumn, with mice typically transporting them tens of metres, whereas jays may travel hundreds of metres. Trees in both the naturally regenerating areas grew rapidly, despite the presence of roe deer and the invasive muntjac when the second woodland was establishing itself, and a series of droughts over the years. Although deer can badly damage young trees, they have been shown to be effective seed dispersers for a number of species, especially those with small hard seeds that are most likely to survive their digestive tract. The impact of deer may therefore be more complicated than is generally realised and, at low densities, they may actually assist the spread of forests.

Traditionally, most studies on seed dispersal have concentrated on birds and small to medium-sized mammals, but brown bears have also been found to be extremely effective seed spreaders. They are omnivorous and, as they roam, they eat all the nuts, fruits and grains they can find. Bears will also kill deer but, if there is plenty of other food available, they tend not to bother. The excrement from a single brown bear has been found to contain several thousand seeds, which germinate much better than those that have not passed through the animal's gut. In addition, brown bears usually defecate next to their resting sites, where they dig and create areas of open soil, creating ideal conditions for seeds to grow. While deer and other hoofed mammals feed primarily on herbs and leaves, with fruits representing less than 5 per cent of the total volume of their diet, bears will consume many different fleshy-fruited plants, including species with large seeds. Large fruit-eating species which range over sizeable distances, like brown bears, are now considered to be particularly important in connecting plant populations, increasing gene flow through the seeds they disperse. In fact, it might even be said that the main ecological function of brown bears is spreading seeds.

The role of humans in the spread of these early forests was highlighted in 1976 by the archaeologist David Clarke, who suggested that hazel nuts were a far more important part of the Mesolithic diet than anyone had previously realised. Another archaeologist, Francis Pryor, best known for his association with Flag Fen, a Bronze Age site near Peterborough, and appearances on the Channel 4 television series *Time Team*, has stated that in his experience 'most archaeologists find different links, different pathways, that fire their imagination and lead them directly to the past'. For some it is pottery, flints or animal bones. For Pryor it was hazel nuts, excavations of sites dating between 9,000 and 4,300 years ago often revealing large quantities of roasted hazel-nut shells. His conclusion was that Mesolithic people must have effectively farmed the nuts, and, like David Clarke, he could not understand why this important source of nutrition had been overlooked by so many archaeologists. It now seems that after the glaciers retreated people spread rapidly across Europe, bringing hazel with them, much as introduced peaches were spread across North America by indigenous people in a few decades. The nuts contain around 60 per cent fat and 20 per cent carbohydrates, with a wide range of proteins, vitamins and minerals. As a result, a few handfuls can cover the majority of a person's daily energy needs. Hazel was also used for tools and firewood, and thatched huts were often constructed from its timber. It seems therefore that the people of Mesolithic Europe relied more on hazel than on any other single plant.

It has also been proposed that the spread of oaks was assisted by people, as well as birds and small mammals, and that intricate relationships between oaks and humans developed due to the mutual benefits. Like hazel nuts, acorns were an invaluable food resource, and there are historical texts describing the regular consumption of acorns up until the Greek and Roman periods. As with hazel, there are intriguing similarities in the speed at which people and oaks colonised Europe after the last glaciation. They are too wide-ranging to be mere coincidence, suggesting that people may have transported acorns as food reserves, while migrating northwards as the climate warmed. The shared history of humans and oaks generated cultural and emotional relationships that were later incorporated into religious beliefs.

We now know that, as well as a practical relationship with oak as a source of food, people in the Late Mesolithic also had a cultural association with the tree. During the construction of the Maerdy wind farm in south Wales in 2021, the archaeologist involved, Richard Scott Jones, recovered several oak posts from waterlogged peat deposits. Following the cleaning and inspection of these timbers off site, in the hope of discovering evidence of possible tool markings, it was discovered that the surface of one of them was covered with carved decorations. The patterning along one of its sides took the form of parallel running zigzags, or chevrons, with a concentric oval motif at one end which has been interpreted as a representation of an 'eye'. If this is the case, then there may have been another eye on the opposite side of the timber, which is now lost.

Radiocarbon analysis subsequently showed that the wood was 6,270 years old, about 100 years older than the deposit in which it was found, suggesting that it had been deliberately brought to the site. The post measures approximately 1.7 metres in length and 0.26 metres in width and appears to have been rounded at one end and tapered at the other end, perhaps being inserted into the ground to mark a tribal boundary, a hunting ground or a sacred site. The only other known decorative art of a similar age and design survives on Neolithic pottery, or on standing stones. In Wales, examples of this type of abstract design are found carved into a number of stones in Neolithic passage graves on Anglesey. Most of the archaeological evidence from the Mesolithic relates to stone tools, so the discovery of this intricately carved wooden post provides an exciting insight into the culture of Late Mesolithic Britain.

Now on show in the new Gweithdy (Workshop) gallery in the National History Museum at St Fagans in Cardiff, the object was initially thought to be the earliest known example of art on timber

*A fragment of an ancient forest: the Mesolithic oak post in the National History Museum at St Fagans in Cardiff, showing the carved zigzags or chevrons.*

ever recorded in Europe. In 2019, however, another piece of oak was found in a trench in Boxford, Berkshire, which was being dug for the foundations of a new workshop. Derek Fawcett, a retired surgeon, was having the workshop built for his woodturning hobby, and initially he considered using the timber to make wooden bowls. But after washing it down he noticed some curious carvings and realised that this was something unusual. He contacted a local archaeologist, who in turn got in touch with Historic England, and the timber was carbon-dated. In 2023 it was announced that the oak was between 6,625 and 6,660 years old, some 400 years older than the Maerdy example. As with the other oak post, the purpose of the markings is unknown, but Historic England felt they were similar to decorations on Early Neolithic pottery and decoration on the Shigir Idol, a wooden sculpture found in the Ural Mountains of Russia, which at 12,500 years old is believed to be the oldest example of carved wood in the world. The Boxford oak post has been donated to another museum, the West Berkshire Museum in Newbury, where it is also destined for display.

One of the best-known representatives of our Mesolithic ancestors is 'Cheddar Man', a skeleton discovered in 1903 at Gough's Cave in Cheddar Gorge, Somerset. This is the oldest almost complete skeleton of our species, *Homo sapiens*, ever found in Britain. The classic Mesolithic campsites of Star Carr in Yorkshire and Thatcham in Berkshire, occupied by people like Cheddar Man, have, like the bone from Heaning Wood, been radiocarbon-dated to around 11,000 years ago, only a few centuries after the retreat of the glaciers. The sparse human population at the time survived largely by hunting and fishing, living in semi-permanent locations that were revisited seasonally, or for longer, over several generations. Their impact on the vegetation was originally assumed to have been limited, but, based on his work in the North York Moors National Park, the geographer Ian Simmons has suggested that Mesolithic people altered their landscape through the use of fire.

Charcoal from fires has been found to be frequent in both coastal areas and the uplands, suggesting that Mesolithic people were extending areas of the forest edge in both locations. Although Oliver Rackham stated that it is practically impossible to burn deciduous forests in Britain, archaeologists have shown that the charcoal horizons exist and are sometimes widespread, so forests must have been burnt, either by humans or in wildfires. Burning created open areas that attracted animals that could be hunted for food, especially, as in the case of Star Carr and Thatcham, if these sites were near sources of water. In recent decades, therefore, our understanding of the ecological context of Mesolithic people has changed from the idea that their influence on the forests was only slight to an acknowledgement that they may well have had a significant and lasting impact on the vegetation. It was a gradual process, but the repeated nature of these activities and the increasing human population probably resulted in a patchwork of open spaces and closed forest some 6,000 to 4,000 years ago. This landscape mosaic is something that Simmons views as the most important environmental legacy of the Mesolithic.

Despite the activities of people in this period, the traditional interpretation of these early forests, supported by Sir Arthur Tansley, was that, as mentioned earlier, they were quite dense, with a closed canopy. But in the late 1990s researchers started to question this assumption. It was suggested that the forests were more open than previously suspected and that, alongside humans, grazing animals had a key role in maintaining their structure, much the same as straight-tusked elephants and narrow-nosed rhinoceroses had done up until 115,000 years ago. One of the key people involved was the Dutch ecologist Frans Vera, whose book *Grazing Ecology and Forest History* was translated into English in 2000. Vera argued that the impact of grazing animals on the landscape that evolved in Europe after the retreat of the ice had been largely overlooked and we had simply forgotten about the megafauna that would have played a large part in the ecology of the forests. It is impossible to reconstruct the population densities of large herbi-

34 *Forgotten Forests*

vores in prehistoric times, but Vera argued that their impact on forest structure is evident from the pollen record, and that, before humans began to have a significant impact, animals such as European bison, elk, horse, aurochs (wild ox), beaver and wild boar, together with red deer and roe deer, would have been present in huge numbers, similar to the number of mammals that can still be seen today in parts of Africa. He went on to suggest that the different grazing methods of the various animals would have produced a complex mosaic of habitats, resulting not in a species-poor closed-canopy forest but in a dynamic, shifting landscape of open-grown trees, emerging scrub, grazing areas, groves and thorny thickets.

In summary, Vera produced a model of the forests as a dynamic system driven by grazing pressure, in a cycle from high forest, through dieback to open pasture, with regeneration taking place along the margins of open areas in places protected from heavy grazing by spiny and unpalatable shrubs, as in the fields next to Monks Wood. Remarkably, the English Romantic poet William Wordsworth had already described the process in *A Guide Through the District of the Lakes in the North of England*, which was published in 1835:

> . . . *let us again recur to Nature. The process by which she forms woods and forests is as follows. Seeds are scattered indiscriminately by winds, brought by waters and dropped by birds. They perish, or produce, according as the soil and situation upon which they fall are suited to them: and under the same dependence, the seedling or sucker, if not cropped by animals (which Nature is often careful to prevent by fencing it about with brambles or other prickly shrubs) thrives, and the tree grows, sometimes single, taking its own shape without constraint, but for the most part compelled to conform itself to some law imposed upon it by its neighbours.*

Equally, an early-seventeenth-century command to forest officers directed them to:

*. . . caste acorns and ashe keyes into the straglinge and dispersed bushes; which (as experience proveth) will growe up, sheltered by the bushes, unto suche perfection as shall yelde times to come good supplie of timber.*

The extent to which natural grazers formed part of the forest ecosystem has certainly been underestimated in the past, partly as a result of the relatively poor fossil record. Aurochs were once widely distributed through Europe, north Africa and Asia in the deciduous forests, and were exterminated as a result of forest clearance and hunting, with the last of the species reputedly killed in Poland in 1627. The bones of aurochs, especially the horns, have been found across Britain but they never reached Ireland. In May 2004, for instance, two horns attached to the frontal bone of a skull were discovered at the bottom of the main drainage ditch in the northeast corner of Ardgye Farm, around five kilometres west of Elgin in Morayshire. The Corpus Christi Great Horn, a medieval drinking horn now on display in the library of Corpus Christi College, Cambridge, is supposedly from the last aurochs in Britain. The animals would have been large enough to maintain, if not create, clearings, requiring extensive open areas for grazing, scattered trees and shrubs for browsing and dense forest areas for cover. The additional grazing pressure from deer would also have contributed to keeping areas open.

In 2015 scientists in Dublin successfully extracted genetic material from a remarkably well-preserved bone, discovered in a cave in Derbyshire, which belonged to an aurochs that died around 6,800 years ago. Comparisons of the genetics of the aurochs, traditional cattle breeds such as the Irish Kerry cow and the Scottish Highland cow, and more than 1,200 modern cows, revealed clear evidence of interbreeding between aurochs and early domesticated breeds. The 'heritage cattle' of Britain and Ireland can therefore trace a significant portion of their genetic make-up back to the aurochs that once roamed Britain. But they are all small compared to aurochs. With a shoulder height of up to 180 centimetres in bulls and 155 centimetres in cows, aurochs were one of the largest animals around at the time, with massive horns that reached up to 80 centimetres in length.

Until recently, the nearest equivalent we probably had to aurochs, alongside the Kerry cow and the Highland cow, were the white cattle to be found at Chillingham Castle in Northumberland. In 2002, however, in a perceptive article in the *Journal of the Folklore Society*, Jessica Hemming effectively demolished the myth, actively promoted by the estate, that the cattle are the sole survivors of the herds of wild cattle that once roamed the forests of Britain. Instead, the animals must undoubtedly be descended from either domestic or feral stock. They do look, to some extent, like miniature aurochs, but that is because they have not been selectively bred for beef or milk. Cattle that have been left to their own devices will tend to revert over time to their ancestral types. There are certainly medieval accounts of wild forest cattle, but as turning domestic stock loose in the forests was common in the Middle Ages there would been plenty of opportunities for herds to form.

In 2024, however, the rewilding charity Trees for Life released a

*The 'wild' white cattle of Chillingham in an area of woodland. Along with the Irish Kerry cow and the Scottish Highland cow, they are one of the nearest visual equivalents to the extinct aurochs, but are much smaller.*

herd of tauros on the Dundreggan estate near Loch Ness, in order to study how they could help to restore natural landscapes. Created by Dutch scientists by interbreeding ancient cattle breeds that are genetically close to the aurochs, tauros are similar in size to the extinct animals. Heck cattle, an earlier attempt to breed an animal similar to aurochs, were originally associated with Nazi Germany and are generally aggressive in comparison to the milder tauros.

In order to test Vera's theory on the impact of grazing animals in the wild wood, Nicki Whitehouse, a palaeoecologist at Queen's University Belfast, and David Smith, a specialist on environmental archaeology at the University of Birmingham, decided to investigate an overlooked resource: fossil beetles. Beetles are an excellent source of environmental data because it is relatively easy

*The ancient Jack O' Kent's Oak in the wood-pasture at Kentchurch Court, Herefordshire, in April 2023, just before the leaves appeared.*

to identify individual species from their remains and, since they only occur in specific habitats, they provide a clue to ancient landscapes. Some beetles, for example, live in rotten wood in dense forests, while others prefer more open areas and grassland, and dung beetles are found in areas grazed by large animals. The proportion of beetle species in a particular time period therefore allows scientists to reconstruct past habitats in some detail.

Nicki and David looked at collections of beetles from different parts of Britain, to see how beetle communities changed between the last glaciation and 4,000 years ago. From their studies it was clear that between 11,500 and 8,000 years ago the fossils mainly represented species of open areas and pastures, with only a few forest types and hardly any dung beetles. At the end of this period though, as the trees returned in strength, beetles typical of the forest environment became more abundant and grassland species declined, indicating an overall closing of the forest canopy. As we will see in the next chapter, trees from the Mesolithic are also preserved in the submerged forests found around the British and Irish coasts. They are invariably tall straight-trunked specimens, sometimes 10–15 metres to the first branch, a form characteristic of growth in a closed forest, in contrast to the low-branched forms which characterise the 'parkland' trees of more open landscapes. The composition of forests though is never uniform, and they consist of a mix of species that varies over time due to the changes in climate and the fact that plant communities are dynamic.

Reconstructing past habitats using the remains of beetles therefore requires caution, as a high percentage of beetles associated with rotten wood does not necessarily indicate a dense forest. The richest places for these species in modern Britain are in fact open landscapes with well-spaced large old trees, such as Moccas Park and Kentchurch Court, home of the legendary Jack O' Kent's Oak, in Herefordshire – Jack being an English folklore character well known for his sorcery and ability to trick and outwit the devil.

*Grazing animals present in Europe some 11,000 years ago after the last glaciation*

| Species | Northwest Europe | Britain | Ireland |
|---|---|---|---|
| Wild boar | x | x | x |
| Red deer | x | x | x |
| Roe deer | x | x | |
| Elk | x | x | |
| Reindeer | x | x | |
| Horse | x | x | |
| Aurochs | x | x | |
| Beaver | x | x | |
| Bison | x | | |
| Fallow deer | x | | |

'Wood-pastures' like Moccas and Kentchurch are very similar to the landscape which Frans Vera visualised as being created by grazing animals. Vera's hypothesis though is now thought by many experts to place too much emphasis on a single disturbance factor, grazing animals, rather than considering all the relevant aspects. It is now considered, for example, that natural fires, although they may be infrequent, were probably the principal cause of gaps in the forest canopy, along with storms, and that herbivores simply perpetuated these gaps. Vera's argument also assumes that the disturbance was evenly distributed. This certainly would not be true of grazing animals, the activities of which would invariably be concentrated near water bodies, rivers and lakes, forest edges and along migration routes, such as the passes connecting valleys. In other areas, where the disturbance was less, or minimal, the dense forest indicated by much of the environmental record would be present.

This conclusion, that grazing animals played only a minor role in shaping the structure of the post-glacial forests, is supported by a study by Fraser Mitchell, Professor in Quaternary Ecology at

Trinity College Dublin, who investigated the situation in Ireland. As the island was covered by ice during the last glaciation, no large grazing animals survived from earlier, warmer, periods. Migration into Ireland following the retreat of the ice would also have been affected by its isolation by the rising sea levels, and this is reflected in the poor fauna compared to the rest of Europe. While Britain had eight large native herbivores in the post-glacial period, including elk and reindeer, Ireland only had two, wild boar and red deer, as the so-called Irish elk disappeared from Ireland, Britain and most of Europe very soon after the end of the last ice age. The similarity between the proportions of oak and hazel in both Britain and Ireland indicates that large grazing animals were not required to maintain these trees in the landscape, as Vera had suggested.

Vera also stated that oak and hazel cannot regenerate under a closed canopy, so the presence of their pollen in deposits suggests that the canopy must have been at least partially open. It has been shown though that the introduction of an invasive mildew has made present-day oak seedlings more light-demanding than their ancestors. A white, powdery covering of mildew on oak leaves is now such a familiar sight that it could easily be dismissed as a normal occurrence. Prior to the early twentieth century, the situation was very different. Before then, mildew was rarely noticed, and it had apparently very little impact on the health of affected trees. The mildew that we know today was first observed in 1907, initially in France, but by 1909 it was being recorded all over Europe.

In the beginning the outbreak was attributed to a mutation in one of the rare, or generally inconspicuous, oak mildew fungi already known. It was caused though by a species that probably originated in the tropics, which leads to stunting, distortion and sometimes death of the affected seedling. The severity of the infection is also being increased by the presence of another closely related species, and since the two species are active in different months of the year, large numbers of spores are released over a long period. The introduction of this powdery mildew into Europe led to high death rates in Pyrenean oak in France, and it is still having a significant impact on forests across Europe.

As well as the large grazing animals described above, these Early Mesolithic forests would also have supported other animals such as the brown bear discussed earlier, alongside wolves, foxes, badgers, pine martens, beavers, hedgehogs and hares. This is the characteristic fauna of a temperate forest, similar to that found today in Poland or southern Sweden, except, of course, for the extinct aurochs. A mammal expert, the late Derek Yalden, suggested that the Mesolithic fauna in Britain consisted of around a million red deer, roe deer and wild boar, along with 99,000 aurochs and 67,000 elk. He also guessed that there might have been 10,000 lynx and

*White-backed woodpeckers, the largest of the spotted, black-and-white woodpeckers, may once have bred in ancient British and Irish forests.*

20,000 wolves preying on the grazing animals, in addition to perhaps 2,000–3,000 human hunters.

The birds that occurred in these forests are more difficult to identify with any certainty, since they are obviously much more mobile than mammals and not so restricted by natural barriers. One of the main problems in comparing ancient bird communities with those of the present is that the small perching birds which dominate habitats today are exactly the species most poorly represented in the archaeological records. For example, the chaffinch is often now the most abundant species in woodlands and, despite the lack of evidence, it seems likely that this was also the case in the Mesolithic. An analysis of Mesolithic and Neolithic deposits at Carding Mill Bay, near Oban on the west coast of Scotland, indicates that willow tits were also once common in the ancient forests there. In addition, there might have been numerous hawfinches, as their massive bills are often found on archaeological sites.

In addition, it has been suggested that white-backed woodpeckers, the largest of the spotted, black-and-white woodpeckers, once bred in Britain and Ireland, as the species occurs widely in eastern and northern European woodlands, as well as in the Pyrenees. Hazel hen, black stork, three-toed and black woodpeckers, Ural and Tengmalm's owls and nutcracker have similar ranges, and the presence of eagle owl, hazel hen and black stork in the British archaeological records indicates that this is a strong possibility. The white-backed woodpecker depends on primeval, or near-primeval, forest due to its specialist diet, predominantly wood-boring beetles and their larvae. Tawny owls and buzzards would probably have been the most numerous predators, reflecting the numbers of wood mice and bank voles to be found on the forest floor.

The development of more closed forest environments around 9,000 years ago is also indicated by the presence of lynx, which survived longest in Scotland until finally becoming extinct around

1,300 years ago. There is though a possible mention of lynx in the medieval Welsh poem *Y Gododdin*, in the area which is now southern Scotland and northeast England. A carving on a ninth-century stone cross on the Isle of Eigg is also said to represent a lynx, although other authorities consider it to be a biblical lion. Whether these were accurate contemporary records, or merely historic references, is hard to tell. Wolves, the last of Britain's top predators, disappeared in the eighteenth century, following centuries of persecution – as we will see later in the book.

In summary, then, it appears that at the end of the Mesolithic period Britain and Ireland were still mainly covered in dense forest, with open areas created by people, or by natural events, which could be maintained by grazing animals. Although large herbivores in the last interglacial period, such as straight-tusked elephants, do appear to have influenced the composition of the forest in the way Vera proposed, this was probably not the case for the forests that grew back after the last glaciation. Vera's argument, while it has certainly stimulated numerous innovative conservation initiatives, such as the well-publicised Knepp Wildland Project in West Sussex, does not therefore quite match the available evidence. But that is the role of a hypothesis, which the dictionary defines as 'a supposition, or proposed explanation, made on the basis of limited evidence as a starting point for further investigation'. On this basis Vera has been extremely successful. It shows that we need to constantly test assumptions about the history of our forests. Oliver Rackham stated in his 2006 book *Woodlands* that 'ancient woodland is not the same as the wildwood' and 'conservationists do no service to woodland if they try to remake it in the image of what they imagine woodland was like, whether on the Vera or the Tansley model. Woodland comes of processes of development and management . . .'

Before we look in detail at the way that woodlands developed under management, however, we need to consider the impact that the warming climate had on Mesolithic life, as extensive areas of forest were drowned under the encroaching tide.

# CHAPTER 2

# *Under the Waves*

*And in summe places when ye sea doth bate*
*Down from ye shore, 'tis wonder to relate*
*How many thousands of theis tree now stand*
*Black broken on their rootes, which once drie land*
*Did cover, whence turfs Neptune yeelds to showe*
*He did not always to theis borders flowe.*

Richard James, *Iter Lancastrense*, 1636

All around the British and Irish coasts are the remains of vast forests that were overwhelmed by the dramatic rise in sea level when the ice melted. It has been estimated that the European landmass was some 40 per cent larger during the maximum extent of the ice sheets, with global sea levels over 100 metres lower than today. Around 2.5 million square kilometres of land was lost as the sea rose, including the area now known as Doggerland which once connected Britain to continental Europe. In the west the Isles of Scilly was previously one landmass, but, between 5,000 and 4,000 years ago, the original island was rapidly submerged by the ocean. Even today the sea between the islands of St Mary's, Bryher, Samson, Tresco and St Martin's is, in places, less than a metre in depth. Between the Isles and Land's End and the Lizard Point in Cornwall lies the lost land of Lyonesse, known in Cornish as *Lethowsow*, which may be more than an Arthurian legend. It is said that the bells of long-submerged churches can be heard ringing beneath the waves on still nights. Similarly, on the other side of England, off the low-lying coast of Suffolk, the ghostly bells of Dunwich are part of East Anglian folklore.

There are many other examples of drowned lands and lost forests around the coasts of Britain and Ireland to be found in old documents. For example, a manuscript in the library of Exeter Cathedral, dated around 1280, records that the Kingdom of Tewthi, son of Gwynnon, King of Kaerrihog, located between Mynwy (St Davids, Pembrokeshire) and Ireland, was submerged by the sea, and that 'no one escaped from it, neither man nor beast, except Teithi Hen and his horse, and for the rest of his life he was sick with fright'. People have been aware of the lost forests around the coast of Wales for so long that they feature in the oldest surviving manuscript written in Welsh, *The Black Book of Carmarthen*, which describes the kingdom of Cantre'r Gwaelod, or the Lowland Hundred. There are various versions of the story, but in one the kingdom is rapidly submerged when a maiden named Mererid lets her well overflow.

Apart from the remains of trees, possible evidence that Cantre'r Gwaelod actually existed is suggested by a map held in the Bodleian Library in Oxford, the information on which is estimated to date from around 1280. Named after its previous owner, Richard Gough, who donated it to the library in 1809, the Gough Map is the oldest map of Great Britain still in existence. Importantly, it shows two islands in Cardigan Bay off the Welsh coast, which are considered to be the remains of the lowland that were later eroded by the sea. Historical maps in general need to be used with caution, but one of the attributes of this map, which is consistently remarked on by scholars, is the relative accuracy of the geography, particularly the shape of the British coastline and islands.

The earliest factual description of submerged forests is probably that of Gerald de Barri, the cleric and historian popularly known as

46                    *Forgotten Forests*

Gerald of Wales or Giraldus Cambrensis, who wrote of tree stumps that were revealed during a storm surge in 1171/72. The wind was so strong that the shores of south Wales were completely denuded of sand and the seashore 'took on the appearance of a forest grove, cut down at the time of the flood'. Before their true nature was understood, trees like this were believed to be the result of the deluge described in the Bible and were therefore called 'Noah's trees'. Some years later, in his *Itinerarium Cambriae* of 1191, Gerald noted another example of the phenomenon at Newgale on the Pembrokeshire coast:

> *We then passed over Niwegal sands, at which place . . . a very remarkable circumstance occurred. The sandy shores of south Wales being laid bare by the extraordinary violence of a storm, the surface of the earth, which had been covered for many ages, reappeared, and discovered the trunks of trees cut off, standing in the very sea itself, the strokes of the hatchet appearing as if made only yesterday. The soil was very black, and the wood like ebony. By a wonderful revolution, the road for ships became impassable, and looked, not like a shore, but like a grove cut down, perhaps, at the time of the deluge, or not long after, but certainly in very remote ages, being by degrees consumed and swallowed up by the violence and encroachments of the sea.*

This theme was repeated a few centuries later by the antiquarian William Camden, who recorded that, again in the reign of Henry II, storms had exposed 'the trunks of trees which had been cut down standing in the midst of the sea with the strokes of an axe as fresh as if they had been yesterday with very black earth'.

In 1904 Thomas Jehu, a Welsh physician and geologist, described the remains of a similar forest in Whitesands Bay, near St Davids:

> *Again about 16 years ago a big storm washed away the sand and exposed roots of great trees in Whitesand Bay. Huge logs of oak trees were carried away by the neighbouring farmers, some of which are still stored, and were shown to the writer. Twigs and branches of hazel were found*

*in abundance, although no hazel grows now near St David's. The writer is also informed that horns of deer were picked up.*

Frederick North, Keeper of the Geology Department in the National Museum of Wales and one of the most active historians of geology in his time, included a photograph of a tree stump and root system at Marros Sands in Carmarthenshire in his book *Sunken Cities: Some Legends of the Coast and Lakes of Wales*, published in 1957. Part of a submerged forest, these stumps can still be seen when low tides and rough seas remove the accumulated mud and sand. They are rooted in peat levels lying below the marine environment and preserved by the continuously waterlogged conditions. There is a similar feature just over the county boundary at Amroth in Pembrokeshire, and there are several other beaches where this phenomenon can be seen, but the stumps and roots of trees are

*The remains of the submerged forest on the beach at Amroth in Pembrokeshire. This is one of the best examples in Wales of a drowned landscape.*

48 *Forgotten Forests*

better preserved at Marros Sands than anywhere else in Wales.

In London, during excavations for a dock in Blackwall, the diarist Samuel Pepys recorded the discovery in September 1665 of:

*perfect trees over-covered with earth. Nut trees, with the branches and the very nuts upon them . . . Their shells black with age, and their kernell, upon opening, decayed, but their shell perfectly hard as ever.*

The excavations had encountered the remains of yet another submerged forest, and a similar discovery was made in 1789 during the digging of the nearby Brunswick Dock. There are many other London examples, including a lost forest at Rainham in the Borough of Havering. A record of this was sent by the Reverend William Dereham, Vicar of Upminster, to the Royal Society in 1792. In it he describes how the forest was discovered after a breach in the Thames wall following an extraordinarily high tide four or five years previously, and he notes that 'By lying so long under ground the trees are become black and hard, and their fibres are so tough, that one may as easily break a wire of the same size as any of those fibres . . . The soil in which all those trees grew was a black ouzy earth . . .' Many of these trees, like those in Wales, are rooted in peat levels lying below the marine sand (the 'very black earth' noted by Gerald of Wales and William Camden) and preserved by the continuously waterlogged conditions.

Hazel nuts were also mentioned by Joseph Sinel who, in 1902, recorded an 'unusual exposure of the old forest floor' at St Ouen's Bay on Jersey which contained the remains of oak, lime and hazel:

*. . . the fine white sand which usually lies throughout this bay from 5–10 feet thick, had disappeared, and in its place there stretched, as far as the eye could reach – north, south and seaward, an expanse of firm brownish-black peaty soil, which was studded with innumerable tree stumps, most of these just level with the soil, but many hundreds of them projecting above it for 2 or 3 feet. Between these stumps were prostrate trunks and large branches*

*with acorns, seeds of telia [lime, Tilia sp.] and hazelnuts in abundance.*

One of the largest submerged forests in Britain can be found at Pett Level in Rye Bay, between Hastings and Rye in East Sussex. In 1850 the historian William Durrant Cooper wrote about the sunken remains of Dymsdale Forest, as the area was once known, stating that:

*Near Pett, at low water, during spring tides, the remains of a wood may be seen embedded in the sand, consisting of oak, beech, and fir, the former sound and nearly black; and on the whole line of this coast, wherever ditches and dykes have been cut in the marshes, the roots and limbs of forest trees have been met with in vast numbers.*

He also recorded that the forest could only be seen at low water, during spring tides, but less than 200 years later exceptionally low tides are not required to expose the trees, which died due to rising sea levels around 6,500 years ago.

*The sunken remains of Dymsdale Forest at Pett Level in East Sussex.*

50  *Forgotten Forests*

In the far southwest of England, the submerged forest in Mount's Bay, Cornwall, has been known for centuries. In Cornish, St Michael's Mount is called *Karrek Loos yn Koos*, meaning 'Grey Rock in the Wood'. The ancient trees here are rarely uncovered now, except at extremely low tides. The chronicler John of Worcester, an English monk who worked in Worcester Priory, relates that in the year 1099 St Michael's Mount was located five or six miles (8–10 kilometres) from the sea, enclosed in a thick wood, but that on the third day of November the sea overflowed the land, destroying many towns and drowning many people, as well as innumerable oxen and sheep. The Anglo-Saxon Chronicle also records, under the date 11 November 1099, that 'The sea-flood sprung up to such a height, and did so much harm, as no man remembered that it ever did before.' Whether this was a storm surge or a more permanent overwhelming of the land, like that of the Lowland Hundred, is unclear, but no forest surrounds St Michael's Mount now.

In the north of England, Mr G. Holt reported at length in the July 1796 issue of *The Gentleman's Magazine* on a submerged forest at Crosby on Merseyside, which extended more than a mile (1.6 kilometres) towards Formby, writing that:

*What might have been its original extent, either in that or in any other direction, seems at present impossible to ascertain; but vestiges of it are visible dipping westwardly into the sea, which doubtless covers a great part of the land on which a considerable portion of it grew. There are numberless trunks of trees standing upright, some feet above the surface, in the very place in which they must have grown, with their prodigious roots extending into the ground in all directions in their natural positions.*

Numerous submerged forests have also been found in Scotland. The *Inverness Journal* of 21 June 1844 records the discovery of a drowned woodland at the bottom of Loch Oich, the central and smallest loch within the Great Glen and a major part of the

Caledonian Canal. Under the combined circumstances of drought and reconstruction work on the canal, the water level of the loch had fallen to a lower level than 'in the memory of man', revealing 'what may be termed a submarine forest'. The trees were removed from the course of the channel, as described by the *Journal*:

> *Some hundreds of trees of all sizes have been dragged out from their watery bed, where they have lain for centuries, consisting chiefly of the finest black oak – some of the blocks 3½ feet in diameter, and other logs 25 to 30 feet in length, and several of them in high preservation, others charred by fire.*

The newspaper also mentions that in amongst these remnants, 'doubtless of the ancient forests of Caledonia, were found a few logs artificially hollowed out, apparently to serve the purpose of canoes'. We will come back to these canoes, now usually called logboats, in a later chapter. Like the drowned trees, they are preserved samples of ancient forests.

There are still discoveries to be made today. As recently as 2018 a local resident, Ann Monk, noticed a partially fossilised tree protruding from a tidal pool at Lionacleit on the west coast of Benbecula in the Outer Hebrides, which led to the discovery of yet another submerged forest. The trees here are the remnants of forests that were once widespread across the Western Isles. At their peak, some 10,000 to 7,000 years ago, they consisted of a mixture of birch, hazel, willow and oak. Around a thousand years later, however, the forests began to decline, due to a combination of rising sea levels, a wetter and windier climate and human activity, and by 2,800 to 2,500 years ago the islands were mainly treeless.

Other long-lost forests have been found on Berneray, the southernmost island in the Outer Hebrides, and in the Bay of Ireland, near Stromness on Orkney. An oak post found here is around 6,500 years old, making it the oldest timber to be found in Scotland so far. It has been suggested that it may have been erected to direct travellers, marking the Loch of Stenness and a stream at the Brig o' Waithe that would have been suitable for beaching boats travelling from Graemsay and Hoy. At Berriedale on Hoy is a fragment of the last remaining forest in Orkney. Renowned as the most northerly native woodland in Britain, it survives in a steep gulley in the exposed moorland, being part of the RSPB's Hoy nature reserve. Apart from the trees – downy birch, rowan, aspen, hazel and willows – the wood has a rich ground flora, which includes mosses, fungi and lichens.

Even very small islands in the Hebrides contain evidence of these lost forests, as shown by Charles Elton's exploration of the Isle of Pabbay in the Sound of Harris in August 1935. Elton, who established the Bureau of Animal Population at Oxford University,

*The radially split oak post found in the Bay of Ireland near Stromness on Orkney is the oldest timber found so far in Scotland, some 6,500 years old.*

was attracted to Pabbay by what he considered to be the 'markedly woodland aspect of the mammal fauna' on a treeless island. Another factor was the description of the submerged forest by Martin Martin, 'a private gentleman who lived in Skye and voyaged among the islands' in the late seventeenth century. Martin reported that 'The west end of this island, which looks to St Kilda, is called the wooden harbour, because the sands at low water discover several trees that have formerly grown there.' A century later, Sir John Sinclair described the same forest:

*Where the sea ebbs out in spring tides to a great distance, there are visible, at the very lowest ebb, large trunks of trees; the roots of which, spread out widely and variously, are fixed in black moss, which might be dug for peat to a great depth.*

There were also extensive forests around the larger islands of Lewis and Harris, as well as in parts of the Sound of Harris now submerged by the sea.

Another forgotten world lies off the east coast of Ireland, but there are far fewer submerged landscapes in Ireland than in Britain, due to the fact that during the period of the lowest sea levels the extent of exposed land was quite limited, probably extending no more than 30 kilometres out from the present coastline. The profile of the seabed in the Irish Sea is such that the largest expanses of land are on the British side. The majority of the Irish forests exposed at low tide are therefore situated in sheltered bays and estuaries, such as Strangford Lough and, on the west coast, the Shannon estuary. In Galway Bay, storms in 2014 revealed a forest, extending out into the lagoons and marshlands, that pre-dated the formation of the bay. The stumps of oak, pine and birch found here, along with others in County Mayo and County Clare, have been carbon-dated to between 7,400 and 5,200 years ago, with some of the trees being nearly 100 years old when they perished.

*The remains of a tree in a drowned forest exposed by storms at Spiddal, County Galway, in March 2014.*

Evidence of rising sea levels towards the end of the last glacial period has also been discovered on the County Dublin coast, where a 6,000-year-old forest is visible between Killiney and Bray. The trees were first recorded about 100 years ago and again in 1999, and were revealed once more after a storm in 2001 when tree stumps and fallen timber were visible on the coast north of Bray.

There are also sites located on more exposed Irish coastlines, such as Portrush on the north coast and various localities on the Atlantic-facing west coast, which are periodically exposed after beaches have been stripped of sand after storms. In 2019 ferocious tides and violent storms revealed evidence of a vast forest floor thousands of years old beneath Claycastle beach, near Youghal, County Cork. The *Irish Examiner* newspaper declared that 'In recent weeks, the receding waters have delivered an enthralling glimpse of the ancient terrain, before the rolling sea restored sands and secrecy to the subaquatic wonder.' Such events are not uncommon along Ireland's coastline, and historical records have frequently referenced the east Cork town's submerged forest. In 1774, Charles Smith referred to the strand having been 'entirely divested of all its sand and gravel' by 'violent high winds' that exposed 'quantities of roots of various trees', including 'fir and hazel'. Equally, on a visit to Youghal in 1903, the Royal Society of Antiquaries of Ireland recorded that 'an immense submerged forest lies underneath the strand, which extends from "Clay Castle" towards Knocadoon'.

These are just a few of the many observations of submerged, or drowned, forests but, remarkably, no serious study of them was made until 1913 when Clement Reid, a geologist, published a book on the subject. *Submerged Forests* was the first attempt to survey the ancient land surfaces and forests that lie underwater along our coasts and estuaries. His work to identify the extent of the submerged land led him to study the area east of the Humber, where bones from extinct animals had long been dredged up by fishing trawlers. One area of the North Sea in particular caught his attention, the shallows of Dogger Bank. In fact, Reid's map of what is now known as Doggerland turned out to be remarkably close to what is currently known about this vast submerged landscape. Reid's studies subsequently inspired the archaeologist Grahame Clark when he was considering the feasibility of contact between the Early Mesolithic peoples of northwest Europe and eastern England. Confirmation that people were present in this landscape occurred in 1931 when the fishing boat *Colinda* discovered a harpoon point embedded within a large block of sediment pulled up from the seabed.

Although most date from the Mesolithic through to the Bronze Age, the exact history of the submerged forests is still not clear. Even the sites around the Welsh coast do not represent a single phase of flooding. Radiocarbon dates from trees at Ynyslas in Cardigan Bay, for example, suggest that they died around 5,500 years ago, while those just over a kilometre to the south, at Borth, died some 2,000 years later.

Wherever they occur around our coasts, submerged forests are

56                              *Forgotten Forests*

a unique resource, providing another window into the landscapes of Britain and Ireland in prehistory. A flaw of previous studies has been that they have tended to focus on a single method for reconstructing these environments. A study in 2005 by Scott Timpany of the submerged forest along the coastline of the Severn estuary was one of the first to assemble a detailed picture of the habitat, including human interactions with the forest. Using evidence from pollen, microfossils such as fungal spores, dendrochronology and microscopic fragments of charcoal, Timpany was able to identify three broad habitat types: dense oak-dominated, high-canopied deciduous forests from the Mid- to Late Mesolithic; alder-dominated wetlands from the Late Mesolithic to the Neolithic; and birch woodland from the Bronze Age. Another excavation at Woolaston in Gloucestershire, on the north side of the estuary, revealed the remains of six large oak trees. In contrast to the long straight trunks of trees found elsewhere in the submerged forests, these oaks had branches low down on their trunks and appear therefore to have grown in an open, park-like landscape.

The remains of terrestrial animals have also been excavated from these deposits. There are some striking examples from Pembrokeshire, and similar finds have been made in many other places. In 2014, for example, when a storm scoured the beach and moved the great shingle bank at Newgale, it revealed more tree stumps, together with human footprints. The scene was remarkably similar to that described by Gerald of Wales in the twelfth century. The footprints in the exposed peat, which probably date from the Mesolithic, suggest that people may have been tracking animals, perhaps an aurochs. Following the same storm, Shaun Thompson, a local resident, also found the horns of an aurochs, together with fragments of its skull, at Whitesands beach near St Davids. Exactly 100 years earlier, aurochs horns had also been discovered at Wiseman's Bridge, between Saundersfoot and Amroth, and these are now in Tenby Museum. In the 1930s, the 'greater part' of an aurochs skeleton was dug up on the shore about three kilometres from the earlier site, and this is now in the National Museum of Wales. Other remains of animals have been excavated from the deposits around the Pembrokeshire tree stumps, including red deer and brown bear from Whitesands and a pig from Lydstep.

Some of the most extraordinary finds to date from the Late Mesolithic have been made at Lydstep, providing a rare snapshot of a fleeting moment in prehistory. In 1917 the skeleton of a wild boar, dated to 6,300 years ago, was found trapped beneath a tree trunk, with two broken flint points in its neck. It appears that it eluded its hunters, only to die later of its wounds in the cover of the forest. Although many animal bones have been retrieved from the submerged forests, it is very rare to find clear signs of hunting such as this. More discoveries were made here in 2010 when a local resident contacted Dyfed Archaeological Trust to report footprints on the beach. Red deer hoof prints were preserved in the surface of a solidified peat deposit that once formed the floor of a shallow lagoon. Human footprints, including those of children, were deeply embedded in the peat as if the people had stood patiently in one place, and it is thought that they might have been a hunting party concealed in reeds near a watering hole. The hunters might have gone hungry that day, but an alternative interpretation of events is that the pig did not escape and its body was used as a votive offering at the water's edge, pinned down by the tree.

From finds such as these it is clear that some of the best evidence of past animal and human behaviour lies below, or close to, sea level. In the intertidal muds at Formby, near where Mr Holt recorded the submerged forest in 1796, is one of the world's largest known concentrations of prehistoric tracks. Many of the beds even retain prints made by the feet of oystercatchers and other birds. Since these impressions are just a few millimetres deep, their preservation over many thousands of years shows that erosion of the surfaces here has been minimal. The oldest beds, towards the south of Formby Point, are Mesolithic, with humans and seven other large mammals represented: aurochs, red deer, roe deer, wild boar, wolf or dog, beaver and lynx. The waterlogged beds containing many deep impressions of aurochs wallowing through the mud. In total, over a seven-year period, hundreds of animal and human footprints (representing 593 individuals, 401 large animals and 192 humans) were documented. These Merseyside footprints provide a unique window into a shared landscape and ecosystem of animals and humans, since the footprint record places them definitively in particular habitats at particular times. The human footprints at Formby are contemporary with trackways recorded at Goldcliff East in the Severn estuary, where 270 human footprints and 21 individuals have been identified in the intertidal muds. The animals recorded by the footprints are very similar to those at Formby, with red and roe deer, aurochs, wolf or dog, crane and other birds, including heron.

Overall, the footprint beds show that, as global sea levels rose rapidly after the last ice age, humans formed part of rich intertidal ecosystems, living alongside other large animals. Following this period there was a striking fall in the populations of large mammals, illustrated by the fact that human footprints dominate the Neolithic period and later footprint beds. This decline could be the result of several factors, including the loss of habitats following the rise in sea level and the development of agriculture, as well as hunting pressures from the growing human population. The research has shown how sea-level rise transforms coastal landscapes and degrades, and disconnects, ecosystems.

Submerged forests, however, are not just a historical phenomenon. Observations show that the global average sea level has risen by about 16 centimetres since the late nineteenth century, and the best estimate of the rate of global average rise over the last decade is 3.6 millimetres per year. This sea-level rise has been driven by expansion of water as the oceans warm, melting of mountain glaciers across the world, and massive losses from the Greenland and Antarctic ice sheets. As mentioned earlier, changes in sea level at any particular location also depend on a variety of other factors, including whether land weighted down by previous ice sheets is rising or sinking, and whether changes in winds and currents are piling ocean water against coasts, or moving water away. The general trend though is upwards, and more forests will be drowned as a result. *The State of the Cryosphere 2022*, published to coincide with COP27, the climate negotiations in Egypt, highlights that 'We cannot negotiate with the melting point of ice.' Our planet's melting ice pays no attention to climate pledges and responds only to the level of carbon dioxide in the atmosphere and the resulting warming. Ice loss and irreversible sea-level rise is occurring faster and at lower temperatures than previously forecast.

While there are few substantial woodlands left on the British and Irish coasts, an indication of what must have happened in these islands in the past comes from the United States, where rising sea levels are today creating 'ghost forests'. Coastal habitats along the entire Atlantic coastal plain, from Maine to Florida are slowly being inundated, and huge swaths of forest are dying as a result. In North Carolina, in particular, the changes have been dramatic, the coastal region witnessing a rapid and widespread loss of trees and the wildlife which the forests used to support.

While natural processes were responsible for submerging the ancient forests, people in the Neolithic were the first to make serious inroads into the remaining forest cover of these islands, mainly through clearing land for agriculture. They began a process of change in Britain and Ireland which has continued up until the present day.

# CHAPTER 3

# *Axes and Agriculture*

*Our understanding of the extent of forest impacts in the Neolithic is still debatable in many contexts. Different pollen sources will produce different qualities of information that are not necessarily easy or possible to reconcile.*

Gordon Noble

According to some archaeologists, the Mesolithic ended violently. A very high percentage of the skeletons recovered from burials at this time show evidence of aggression. It has been suggested that the violence arose because of social pressures resulting from competition for resources, as the incoming Neolithic farmers competed with the Mesolithic hunter-gatherers for land. Other researchers think that the increase in cases of violence is related merely to a much higher number of burials and more complete skeletons. But there is no doubt that while Mesolithic people only altered their landscape in a limited way, the evidence for forest clearance in the Neolithic is much more common and less ambiguous.

Mainly driven by the migration of people from mainland Europe, the Neolithic was one of the great transformations in human history, with innovations such as the introduction of rectangular houses, stone tombs for the dead and the domestication of plants and animals. As a result, some 6,000 years ago there were remarkable changes in landscapes, societies and technologies, and the beginning of a move from a wild, forested, world to one of agriculture and more settled communities. In little more than 80–100 human generations everything changed. And we must remember that generations then were much shorter, and people therefore younger, than today. If people survived until they were fifteen years old, they were usually halfway through their life. All of these dramatic changes associated with the Neolithic took place in an environment that was radically different to that found in almost all areas of Europe today. Many landscapes were still dominated by forests, with giant oaks and other trees towering over human activity in the landscape below.

As Gordon Noble has pointed out, working with the environment to create conditions suitable for agriculture would have been one of the major challenges in establishing this new way of life. Creating plots for horticulture and grazing for animals would have required the removal of trees, involving considerable effort and constant maintenance. Indeed, the environmental evidence for this period shows that at times the battle against the 'ever regenerating forest' was lost, with the trees taking back areas that had been hard won. The forest was far from a passive backdrop to Neolithic life. Evidence of actual settlements is scarce, but near Bangor, in north Wales, two large timber buildings were built close to a major complex of ceremonial monuments. In the uplands nearby, pollen studies from deep peat deposits show, yet again, evidence of fires and a decline in oak, elm and hazel, possibly related to clearance for grazing and growing crops. Despite these profound changes, the relationship between forests and people continued to be an important part of everyday life, in many ways becoming more entwined than ever.

One of the most well-known wooden structures of the Early Neolithic is the Sweet Track in the Somerset Levels, whose construction dendrochronology has dated, remarkably precisely, to 3807 or 3806

BCE. Named after Ray Sweet, who discovered it while cleaning out a ditch, the causeway consists mainly of planks of oak laid end-to-end, supported by crossed pegs of ash, oak and lime driven into the underlying peat. When the track was constructed, this was a landscape of open water, reed-swamp, wet woodland and raised bog, a place that was difficult to cross on foot. The planks, which were up to 40 centimetres wide, three metres long and less than five centimetres thick, were cut from trees which were up to 400 years old and a metre in diameter. They were felled and split using only stone axes, wooden wedges and mallets. An even earlier trackway, called the Post Track, was built on the same line as the Sweet Track in 3838 BCE and is the oldest such trackway that we know of. Other, much simpler, tracks were made of bundles of brushwood laid along the line of the route and pegged in place using small stakes. Today these causeways are located in Shapwick Heath National Nature Reserve and they have been preserved by covering them once again with the wet peat. It is still possible, however, to walk along the line of the Sweet Track on a replica section.

*A replica of the Neolithic Sweet Track running through wetland at Shapwick Heath National Nature Reserve, Somerset.*

Closely associated with forest clearance is a well-known decline in elm, which is visible in numerous pollen samples. This phenomenon, probably the most-studied, best-dated and least-understood event of its time, was once assumed to be a direct consequence of the early stages of transforming areas of the forest into a farmed landscape. Elm is one of the earliest trees to open its buds in spring, and the high phosphorus and calcium content of the young leaves makes it an excellent forage for livestock. There has long been a tradition of feeding elm leaves to livestock, and in parts of Norway elm trees still provide fodder for animals. It has been suggested therefore that elm branches were cut by Neolithic farmers in early spring to feed their animals. Cattle are particularly partial to elm leaves, and the Roman author Cato records that elm leaves were routinely fed to cattle and sheep. An early Irish text also describes the elm as 'sustenance of cattle' and 'friend of cattle', so it is likely that the practice was once widespread. Mature elm trees across the world were heavily lopped by people using simple hand tools, and the damage inflicted in this way resulted

*The Romanesque wooden ceiling in St Martin's Church in Zillis, Switzerland, which was painted around 1100, is one of very few to have been preserved in Europe. One of the many wooden panels illustrates the lopping of elm.*

in the near disappearance of the species from areas such as the mountain forests of India. Elm bark may also have been used for human food, since it contains starch, proteins, fats, oils and sugars. Indeed, there is documentary evidence of the practice in Norway until 1895 and of 'chewbark', elm bark collected by children, in Northumberland in 1853. It is best gathered in February or March, using bark stripped from branches that are four years old or younger.

It is uncertain whether Neolithic elms were affected by cropping for forage, selective felling to create small fields, browsing by livestock, or the introduction of the fungus that causes elm disease, perhaps worsened by climate change. It has been suggested, for instance, that the reduction in temperatures at this time may have resulted in elm seed becoming infertile. While wider studies of the elm decline in lowland Britain have found that the majority of cases examined could be associated with people, it was probably the interplay between these factors, rather than any one in isolation, that prompted the widespread and catastrophic decline of elms in this period. A re-analysis of the timescale of the elm decline in Ireland suggests that, while in some locations it is associated with the earliest evidence for farming, the 'start' of the elm decline here covered almost a millennium.

Elm disease, now commonly called 'Dutch elm disease', as it was first described in the Netherlands by Dutch pathologists in the 1920s, is a highly destructive disease of elm caused by two related fungi. It is spread from tree to tree by elm bark beetles, which breed in the bark of cut, diseased or otherwise weakened elm trees and then disperse to other trees. In the late 1980s a similar disease swept through Europe and provided an opportunity to observe the effects of the decline of elms on the pollen record. Pollen analysis of soil profiles from a woodland once rich in elm showed a decline of elm pollen in similar proportions to that found in the Neolithic and an increased amount of pollen from weed species, as a result of the opening of the woodland canopy

– confirming earlier suspicions about the cause of the prehistoric decline.

Whatever caused the loss of elm, it signals another significant change, the first introduction of domestic livestock. Four species were initially involved, sheep, goats, cattle and pigs. Cattle and pigs, and possibly goats, had wild relatives, but sheep were entirely new in these northern landscapes, and their introduction had consequences that we are still living with today.

Despite the negative impacts on natural habitats, the importation of domestic animals probably relieved the hunting pressure on native species. Excavations of archaeological sites from this period all show the strong dependence of these early farmers on their livestock and, conversely, how unimportant wild animals were now as a source of food. The attitude to predators also changed fundamentally, with wolves, lynx and brown bears regarded as threats to domestic animals, rather than as sources of fur and, in the case of bears, meat.

*The area around Stonehenge in Wiltshire seems to have been kept clear by grazing animals in the Neolithic, maintaining views to the monuments, while other areas were often still forested.*

66 *Forgotten Forests*

Pollen data from southwest England following the elm decline indicate that the forest grew back in many areas from which it had disappeared, although elm did not always recover to its former levels. Thereafter the forest was only occasionally affected by people, and only then on a small scale, until the very Late Neolithic and Early to Middle Bronze Age. It would appear, therefore, that a pattern of shifting agriculture and small-scale pastoralism was maintained. The Wessex Downs in southern England seem to be an exception, however, as analysis of snail shells from buried soils indicate the presence of open grassland throughout this period. It is likely that herds of cattle and sheep kept the area clear of trees, maintaining views to the funerary and ritual monuments that are common here, including Stonehenge. In Scotland and northern England, the pollen record suggests that there was little change in the overall composition of forests during the Neolithic, in spite of some evidence for the expansion of heathland in the uplands and limited clearance in lowland areas.

In the Late Neolithic the wild wood gave way to a more open landscape containing small-scale clearings, abandoned clearings, stands of secondary growth and still undisturbed primary forest; but closed forest canopies survived, in some localities, well into the Bronze Age. A study of an Early Neolithic timber building at Crathes in Aberdeenshire has suggested, however, that larger clearances do not show up well in regional sources of pollen. The evidence here indicates that a large and unusual timber hall existed in a clearing that could have been as much as two kilometres wide. The building itself was constructed using very substantial oaks and other mature trees, suggesting that dense, old-growth, forest was still located nearby. Indeed, while Neolithic communities were having a definite impact, the presence of species of woodland insects that are now extinct, or occur only rarely today, suggests that the forest at this time was still extensive. This 'old forest fauna' was characterised by insects associated with over-mature trees and dead wood, such as the maple wood-boring beetle, a species of death-watch beetle that now occurs only in Windsor Great Park and a few other localities.

While the study of pollen deposits and other material, including insect remains, has been successful in identifying the impact that Neolithic communities had on the natural environment, there has been surprisingly little discussion about the social impacts that this new relationship with the forest would have involved. Clearance obviously meant the destruction and felling of numerous trees, many of which would have been significantly older than the human communities responsible. Overall, the evidence suggests that land-scapes in this period were quite fluid, with forest cover receding and regenerating over time at different speeds in different regions, providing a certain 'rhythm' to Neolithic life.

Gordon Noble was one of the first to question why people started cutting down forests when past generations had lived in relative harmony with the environment for millennia, and why, once commu-nities began felling trees on a large scale, they started building monuments constructed from them that had little practical function and probably took up significant areas of newly cleared land. Those questions are still relevant today. The incorporation of trees and the use of timber in Neolithic monuments is not really surprising, however, in a world where trees were the major feature in the land-scape. Trees were harvested on an unprecedented scale, with the construction of the monuments alone having a major impact on the surrounding environment. The emphasis on forest clearance in this period is undoubtedly why such significance was attached to stone axes and why such great efforts were made to procure, exchange and deposit them in special locations. The felling of trees was a recurring, and repetitive, task for numerous communities, and the power and symbolism of the axe undoubtedly derived from its effectiveness in transforming the environment. As in the Mesolithic, fire also played a role in altering the land, and there is increasing evidence of the burning of tree trunks in a number of places. It seems nevertheless that the demand for timber for fuel and construction had no overall impact on the forests, because the amount needed was much smaller than the natural growth. If there was any deforestation, or changes in the forest cover, it was probably caused by animal and crop husbandry and not by the exploitation of timber.

The wooden monuments constructed in the Neolithic may have been a way of addressing this changing relationship between forest and people. Timber was being used in highly structured and symbolic ways and not merely as a simple building material. It has even been suggested that the monuments may have been regarded as alive, perhaps even as beings in their own right. One of the best-known timber monuments is Woodhenge, a Late Neolithic structure built around 4,500 years ago, about the same time as Stonehenge and about three kilometres to the northeast. Originally Woodhenge consisted of six concentric ovals of massive posts, surrounded by a bank and ditch. The site was discovered by aerial photography in 1925 and excavated in 1926–27 by archaeologists Ben and Maud Cunnington, who marked the positions of the wooden posts with concrete pillars. The deepest postholes were up to two metres deep and because of this are believed to have held posts which were as high as 7.5 metres above ground. Each post would have weighed around five tonnes, and their arrangement was comparable to that of the bluestones at Stonehenge. Interestingly, both monuments have entrances oriented approximately to the summer sunrise, and the diameters of the timber circles at Woodhenge and the stone circles at Stonehenge are similar.

Many of these early timber henges must have resembled a forest of tall trees, but the erection and later removal of posts appears to have been an essential part of the ritual, and it is unlikely that the excavated postholes signify posts that were all in place at the same time. At the Neolithic Sanctuary on Overton Hill near Avebury two of the seven circles seem to have consisted of repeatedly renewed oak posts, possibly carved or painted, which were set into pits in the chalk.

While the Irish Neolithic is best known for the massive megalithic

# Axes and Agriculture

tombs at Newgrange, Knowth and Dowth, situated alongside the River Boyne in County Meath, excavations in the 1990s at Ballynahatty, in County Down, uncovered a huge Late Neolithic timber circle complex. It consists of a double outer ring of postholes, enclosing an area 100 metres by 70 metres, and a double-ringed inner enclosure, 16 metres in diameter, which encloses four large corner postholes and a central platform. In 2017 a geophysical survey in the Boyne valley also revealed a large monument comprising a passage enclosed by a rectangular arrangement of wooden posts, which were surrounded by rings of smaller timber posts. The complex aligns with the sunrise during the winter solstice.

Five circles of oak posts, with a massive oak pillar in the centre – which would have been visible for miles – also once formed part of a ceremonial complex at Navan Fort in County Armagh, the site of the legendary court of Eamhain Mhacha. The Irish folklorist Dáithí Ó hÓgáin saw this oak pillar as an example of a 'world-tree' at the sacred centre of the community's territory which had the function of linking the earth with the sky. This tradition, of a central tree in a ceremonial site, was carried forward into the Iron Age, and at Bubbenhall in Warwickshire a single tree seems to have stood within an enclosure some 20 metres across. At Uley, in the Cotswolds, a tree, or alternatively a post, marked a similar centre on West Hill. Here the sacred tree may have been a yew, since in the late eleventh century the place-name was recorded in the Domesday Book (a record of the 'great survey' of most of England, and some parts of Wales, which was completed in 1086) as *Euuelege*, probably meaning 'clearing in a yew wood'.

While these monuments were constructed using huge felled trunks, there is also evidence that, in the Neolithic, people deliberately incorporated living trees in their structures. At Carsie Mains in Perthshire, Scotland, excavations in 2004 revealed an unusual construction. A rectangular timber structure and a small timber circle once stood here, and at one end of the rectangle a large hole was found where a tree would have been – so the building appears to have surrounded a living (or dead) tree. The timber circle itself may also have surrounded a tree and some of the outer ring of posts seem to have been live trees, rather than cut timber. So trees, perhaps the ones felled during the clearance of the area, were used to construct monuments that surrounded living specimens. Additionally, the structure itself covered the remains of dead trees, which undoubtedly remained visible. It has been suggested therefore that the two timber features were built during a period of forest regeneration, in an area where trees were both deliberately removed and conserved.

A similar approach can be seen in a modern building constructed at the Yorkshire Sculpture Park, near Wakefield, by the artists Heather Peak and Ivan Morison. It is the first sculpture commission in a pioneering arts programme, the Oak Project, which is

Silence – Alone in a World of Wounds, *a modern building at the Yorkshire Sculpture Park that includes living trees in its construction, in the same way that Neolithic people sometimes incorporated them in their structures.*

designed to 'create kinship with nature in response to the climate emergency and environmental crisis'. *Silence – Alone in a World of Wounds*, which takes its title from a famous quote by the great American ecologist Aldo Leopold, shares space with nature, being constructed from earth, timber, heather, paper and living trees. As weather and time cause its decomposition, over the years the structure will be gradually reclaimed by nature, leaving only a trace in the ground.

Timber, by its very nature, is inevitably affected by decay – and in the case of the great timber monuments we are confronted with an 'archaeology of absence', represented by circles of postholes rather than the actual posts themselves. If they had survived until today the Sanctuary on Overton Hill or the ceremonial complex at Navan Fort, along with many others, would be seen in the same light as Stonehenge, or the remarkable structures in Orkney – as spectacular monuments from the past. But, as it is, they are difficult to interpret. Remarkably, however, two timber monuments from prehistory have survived in Britain, and they were constructed only a few centuries after the end of the Neolithic.

In the early spring of 1998, John Lorimer, an amateur archaeologist and beachcomber, was catching shrimps with his brother-in-law at Holme-next-the-Sea on the north Norfolk coast. During their visit they found a Bronze Age axe head in the silt, but at first did not know what it was. Intrigued, Lorimer visited the area repeatedly, eventually finding a lone tree stump that had been unearthed on the beach, which was unusual in that it was upside down. He informed Norwich Castle Museum and the area was eventually excavated. Initially there was little media interest, but this changed on Saturday 9 January 1999, when *The Independent* newspaper ran a front-page story by their environment correspondent, Michael McCarthy, referring to the discovery as the 'Stonehenge of the Sea'. This sparked articles in rival newspapers, repeating the comparisons to Stonehenge, despite the two being completely different, and the site became known as 'Seahenge'. It became famous when Pagans objected to the decision by English Heritage to dig up the whole structure, remove it from the beach and preserve it.

As a result of the excavations, we now know that in the spring of 2050 BCE, during the Early Bronze Age, a very large oak tree was felled and its stump half-buried with the roots uppermost. The stump weighs well over a tonne, so digging it out of the ground and then hauling it to its final position, using rope woven from honeysuckle, would have been a huge task. The surface of the stump was shaped and trimmed using bronze axes, and it is possible to see the individual marks left by these tools. Each axe left its own unique 'fingerprint' and, as a result, archaeologists have estimated that over fifty different axes were used, indicating a communal or ritual element to the activity. About a year later, some smaller oaks were felled, and from these 56 posts were cut and arranged in a circle around the upturned central stump. The monument, described by some archaeologists as one of the most significant

*Seahenge on the beach at Holme-next-the-Sea, Norfolk, before it was removed in the interests of preservation.*

ever discovered, may have been a ceremonial site, or 'excarnation' site, where, after death, bodies would be exposed to the elements to hasten the process of decomposition and help the spirit on its way to the afterlife.

In 1999, while Seahenge was being excavated, a second structure was discovered about 100 metres away from the original site. The second circle was much bigger and had two oak logs in the centre, with other posts and a wickerwork fence surrounding it. It was dated to 2049 BCE, the same date as Seahenge. This is the only known case in British prehistory where we know that two monuments were built at exactly the same time. But while the timbers of the external circle at Seahenge had retained their bark, creating the illusion perhaps of a giant tree trunk, the bark on the timber circles here had been removed. Although discovered on a beach, both monuments were originally located in a very different environment. At the time they were constructed, the area would have been saltmarsh. There was mixed oak forest nearby but the area was becoming waterlogged and the oak trees used to construct the monuments show signs of struggling to survive in the increasingly wet conditions. In the following centuries the saltmarsh was covered by freshwater reed-swamp, colonised by rushes and alder trees. This created a thick layer of dark peat, which covered the remains of the timbers, ensuring their preservation. Over the last 3,000 years, the sea has encroached on the land, as the protective barrier formed by the sand dunes moved steadily inland.

The transition between the Neolithic and the Bronze Age seems, potentially, to have been as dramatic as that between the Mesolithic and the Neolithic. A study published in the journal *Nature Communications* in 2023 revealed how researchers re-examining bones from the Levens Park ring cairn in the Lake District found that four people buried within the cairn had been infected with the plague. Dating to around 2000 BCE, this is the earliest known instance of the disease in Britain. Some studies have suggested that there was a 90 per cent decline in the population between 2200

74                  *Forgotten Forests*

and 1800 BCE, due to war, famine and invasions from the continent. With the addition of a major outbreak of plague, the situation for Neolithic people at this time seems to have been rather bleak.

At the start of the Bronze Age, Britain was still largely forested, although the activities of Neolithic people had permanently altered its composition and distinct regional differences had begun to emerge. But further change was coming. In north Wales, for example, the world's largest Bronze Age copper mine, on the Great Orme, is estimated to have consumed between 400,000 and 600,000 tonnes of timber over a 1,260-year period. Copper mining in this period used a lot of firewood, both for the smelting process and for the repeated 'fire-setting' inside mines to shatter the rockface, allowing the removal of a layer using stone hammers and antler-horn picks. Archaeologists have suggested that all this timber must have been produced by the systematic coppicing of large areas of nearby woodland. Discovered in 1987, during a scheme to landscape part of the headland, the mine is one of the most astounding archaeological discoveries of recent times. There are uncertainties, however, about the demand for timber at any particular time in the mine's development. A 'golden period' of ore production between 1600 and 1400 BCE has been proposed, followed by a 'twilight period' lasting many centuries, during which only small amounts of ore were produced. Unfortunately, little detail is known about the local environment during this period, and the composition of the forest which was being exploited is still not clear.

Interestingly, two Irish botanists, Micheline Sheehy Skeffington and Nick Scott, have recently suggested that this ancient woodland management is the key to understanding the current distribution of the strawberry tree in these islands. Today strawberry tree is a common garden shrub, but it has an unusual natural distribution, being mainly confined to the counties of Cork and Kerry and the south side of the Great Orme. These are all areas associated with Bronze Age copper mines. There are also populations along the Menai Strait, which separates Anglesey from the mainland. A genetic study of strawberry tree in Spain has shown that it is not a native species, in either Britain or Ireland, as was once thought. Instead, it was introduced by the so-called Beaker people, as they moved along the Atlantic fringe from their origins in southern Iberia. This movement of people, carrying the strawberry tree with them, is described in Irish mythology, a body of work which is far more extensive than anything known for Britain and which is exceeded in length only by the Egyptian and Jewish chronicles.

The *Fiannaíocht*, the Fenian cycle of legends, for instance, includes the story of the pursuit of the lovers Diarmuid and Gráinne by Oisín and the Fianna. The narrative includes the following, in translation: 'And the provisions they brought with them from fair-cultivated Tír Tairngire were crimson nuts and strawberry tree berries and fragrant berries.' Early English scholars dismissed Irish legends as merely fabricated tales, and even today these myths are sadly given little credence, even by Irish academics. In Charles Nelson's *The Trees of Ireland* this reference to the strawberry tree is described as 'fabulous', but it now appears to be extremely accurate. The 'crimson nuts' would have been sweet chestnuts.

In its native habitat around the Mediterranean, the strawberry tree is a typical species of open scrub woodland, a habitat that is subject to frequent fires. As an adaptation to fire, the species has an underground 'lignotuber' from which it can regrow, similar to the related heathers and rhododendron. Indeed, another Irish botanist, David Webb, described the strawberry tree as 'almost immortal'. Its ability to sprout repeatedly from its lignotuber base means that it coppices well, and, as a pioneer species that can rapidly invade suitable areas, its spread would have been encouraged by repeated coppicing of timber for the copper mines. This is no more than a hypothesis at this stage, but if it is confirmed by further studies then the strawberry tree would join a strange mix of species, including the Kerry slug and Kerry lily, that have been introduced to Ireland by human migrations in the distant past.

Changes, with natural causes this time, were also occurring in the fenland basin of East Anglia. This was once covered by dense oak forests, but a rise in sea level caused the rivers to back up and flood the fens, killing the trees – which then fell onto the forest floor. Described by Sir Harry Godwin, once the main authority on the fenland, as the 'Fen Clay marine transgression', this flooding resulted in a 'buried forest' covered by peat. Oaks, generally known as 'bog oaks' are abundant here, along with numerous yew trees. Often stained black by the reaction of iron in the groundwater with the tannins in the wood, they have a reputation for toughness, and many are of a colossal size. Some of the trunks have been measured at 30 metres or more before the first branch and are over a metre thick. Radiocarbon-dating of their outer rings indicates that they died over 4,500 years ago, a date which fits with the Neolithic artefacts often found alongside them. The first trees which fell into the silt are in a far better condition than those which were exposed for longer and therefore subject to insect infestation

*The great capricorn beetles, one of the largest beetles in Europe, found in a fragment of an ancient bog oak dug up in an arable field in Cambridgeshire in 1976.*

and fungal disease. It is not unusual still for farmers to encounter one or two of these trees during ploughing, and in some areas numerous oaks were found lying across each other. These examples, and others, indicate the extraordinary grandeur and density of these high forests. The bog oaks and yews are important in the story of our forests, since they provide hard evidence for the physical structure of these ancient habitats, which is difficult to determine from pollen samples alone.

A glass-topped box in the Natural History Museum in London literally provides a window into the past history of these forests, containing as it does a fragment of an ancient bog oak dug up in the fens at Ramsey in Cambridgeshire in 1976. Dated to around 3,785 years ago, it contains several large tunnels made by the great, or oak, capricorn beetle. This beetle is a member of the longhorn family, recognised, as the name suggests, by their extremely long antennae. Seven species of capricorn occur in Europe, and they are so called because their strong curved antennae are considered to resemble the horns of an ibex, or capricorn, a wild goat that lives in the Alps. One of the largest beetles in Europe, the great capricorn has a body length of around 4–5 centimetres, excluding the antennae, which are much longer in the males.

Amazingly, the tunnels in the bog oak still contained two adult capricorn beetles, which are now preserved in the museum and look almost as fresh as modern specimens. The discovery of these longhorn beetles has provided new insights into the climate and conditions of the forest in the Late Bronze Age. Max Barclay, Curator of Beetles at the museum, said at the time that 'These beetles are older than the Tudors, older than the Roman occupation of Britain, even older than the Roman Empire. These beetles were alive and chewing the inside of that piece of wood when the pharaohs were building the pyramids in Egypt.' Some years earlier, in 1965, another less well-preserved specimen was found in a partly submerged bog oak near Ely, but the species is now extinct as a breeding species in Britain.

The great capricorn is, however, occasionally imported with timber from Europe, and there are scattered records of live specimens from timber yards and other similar localities. In June 2008 Hampshire Museums Service received a female which had been found crawling along a garden path in Sherfield on Lodden, near Basingstoke. This spectacular insect had probably emerged from a building constructed of imported oak. The species has also been recorded from the New Forest, and emergence holes in trees have been found there, but these probably only reflect a temporary colonisation. One of the most recent records is from Essex in July 2013, where a great capricorn was 'knocked out of the air by a blackbird'. The beetles are poor flyers though and very rarely travel more than 500 metres from where they emerge as adults.

The beetle is both a lesson in the interconnected nature of forest life and yet another reminder of the incredible richness we have lost. A recent study by researchers at the University of Wrocław, Poland, for instance, has revealed that, like earthworms, woodpeckers and beavers, they are 'ecosystem engineers', shaping and

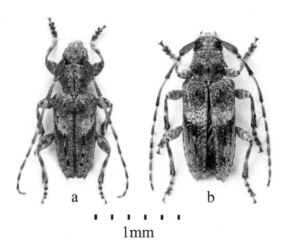

*The original specimens of* Pogonocherus caroli, *a native British beetle first discovered in Scottish pine forests in 2017. (a) is the male and (b) is the female.*

indeed creating habitats which are then used by other species. The larval stage of the beetle can last up to five years, and during this time they excavate large galleries in the timber, up to 40 centimetres in length and often ending in an oval cell around 10 centimetres wide. These galleries are very durable and can persist for decades after the adult beetle has left them, becoming important microhabitats for a variety of other animals, including common lizards, sand lizards, slow worms, snakes and even bats. Ecosystem engineering is one of the most important factors shaping the natural environment, but it is rarely studied by naturalists, or taken into account in conservation initiatives.

We may have lost the great capricorn, but in 2017 Martin Rejzek, a researcher in biological chemistry who collects insects as a hobby, found what generations of British entomologists had missed: *Pogonocherus caroli*, a native British beetle which lives in the ancient Scottish pine forests. Max Barclay considered that, as the beetle has specific habitat requirements, its discovery puts the 'biodiversity seal of approval' on these forests. If the beetle was a recent colonist, it would have first been seen spreading through pine trees in southern Britain, rather than being restricted to sites in Scotland.

Despite their importance as indicators of past habitats, Oliver Rackham noted that the bog oaks found in the fens 'are only a minute and unrepresentative fraction of all the trees that grew in prehistory; they lived in unusual places and died violent and unusual deaths, being killed by a sudden rise in the water-table'. Nor were all the species preserved. In the Fens there are bog oaks, bog pines and bog yews but no bog limes or bog hazels, even though the pollen evidence is that lime and sometimes hazel were more abundant in this part of Britain than oak, pine or yew. It has been suggested therefore that lime and hazel, which rot more easily, had disintegrated before the expanding peat could cover them. But without this information from the trees found in bogs, we would only be guessing as to what these ancient forests looked like.

The surviving ancient woodlands provide many clues, but they are not a random sample. In particular, they occur mainly on land which was considered too poor for agriculture. Only a few are on fertile land, and almost none are on flood plains, which would have been the best land for growing crops.

An article in the *Illustrated Sporting and Dramatic News* in 1942 graphically described the finding, destruction and disposal of bog oaks in the Cambridgeshire Fens during the Second World War:

*In 1631 the Earl of Bedford, with a company of promoters called the Adventurers, set out to drain the Fens. To-day the 8-ft.-high rushes on Adventurers' Fen are being cut and battered by great, crawling tractors; the bog oaks are being riven by explosives; teams of land girls with tractors and harrows are gathering the rubbish and huge fires are burning. By the autumn the green fen will be a black patch as level as a billiard-table and the seed-drills will be putting in the winter wheat.*

According to the article, the bog oaks were up to 110 feet (34 metres) long and were resting on the subsoil, 3–5 feet (1–1.5 metres)

*The bog oak 'Table for the Nation' in the Lady Chapel of Ely Cathedral in March 2023.*

deep. The trunks lay in roughly the same direction and seem to have been laid low by a great prehistoric storm. The area known as Adventurers' Fen was much loved by the wildlife artist Eric Ennion, who wrote a book about the area and its wildlife. In 2001 the National Trust bought Burwell Fen Farm, and the area is now being restored to reedbed and marsh, with Ennion's book as a guide to what the area could be like once again.

Over the years many thousands of tonnes of these extraordinary sub-fossilised trees have been excavated and burnt to enable continued cultivation of the Fens. Indeed, in the absence of woodland, bog oak was an important asset for the farm workers and local villagers. Until quite recently, when central heating became common, the woody smell of burning bog oak was common in the villages. The better pieces of bog oak could be valuable for the fen farmer, and there was a good market for those pieces that could be made into furniture and carved decorative items such as jewellery. Bog oak has been used for small turnings and inlay details in furniture for hundreds of years, mainly because it was the only native black timber available. Indeed, one woodworking business in Kent is apparently still regularly milling, kiln-drying and making furniture from the oak. The oaks must be dried artificially to ensure a consistent rate of moisture extraction, a process which reduces the width and thickness of each plank by around one-third as it loses water.

A bog oak that has been transformed into a large sculptured table was unveiled at Ely Cathedral in May 2022 in honour of Queen Elizabeth II's Platinum Jubilee. The 13-metre-long table, large enough to seat fifty people, has been described as 'a table for the nation'. The Fenland Black Oak Project involved a team of craftspeople working to preserve the tree after it was unearthed in March 2012 by a Fenland farmer who hit an obstacle while ploughing a field. Cabinet maker and black oak specialist Hamish Low was immediately contacted to assess the viability of its preservation. Not only was this exceptional specimen considered suitable for preservation, it was also decided that its extraordinary length should be retained. The understructure of the table was constructed in bronze to reflect the fact that archaeologists refer to the centuries after 3000 BCE as the transition between the Stone and Bronze Ages.

The oldest accurately dated sample of bog oak in Britain and Ireland, however, is from a tree found on a farm in County Waterford by the landowner, Tom Joe Murphy, who unearthed it in 2016 when he was draining part of his land on the banks of the River Bride, near Knockanore. The blackened trunk, weighing over half a tonne, is all that is left of a once majestic oak that tumbled into a bog over 3,500 years ago. In 2018 Murphy sent a slice of the trunk to Queen's University Belfast for dating by research fellow David Brown. Amazingly, the analysis showed that the tree died late in 1048 BCE, or early in 1047 BCE, when it collapsed, possibly due to a storm. It was possible to be this accurate because the sapwood is complete and the bark surface was

*Tom Joe Murphy with the Knockanore Bog Oak, which died over 3,500 years ago, making it the oldest dendrochronologically dated bog oak in Britain and Ireland.*

present on the sample. Like other bog oaks, it was covered quickly with peat, which preserved the wood. The tree ring measurement taken from the sample was 605 years, indicating that the tree started growing in 1652 BCE. It is therefore an incredibly ancient tree and an important relic of the early forests which covered Ireland at this time.

A prehistoric storm also felled a yew tree which was found in 2018 during excavations in Dagenham. This part of London, alongside the River Thames, was once covered with forests but, again, rising sea levels flooded the area, drowning the trees. It seems that the yew died while it was standing, before a northwesterly gale caused it to fall into peat, where it was preserved by being waterlogged and sealed under silty clay. The find was especially important because the tree shows evidence of being hollowed out and cut using metal tools. Radiocarbon-dated to 2470–229 BCE, it belongs to the very early Bronze Age, when, for a period of only 300 years or so, copper tools were being used. This was a huge technological change from the previous use of stone and flint and a precursor to the development of bronze, an alloy of copper, tin and other metals. Archaeologists have suggested that the yew was intended to be a small boat, a coffin or even a drum, but it appears to have been discarded when faults were found in the timber. This part of the Thames estuary is rich in prehistoric finds, the most famous of which is the Dagenham Idol, a wooden human figure carved from Scots pine. It was found in 1922 during excavations for sewer pipes, only 750 metres west of where the yew was discovered. One of the oldest human representations found in Europe, it has been dated to the same period as the yew tree, so it is possible that the people who worked on the tree knew about it. Other Bronze Age wooden structures have been discovered in the area, including trackways similar to the Sweet Track in Somerset.

Between 3000 and 2400 BCE the cooler and wetter climate in Scotland also caused the water table there to rise, drowning the pine forests that had grown on the surface of blanket peat. Having advanced over the drying peat bogs as far as the north coast of Caithness and west to the islands of Skye, Rum and Lewis, there was a dramatic collapse in the range of the forest. Both in the newly occupied areas and in its Highland heartlands the species shrank back to much the same area that it occupies today, leaving substantial areas without large trees.

Like those found in the Fens, peat layers all over the Highlands contain the remains of tree trunks and stumps, and many Scottish legends seek to explain their presence. Their loss in Sutherland was attributed to a dragon, the 'Beast of the Charred Forests', which stalked over northern Scotland, incinerating trees as it went. This terrifying and powerful monster was said to have been born from a fire that burned for seven years, and to have lived throughout its life in fire. It met its match though when it encountered Saint Gilbert, Bishop of Caithness in the thirteenth century and the founder of Dornoch Cathedral, who promptly killed it with an arrow. The presence of apparently burnt pine stumps in the peat is said to be evidence of the Beast's ravages. In the Outer Hebrides, tales are told of a Norwegian princess who was said to have burned the pinewoods – the remnants of which can be seen in the peat near Scaladale at the head of Loch Seaforth – in anger at a foreign prince who spoke admiringly about the Harris woodlands, and not at all about her! It was thought that the trees were felled by people, since metal axe marks, later dated to the Early and Middle Bronze Age, had been found on pine stumps and branches, but the trees themselves were dead before any axe was used on them. The Scots pines of Lewis and Harris were the victims of one of the most dramatic climatic and environmental changes that Scotland has experienced since the retreat of the glaciers.

While in areas like East Anglia and Scotland whole forests were felled by environmental changes, elsewhere the Bronze Age is typified by temporary clearances in the valleys and lowlands, rather than permanent deforestation. Lime trees may have been selectively felled, possibly because they were an indicator of soils suitable for agriculture. In the uplands the impact was more noticeable, and there is evidence for large-scale clearance in places that are now designated as National Parks, such as Dartmoor, the Lake District and the North York Moors, exploitation reaching a peak towards the end of the period. Extensive areas of oak forest were cleared. This was a direct consequence of the introduction of metal, the bronze axe being a far more efficient tool for felling trees than its polished stone predecessor. At the same time, increasing numbers of sheep and cattle grazed the high ground, which prevented the forests recovering. Later on, in the middle of the Bronze Age, the climate began to deteriorate and people retreated from the uplands, taking their animals with them. and bogs and heathland spread over the former grazing areas. This pattern of forest clearance and the spread of heathland and bog also occurred in Ireland, with large areas of peat developing.

The full range of forest mammals present in the Mesolithic survived into the Bronze Age, with one exception, the elk. Shortly afterwards, aurochs also disappeared, and there are no records of the species anywhere in Britain after the Early Bronze Age. It is interesting that most of the later finds are from archaeological sites in England, so it seems that far from surviving longer in Scotland, as has been often claimed, they died out earlier in the north than the south. The extinction of the aurochs and a parallel decrease in the remains of wild animals found on archaeological sites must undoubtedly be a result of the increasing destruction of the forests. Red deer probably also declined due to the loss of their forest habitat, the species adapting to open moorland and, in the process, becoming smaller as a result of poorer nutrition. At this time, there was also an increase in species adapted to 'edge habitats', such as foxes, which were able to subsist on a variety of food. The spread of permanent agriculture on fixed fields, along with continued grazing by domestic animals

86                                    *Forgotten Forests*

in the remaining forests, also contributed to the pressure on native mammals.

In Ireland by the end of the Bronze Age, about 2,500 years ago, most of the hills had been cleared of forests by a combination of burning and cultivation, with blanket bogs replacing the trees. In the lowlands, clearance for cattle grazing continued, but the climate deteriorated and cultivation was replaced by forest regrowth. The climatic deterioration which began in the middle of the Bronze Age continued into the Iron Age, and, as a result, by this time there was much less forest remaining in many parts of Britain and Ireland. In particular there was a marked contrast in Britain between the south-east of England, which was already settled and farmed, and the rest of the country, where the forest was still more or less intact, apart from open moorland in the uplands, as described earlier. As the Iron Age progressed, however, large areas of forest were felled and the land farmed, often for long periods. *Culhwch ac Olwen*, the earliest Arthurian tale in Welsh, includes a graphic description of forest clearance by slash-and-burn agriculture. Before Culhwch can marry Olwen, he must first complete forty impossible tasks for her father Pencawr, the Chief Giant. He sets Culhwch his first task as follows:

> *Dost see the great thicket yonder? . . . I must have it uprooted out of the earth, and burnt on the face of the ground so that the cinders and ashes thereof be its manure; and that it be ploughed and sown so that it be ripe in the morning against the drying of the dew.*

The introduction of iron, the plough and an increasing number of sheep, allied to a fast-deteriorating climate, did not favour the regeneration of forests after they were cleared. Their disappearance in the Iron Age on a large scale is therefore a defining feature of the period. It produced a number of secondary effects, including soil being washed into rivers, a change in soil types, and the development of blanket bog in places where the forest cover had broken down. The removal of the trees even altered the course and flow of rivers. Studies of the Ripple Brook, near Tewkesbury on the River Severn, for example, suggest a time lag of 300–400 years between forest clearance and the deposition of sediments on the floodplain. Lowland floodplains had been relatively stable from the Late Mesolithic to the Late Bronze Age, a result of the presence of alder and hazel woodland, combined with less flooding than occurs at present. When these woodlands were cleared, along with the trees in the upper reaches of the watercourse, the build-up of sediments effectively fixed the course of the brook.

As well as being a destructive act, the felling of trees may have been seen as an act of renewal, through their transformation from tree to timber, which could then be used in many different contexts: perhaps as roof beams for a house, or to construct a boat. In August 1964 a very large piece of wood was dredged out of Poole Harbour in Dorset. It was located in 6–7 metres of water on the edge of the main shipping channel, 75 metres off

*The Poole logboat, now in Poole Museum, was constructed around 1,727 years ago from a huge tree, estimated to be at least 280–350 years old.*

88  *Forgotten Forests*

the current eastern shore of Brownsea Island. Two weeks later, divers from Bournemouth and Poole Sub-Aqua Club found another huge piece of timber. Laid side by side the two pieces formed the near-complete bottom of a prehistoric boat, some 10 metres long and hewn from a single oak log. The presence of substantial knots and a marked spiral grain, together with the fact that annual growth rings in the hull are fairly narrow (around two millimetres wide), as well as the boat's size, indicate that the vessel was constructed from a huge tree, at least 280–350 years old, with the first really substantial branches appearing as high as 9.5 metres above the ground. Radiocarbon dating revealed that it had been constructed in the Iron Age, around 295 BCE, and it is of great interest as very few prehistoric logboats have survived from this period.

The tree, a large old oak growing in dense woodland little affected by human activity, was, even by the standards of the trees modelled from the timbers found on other logboats, exceptionally large. It was surpassed in size though by the tree used to build a giant logboat that was found at Brigg in Lincolnshire in April 1886, by workmen constructing a gasometer alongside the River Ancholme. This boat was made from a single oak log 14.8 metres long and 1.4 metres wide. The felling and shaping of both logboats would have been a major undertaking, using small iron-bladed axes, wedges, levers and mallets. It has been estimated that at least five people, and possibly ten, would have been involved in the construction of the Poole logboat, which probably produced around five tonnes of firewood as a by-product.

Another large logboat, the Hasholme logboat, a Late Iron Age boat discovered in 1984 in East Yorkshire, was also constructed from a very large oak tree. After measurements of the hull were taken, it was estimated that the parent log was approximately 14 metres long and at least 5.4 metres in circumference. Based on the size of the oak and other measurements, it was suggested that this tree was between 810 and 880 years old when it was felled. Oaks

*Axes and Agriculture* 89

of such advanced age and size develop a rot known as 'brittle heart', which originates at the base and spreads upward. In the case of Hasholme, this rot had spread almost to the very top of the trunk. This meant that it was much easier to hollow it out, although the openings on both ends had to be closed and made watertight. It seems therefore that it was a deliberate choice to select a tree with extensive rot along its entire length, to save time in construction.

On 12 December 1881, the Society of Antiquaries of Scotland recorded the following donation to the National Museum of Antiquities of Scotland:

*Canoe, of oak, hollowed out of the bole of a tree. It measures 16 feet 3 inches in length, 3 feet wide at the stem, 2 feet wide at the bow, and 2 feet in depth of the side. It was discovered in 1874 by the accidental change of the course of the River Conon, opposite Dingwall. There had been a great flood, which carried away the sandhills and excavated a new channel at the point where a strong tidal current meets that of the stream. The canoe was found sticking out of the silt, about 8 feet below the surface of a bank of gravel.*

Prehistoric logboats like those found at Poole, Brigg and Hasholme are relatively rare, with most of the surviving examples dated to the medieval period. An analysis of the tree-ring pattern indicates that the Conon logboat was probably fashioned in the late thirteenth, or early fourteenth, century from a mature oak some 300 years old. Oaks of this age were also used to line wells in Elgin, and for the roof of Darnaway Castle, so there were clearly significant amounts of mature timber available at this time. In general though, the Scottish logboats are notably shorter than the English and Welsh examples, reflecting the scarcity of substantial lengths of oak.

Majestic oaks like those used to construct prehistoric logboats would have dwarfed even large modern trees and, along with bog oaks, provide a glimpse of what the lowland old-growth forests that used to cover vast areas of the countryside would have looked like. There are almost no trees like this left in Europe, since the primary forests have disappeared completely, but we can get an impression of what they looked like from a small number of forest areas that have had no major human impact for centuries. One of the best known of these is the Białowieża Forest World Heritage Site, a vast forest complex consisting of the remnants of several primeval forests: Białowieża Forest itself, Ladzka Forest, Świsłocka Forest and Szereszewska Forest. Home to the main European population of bison, our largest surviving land mammal, it straddles the border between Poland and Belarus. Because of its unique value, Białowieża Forest has been designated as a UNESCO World Heritage site and a Natura 2000 site and is protected by the EU Birds and Habitats Directives.

The forest contains a number of large, ancient pedunculate oaks, many approaching 40 metres in height. Many of these are named, such as the Tsar Oak, which died in 1984. Over 41 metres high, it still stands on the edge of the valley of the Leśna Prawa river.

*A fallen tree in the Białowieża Forest, Poland.*

*Axes and Agriculture* 91

Even though the trunk is totally devoid of bark and some of the branches have broken off and lie at the base of the trunk, it remains an impressive sight. In contrast, the Emperor of the South is 40 metres high and is still in good health. Large areas also consist of bog, marsh and alder swamp, and it is an amazingly dynamic environment, with storm events and the actions of humans and animals creating small clearances, but these rarely endure for any length of time. The composition of species here is not an exact replica of the forests that existed in prehistory in northern Europe, but it provides a closer model than the lightly wooded areas that exist today in Britain and Ireland. Other similar areas include the Rotwald, near Lunz in Austria, or the so-called Bannwälder, established by the forest administration of Baden-Württemberg, Germany, in the nineteenth century.

Since the emergence of modern humans around 300,000 years ago, the average size of herbivores has decreased 100-fold and carnivores 10-fold, due to the loss of very large animals such as straight-tusked elephants. Sadly, at the current rates of extinction, within 300 years only a few land mammals larger than a domestic cow might survive. Human predation has effectively reduced the size of many species, and, perhaps surprisingly, this includes trees as well as animals. The tree from which the Jubilee Oak table exhibited in Ely Cathedral was constructed is estimated, for example, to have been around 55 metres high, only slightly shorter than the cathedral itself, which is 66 metres high. It was a giant compared to present-day oaks, the largest of which are only about 20 metres in height. While trees in the forests of South America are still large and impressive, we are unlikely to see their like again in Britain and Ireland. The bog oaks and logboats bear witness to what we have lost. At the time of the Roman invasion of Britain, however, there were still extensive areas of ancient forests in both Britain and Ireland, and while the story to date has depended almost entirely on the information provided by archaeology, with the arrival of the Romans it comes into contact with historical sources for the first time.

# CHAPTER 4

# *What the Romans Did for Forests*

*All kinds of wood are found here, as in Gaul, except the beech and fir trees.*

Julius Caesar, *De Bello Gallico*

In 2000, echoing a memorable scene from *Monty Python's Life of Brian*, a BBC documentary series called *What the Romans Did for Us* looked at the innovations and inventions brought to Britain by the Romans. For centuries, Rome's colonial legacy in Britain has been considered through the remains of military frontiers, roads, mosaics and pottery, and the programme reinforced this view, but in recent decades archaeologists have started to examine the environmental changes of the Roman period.

In the course of his Gallic Wars, Julius Caesar temporarily invaded Britain twice, in 55 and 54 BCE, and is said to have considered it to be 'one horrible forest'. In his *Commentaries*, which were propaganda to increase his popularity back in Rome, he commented that the Britons' idea of a town was simply a place enclosed by a rampart and ditch in a thick woodland. In the popular Roman imagination Britain was a place of forest and marsh, mist and drizzle, inhabited by ferocious blue-painted warriors. Only Ireland, which was never invaded by the Romans, was considered to be worse, a country that the historian and senator Tacitus called Hibernia, the Land of Winter.

Caesar's view of Britain as an unending forest is not really accurate, as we have seen from the preceding chapters, and he was almost certainly exaggerating the horrors for his audience, but the Romans generally had negative views about forests. Indeed, they believed that the entrance to Hades, the underworld, was through a forest. Centuries later, in 1320, the Italian poet Dante Alighieri, in his epic poem *The Divine Comedy*, began his journey into the underworld by travelling through a dark, shadowy, wood. Ironically, many Roman gods were associated with individual trees. The chief god of Rome, for instance, Jupiter Feretrius, was worshipped in the form of a sacred tree, in all probability an oak. Trees also became a symbol of conquest. Species considered to be foreign were imported and exhibited in Rome, being incorporated into the cityscape just like the statues looted from territories that had been subdued.

The third, successful, invasion of Britain, which began in 43 CE, was prompted both by the Emperor Claudius's need for a successful military campaign to secure his position and by the desire to exploit the island's natural resources. The Romans also aimed to civilise the barbarians in the name of *humanitas*, which included changing landscapes as well. Tertullian, 'the father of Latin Christianity', described this process at the end of the second century as follows:

> *Surely it is obvious enough, if one looks at the whole world, that it is becoming daily better cultivated and more fully peopled than anciently. All places are now accessible, all are well known, all open to commerce; most pleasant farms have obliterated all traces of what were once dreary and dangerous wastes; cultivated fields have subdued forests; flocks and herds have expelled wild beasts; sandy deserts are sown; rocks are planted; marshes are drained; and where once were hardly solitary cottages, there are now large cities.*

The 'most pleasant farms' were Roman villas. This subjugation and control of nature, the creation of a habitable landscape from somewhere that was considered inhospitable, was a key part of Roman engagement with the world, as the empire sought to control both the people and the land itself. Their relationships with nature were typically aggressive, and they viewed the management of land, and even farming itself, as a noble form of warfare. Imperial landscapes did not tolerate forests, wastes, deserts, rocks and marshes, as these were symbols of barbarism. There were some dissenting voices – the Stoic philosopher Seneca, for example, challenged the levelling of forests and the alteration of nature in general – but the destruction continued relentlessly.

Examples of vanished forests mentioned in the classical literature range from a region of giant trees in Egypt, described by the Roman author and naturalist Pliny the Elder, to the woods of Sicily and Spain, whose loss was chronicled by Diodorus, an

*A scene from Trajan's Column, showing Roman troops clearing a forest at the edge of which more soldiers assemble. The carved figures would once have been painted and held small metal axes.*

ancient Greek historian. Strabo, another Greek, complained that the forests around Pisa were being consumed in order to construct public and private buildings in Rome. Trajan's Column in Rome, erected in the emperor's forum complex by 113 CE as a monument to his successful Dacian Wars in Romania, is decorated with a helical relief that shows the detail of these campaigns. The column's depiction of the Roman army in a foreign landscape includes deforestation or tree-felling scenes, which usually then lead into scenes illustrating the construction of forts. The Roman soldiers are seen taking control of the foreign landscape, moulding it to their purpose, and urbanising their surroundings, in contrast to their Dacian enemies. Trajan's Column neatly summarises the complexity of Rome's relationship with trees, and shows that the Dacian campaigns were not simply battles between an urban emperor and a forest king but, once again, a war on the landscape, with the felled timber swiftly utilised by the empire. In almost every corner of the Roman Empire a dramatic deforestation was taking place, creating, for instance, the most visible, far-reaching, and relatively permanent changes in the Mediterranean landscape caused by human activities in ancient times.

The historian Edward Gibbon, whose six-volume work *The History of the Decline and Fall of the Roman Empire* was published between 1776 and 1788, also used forests to emphasise the savagery and danger of the indigenous peoples. Attacks from barbarians came from forests as a contrast to the civilisation of walled towns and forts. His writing is littered with comments such as 'the crafty barbarians, who had lined the woods, suddenly attacked the legions'. Indeed, the phrase 'woods and morasses' occurs repeatedly throughout his work as a means of emphasising the barbarity of native people compared with Roman civilisation. The clearance of forests and the drainage of marshland were regarded by Gibbon as acts of improvement, just as they were in his own time.

Despite the fact that Rome grew to rely on timber from the

empire, the British forests that were still in existence when the Romans arrived largely survived, probably because of the distance from Rome and the challenge of shipping timber across the English Channel. Elsewhere, timber was regularly transported great distances. Buried in the foundations of an ancient villa in the centre of Rome, for example, are planks from trees that travelled more than a thousand miles from the French forest where they grew, a journey that involved floating them down rivers and transporting them across the Mediterranean.

The distinction in Latin between firewood (*lignum*) and construction timber (*materia*) suggests the critical role wood played in Roman civilisation. Indeed, it was so important that the ancient Romans considered it as signifying matter, or substance, in the modern sense of the word 'material'. Wood was the most important fuel in the Roman world, and, together with stone and cement, remained an essential construction material. Its abundance, or absence, could materially affect a state's ability to wage war and to trade. The importance of wood is also reflected in the *Natural History* written by Pliny the Elder. He recognised the importance of forests for human existence, and devoted Books XII to XVI of his work entirely to trees.

Archaeological excavations of first-century waterfront wharf sites in London have revealed that many were built using Late Iron Age oaks shaped into massive squared quay beams. As mentioned above, the Romans thought nothing of felling some of the ancient forests they had just acquired. For example, in 60 CE, less than twenty years after the successful Roman invasion, Paulinus, governor of the new province, marched on the sacred Welsh island of Mona, now known as Anglesey, with an army. Tacitus famously described the scene as follows:

*On the shore stood the opposing army with its dense array of armed warriors, while between the ranks dashed women, in black attire like the Furies, with hair dishevelled, waving brands. All around, the Druids, lifting up their hands to heaven, and pouring forth dreadful imprecations, scared our soldiers by the unfamiliar sight, so that, as if their limbs were paralysed, they stood motionless, and exposed to wounds. Then urged by their general's appeals and mutual encouragements not to quail before a troop of frenzied women, they bore the standards onwards, smote down all resistance, and wrapped the foe in the flames of his own brands. A force was next set over the conquered, and their groves, devoted to inhuman superstitions, were destroyed.*

Even centuries later, a royal writ issued in 1284 by Edward I to Geoffrey Clement and Brother Madoc, a lay brother of Strata Florida Abbey in the Cambrian Mountains, while disguised as an instruction to protect travellers from ambush, was clearly driven by a wish to destroy significant spiritual groves:

*Appointment to fell the groves (nemora) about the frequented roads in the woods (boscis) and to enlarge the passes through those woods in county Cardigan, as they shall see fit for the security of travellers by the counsel of lawful men of those parts, as the king considers that damages and perils may threaten men passing through divers places within that county unless the groves about the roads be felled as above.*

The locations of the ancient Anglesey groves are unfortunately not recorded – and this is typical of accounts written at the time – but some Roman texts do provide useful environmental data. There are severe doubts nevertheless about the Caledonian Forest referred to by a number of writers, including Claudius Ptolemy, astronomer and geographer of the Roman world, as a major feature of the Scottish landscape. On a medieval map based on Ptolemy's *Geographia*, an atlas of the Roman Empire, there is an area named *Caledonia Silva*. Covered with tree symbols, it stretches from Loch Lomond to the Beauly Firth, but the boundaries are vague and uncertain.

In the *Matter of Britain*, a body of medieval literature and legends associated with Britain and Brittany, the Caledonian Forest is the site of one of King Arthur's Twelve Battles. The battle here is called Cat Coit Celidon, a name derived from the Gaelic *Coile Dun*, meaning 'woodland fortress'. It has been suggested that the army of trees animated by sorcerers in the Old Welsh poem *Cad Goddeu* ('Battle of the Trees') is intended to be the Caledonian Forest. J. R. R. Tolkien was apparently familiar with *Cad Goddeu*, and this may have been the inspiration for the tree-army that engages in battle with demonic forces in the *Lord of the Rings*. Related literature about Merlin, collected in the *Black Book of Carmarthen*, also states that Myrddin Wyllt is said to have retreated to the forest after the Battle of Arfderydd in the year 573. He was fleeing from the wrath of Rhydderch Hael, King of Strathclyde, after the slaying of Gwenddoleu ap Ceidio, who ruled what is now southwest Scotland and northwest England.

Frank Fraser Darling, an English ecologist who was nevertheless strongly associated with the Scottish Highlands, lamented the destruction of what he called the Old Wood of Caledon in his book *Natural History in the Highlands and Islands*, which was published as part of the Collins New Naturalist series in 1947. He mentions that the great Caledonian Forest extended 'from Glen Lyon and Rannoch to Strathspey and Strathglass and from Glencoe eastwards to the Braes of Mar'. Fraser Darling goes on to say that 'The imagination of a naturalist can conjure up a picture of what the great forest was like: the present writer is inclined to look upon it as his idea of heaven and to feel a little rueful that he was born too late to "go native" in its recesses.' The legendary forest is nowadays identified with the relics of ancient pinewoods that survive in a number of Highland glens, and Fraser Darling's imaginary forest appears, unfortunately, to be just that – a fantasy.

Reports and maps from the various military campaigns in Scotland between 71 and 221 CE do describe a large area of uninviting woodland, but it cannot be taken to mean that Scotland as a whole was still heavily forested at this time. It might only be a generalised reference to a heavily wooded and impenetrable region that the Romans encountered in the central and eastern Highlands. While they have left us with the first written descriptions of forests in Scotland, and indeed more generally in Britain, it must also be remembered that these originate in narrative accounts written by a number of commentators, such as Tacitus, who were describing military campaigns. It is important therefore not to place too much reliance on these sources. Like Caesar, these later Roman writers must have had an incentive to exaggerate the wildness and impenetrability of the landscape through which the army was campaigning, in order to add honour to victories and explain away defeats. So, while they created the impression that in their time Scotland was covered by deep and extensive forests,

*The 'Old Work' at Wroxeter in Shropshire, the surviving seven-metre-high south wall of the basilica, is the largest free-standing Roman wall in England. The earliest defences of the city are estimated to have consumed 36,000 tonnes of timber.*

there never was a vast Caledonian Forest in the Roman period, certainly not in the form it has often been described. Indeed, by the time the Romans arrived over half of Scotland's native forests had disappeared, partly as a result of the cooler, wetter climate which had developed, and partly because of human activities.

On their European frontiers the Romans initially built forts using wood, and after their invasion of Britain they constructed several hundred, mostly on a square plan. Trajan's Column testifies to the importance of timber, mostly oaks in this case, in Roman fortifications of the early empire. Reliefs on the column also suggest that a timber rampart-walk and breastwork could be present. In the end, direct Roman occupation of southern Scotland did not last more than forty years, but the empire successfully dominated the country beyond the fixed frontiers for most of that time, employing raids, bribery and the establishment of client states to achieve a level of influence and control. The extent of the indirect Roman pressure on the forests is unknown, but it is likely that they bought timber from areas that lay far beyond the land they occupied.

Roman forts and other military installations certainly required large quantities of wood. Some of these forts, such as the temporary legionary fortress at Inchtuthil, which was situated on a natural platform overlooking the north bank of the River Tay, were large, with sides of 500 metres and covering an area of 20 hectares. It is thought that the fortress required over 100 hectares of forest to supply its walling and other structures. The forest would probably have regrown after the Romans left, since grazing and other pressures were low. Similarly, it has been estimated that the Roman fortress at Chester required 32,000 tonnes of timber for its construction, excluding brushwood for fuelling furnaces and kilns, the equivalent of a minimum of 104 hectares of mature woodland. In Shropshire the early defences of Wroxeter (Viroconium), once the fourth-largest city in Roman Britain and almost the same size as Pompeii in Italy, are calculated to have required the felling of some 36,000 tonnes of timber.

## What the Romans Did for Forests 101

Some useful details of the preparation of structural timbers have been revealed at Caerleon in south Wales, where the framework of an officer's house was built of oak posts of uniform size, with off-site preparation being suggested by the lack of wood chippings. A typical fort in Roman Britain only covered about two hectares, and was built in a clearing of around five hectares. Apart from military requirements, one of the main considerations in choosing a site was a suitable timber supply. Structural timbers alone for an average-sized fort in Roman Britain required felling between six and twelve hectares of mature forest. For about a century and a half, Roman authority rested on these wooden strongholds.

The occupying forces also constructed ships, bridges, temporary roads and siege towers out of the trees they felled, and of course they used wood for fuel, as did the native populations. As timber was a crucial component of Rome's military power, especially when combined with their engineering expertise, the associated trades were highly specialised, including those involved in ship-building. There is a surviving Roman barge in the Arles Museum of Antiquity in France. Around 31 metres in length, and constructed of large slabs of oak, it is typical of flat-bottomed river trading vessels.

Even after the Romans started to use stone to build their forts, timber was still needed for buildings, scaffolding and roofs. They may be famous for their roads, but it was the archaeological excavations ahead of the improvement of a modern road, the A14 from Cambridge to Huntingdon, that revealed evidence of one of the few securely dated Roman timber structures built using elm. The enormous elm posts, carbon-dated to 120–240 CE, had survived in wet ground near the village of Orford Cluny. They would have supported the roof of a large aisled building, perhaps a substantial barn or hall. In the areas around Hadrian's Wall and the Antonine Wall, two major linear fortifications in the north of England and southern Scotland, forests were felled to clear the route and provide the material for their construction. At Fozy Moss

*The 2,000-year-old Roman barge in the Arles Museum of Antiquity in France, constructed from huge slabs of oak.*

in Northumberland the land was almost completely deforested around 125 CE, and the settlements associated with Hadrian's Wall required farmland until the fourth century. Organised agriculture was essential to sustain armies and towns and there was a well-organised market, concerned with the collection, distribution and sale of produce.

Several different iron hand saws were manufactured in the Iron Age, but the Romans developed long two-handled saws for the conversion of felled timber. In addition, the range of Roman forestry implements included the basic *securis*, the woodman's axe, with a convex cutting edge, the sides of the blade more or less concave in profile, and wedge-shaped in section. Heavy long-handled axes were used for felling, and lighter short-handled types for splitting logs, chopping out roots and making stakes. Other forest tools included the *dolabella* (a small short-handled hatchet), the *serrula* (a small saw, often a pruning saw), and the *falx arboraria* (the common billhook with a curved blade, used for lopping trees). It is likely that one of the main uses of the billhooks and slashers was for lopping branches of certain tree species to provide winter feed for cattle. The lopping of elm to provide fodder for livestock was, as we have seen, probably one of the reasons for its decline in an earlier period.

Overall, it appears that there was a further reduction in forest cover in the Roman period but there was also considerable regional variation. In southeast England, for example, it appears that little forest remained, with limited amounts of oak and hazel on the drier land. In central Essex there are two roads, remarkably straight and parallel to each other, about 12 kilometres apart, which are aligned about 25 or 26 degrees east of north. One road, the B184, sometimes called the Suffolk Way, runs straight for six kilometres from the district called The Rodings and continues, less clearly, through Great Bardfield and Finchingfield

*Hadrian's Wall near Housesteads Fort, the most complete example of a Roman fort in Britain. Forests were felled to clear the route of the wall and provide material for construction.*

104         *Forgotten Forests*

heading towards Clare in Suffolk. The other road, which now forms part of the A131 between Chelmsford and Braintree, begins at Little Waltham, north of Chelmsford, and runs straight for almost 20 kilometres through Braintree towards Gosfield, where the straight section ends. Neither road appears to connect with nearby Roman sites, or indeed other Roman roads. They are ancient tracks and appear on a map of Essex drawn by Hans Woutneel, the earliest known London print seller, in 1602. It has been suggested that these roads are a rare example of Roman 'centuriation' or land-surveying, carried out by the *territorium* of the nearby municipality of Colchester. The area between the two roads coincides almost exactly with an area of medium loam soil, a mixture of clay, sand and silt that is fertile, well drained and easily worked. It has been suggested therefore that it represents a site marked out for large-scale deforestation, to prepare the land for agriculture.

From the second through the fourth centuries, the population of Roman Britain has been estimated at approximately 3.5 million people. In his book *The End of Roman Britain*, Michael Jones argued that feeding this number of people would have put considerable strain on the landscape. Up to 240 square kilometres would have been required just to feed the 50,000 or so soldiers stationed in Britain in the first century. As some forests had already been cleared before the Roman invasion, especially in southern England and Wales, there were already considerable areas of cultivated land available. The Romans undertook additional clearances, however, particularly in northern England and the area around Hadrian's Wall, and opened up new arable land in higher areas, while the forests in eastern Scotland, north of the Antonine Wall, were able to regenerate.

Wentwood, near Newport in south Wales, once formed part of a much larger forest stretching between the Usk and Wye valleys, dividing the former county of Gwent into Gwent Uwch-coed ('Gwent above the wood') and Gwent Is-coed ('Gwent below the wood'). It may even have reached as far as the Forest of Dean in Gloucestershire. Pollen studies here indicate that in the Roman period there was a mixed broadleaved forest dominated by oak and hazel, with alder growing on wetter soils. It was an important source of timber for the invading army, large quantities being required to support the military presence at Caerleon and the growing populations at sites such as Usk and Caerwent. Later, between the third and fifth centuries, there is evidence of widespread regeneration, probably reflecting land-use changes as a result of the abandonment of settlements. Most villas and lower-status sites in southeast Wales appear to have been abandoned by the mid-fourth century, including those on the Gwent Levels.

There were other demands on the forests, including the felling of trees to fuel furnaces producing iron. The Romans were themselves an Iron Age culture, though their demands were much greater than what had gone before, with the industrial-scale smelting of a wide variety of metal ores requiring large quantities of wood. As a result, the centres of mining and metal smelting became, at least temporarily, the most deforested areas of the Roman Empire. One of the most important areas of iron production in Britain was the Weald, the area later described in the Anglo-Saxon Chronicle for 893 as 'the great wood which we call Andred'. When the Romans invaded, they found a well-established local tradition of iron making here, using small clay furnaces. With the growing markets produced by the building of towns, villas and farms, the Romans encouraged these native enterprises. In fact, the size and importance of the iron industry here, together with the absence of any large settlements, has led to the suggestion that the region may have formed an Imperial Estate, restricting civilian exploitation. It comprised two main groups of ironworks, a western 'private' zone and an eastern area which was linked to the Roman fleet (the *Classis Britannica*). In addition, the forest probably acted as a boundary between the tribal territories of the Regni and the Cantiaci (or Cantii) who occupied the modern counties of Sussex and Kent respectively and had their capitals at Chichester and Canterbury.

Around 500 tonnes of Roman military ironwork were produced every year from the furnaces in the Weald. At a site near Bardown, where it was calculated that seven or eight furnaces would have been in operation in order to produce the estimated annual output of 40–45 tonnes of iron, some 13–15 hectares of forest would have to be cleared to produce sufficient charcoal. Although coppicing may well have been practised, which would have required a smaller area, the amount of timber that had to be cut and turned into charcoal would remain the same – nearly 6,000 tonnes. A very large amount indeed, compared with the quantity of iron produced but, for the most part, the forest survived more or less intact.

The Romans also brought many new species to Britain, including at least fifty new sources of food, mainly fruits, herbs and vegetables. We will probably never know the full range of plants that they deliberately, or inadvertently, introduced. Amongst the trees, it is

*Sweet chestnut coppice in the Forest of Dean at Beechenhurst, Gloucestershire.*

often said that the two main introduced species were walnut and sweet chestnut, but while sweet chestnut has been regarded as a Roman introduction for at least three centuries, it now seems that this is incorrect. Rob Jarman from the University of Gloucestershire and Historic England examined written reports, together with specimens from museum archives that had previously been identified as Roman. Rob found that most of these species had been misidentified, or that the dates they had been assigned could not be confirmed. During the project, only one example was definitely linked with Roman Britain, peelings from around five sweet chestnuts found at the Roman site of Great Holts Farm, in Boreham, Essex. They were, however, in food waste that also included olives, pine nuts and Mediterranean fish bones, so may have been part of a consignment of exotic food imported from mainland Europe.

It was John Evelyn (1620–1706), author of *Sylva*, the first comprehensive study of British trees, who originally promoted the Roman theory, but while his view was 'formalised' following a crucial debate in the Royal Society in 1769–1771 the earliest written record of sweet chestnut growing in Britain is to be found in a charter dated 1113. In this, Robert de Candos gave land and woodland and other assets to the newly founded Goldcliff Priory in Monmouthshire, and the description of the boundary of the property includes '. . . *ad castaneam, et de castanea* . . .' ('. . . to the chestnut, and from the chestnut . . .'). The second-oldest written record of sweet chestnut, dating from 1145, appears in another charter, this time from Roger Earl of Hereford, granting land (assarts) to William de Dene, '*et nominatem essarta de Chestiard*', in a place called 'Castiard' in the Forest of Dean in Gloucestershire. Since they were being used as landmarks, it seems that sweet chestnuts were very rare trees in Britain, even up to the Norman period, but the species is now considered as an 'honorary native', occurring across southern Britain in semi-natural ancient woodlands on suitably acidic, free-draining soils.

It has also been suggested that what was once the most widespread species of British elm, English elm, derives from a single clone that the Romans transported from Italy to the Iberian peninsula, and from there to Britain, for the purpose of supporting and training vines. Some people consider that the English elm was introduced during the Bronze Age, but it does resemble the elm that was used for vine-training by the Romans. In his treaty *De Re Rustica* (written in about 50 CE), the Roman agronomist Columella advocated the use of elm for this purpose, recommending in particular a barren tree that was vegetatively propagated, the Atinian elm. The clone was probably transported to Britain in the form of root suckers, the combination of elm and vine pollen from the vineyard at Wollaston, Northamptonshire, almost certainly indicating the use of elm to train vines.

Robert Witcher of Durham University has argued that the presence of four grains of elm pollen on a Roman site does not demonstrate that elm was a Roman introduction; nor does its presence at a vineyard mean that elm was used to support vines. He also maintains that the similar distributions of elm and Roman vineyards across southeast Britain are far from conclusive, as the majority of all our introduced species are concentrated in this region. Whatever its origin, the Atinian elm's highly efficient vegetative reproduction and its inability to set seeds preserved this clone unaltered for 2,000 years as the core of the English elm population. In contrast, the native wych elm and southern wych elm are highly fertile and readily reproduce from seed. The outbreak of Dutch elm disease in the 1970s ravaged European elm populations, killing more than 25 million trees in Britain alone, but its greatest impact was on the English elm, and the preponderance of this susceptible variety may have favoured the rapid spread of the disease.

Alongside the ecological changes created by the Romans there were also climatic changes. During the Roman era the weather in Europe was unusually warm, some 2–6 degrees warmer than today. This was why the Romans managed to grow grapes in northern

England. About 40 CE, however, there was a shift to wetter, colder weather in Britain, a deterioration that intensified after the year 450. By the late Roman period, there may have been as much as a 10 per cent increase in rainfall. These new areas of cultivation were increasingly vulnerable as the climate deteriorated, especially in the Highlands. As a result, around the year 400, clearing was discontinued, and numerous fields abandoned, so that scrub spread, and in some areas the forests could partially recover and expand again.

In the mid-1950s the local historian W. G. Hoskins repeated the long-held view that the end of Roman administration was followed by the regrowth, in England at least, of damp forests of oak and ash. Later, this opinion came under attack from researchers who suggested instead that there was relatively little change. Oliver Rackham's view was that woodland certainly increased locally, 'but there is no sign of a general or overwhelming increase'. It appears now that Hoskins was essentially correct, as evidence continues to accumulate of the large-scale abandonment of cultivated land at the end of the Roman occupation and a gradual return to woodland and forest in the fifth and sixth centuries.

For many centuries the area in Northamptonshire later known to the Anglo-Saxons as Whittlewood Forest (the 'wood of Witela') was mainly an open landscape of arable and pasture, with restricted, and probably heavily managed, areas of woodland. Following the departure of the Romans it was abandoned, analysis of pollen samples revealing the regeneration of the woodland in the period 400–600 CE. Its spread across former agricultural land is also demonstrated by the fact that much of the medieval and post-medieval woodland covered the remains of fields, which have yielded significant quantities of Roman pottery. A decline in woodland cover during the early Roman period and subsequent regeneration during the late Roman and early medieval periods, has in fact been reported for many parts of northwestern Europe. Studies of a site in northern Belgium, for example, showed that

110  *Forgotten Forests*

the abandoned fields were first covered with pioneer woodland consisting of willow, hazel and birch, then a secondary forest dominated by oak, and finally a forest containing beech, hornbeam and holly, an evolution that took over 300 years.

Much of the great Northumbrian wood which was called Cocwudu, an early form of the name we now know as Coquet, was probably secondary woodland. Largely formed after the abandonment of pasture and arable lands at the end of the Roman period, by trees self-seeding from established woodland, it covered the area between the rivers Coquet and Wansbeck. It has been suggested by the Bernician Studies Group, which researches the Northumberland landscape, that it formed a 'Dark Age borderland, a territory of brigands, outcasts and wild animals'. Today it is a typical landscape of pastures and fields, small woods, winding lanes and open views, but one with a secret past, like most of the places described in this book.

Whatever the truth, stories of Roman fields and settlements being abandoned and becoming overgrown have entered popular imagination, even being included in children's books. Rosemary Sutcliff, for instance, set three of her four great historical novels for children – *The Eagle of the Ninth*, *The Silver Branch* and *The Lantern Bearers* – during the last years of the Roman occupation of Britain. Together they provide a graphic picture of the decline of imperial power. Similarly, in *The Wind in the Willows* the Badger, who lives in an extensive sett incorporating the remains of a buried Roman settlement, explains that:

*'Well, very long ago, on the spot where the Wild Wood waves now, before ever it had planted itself and grown up to what it now is, there was a city – a city of people, you know . . .'*

*'When they went,' continued the Badger, 'the strong winds and persistent rains took the matter in hand, patiently, ceaselessly, year after year . . . It was all down, down, down, gradually – ruin and levelling and*

*disappearance. Then it was all up, up, up, gradually, as seeds grew to saplings, and saplings to forest trees, and bramble and fern came creeping in to help. Leaf-mould rose and obliterated, streams in their winter freshets brought sand and soil to clog and to cover, and in course of time our home was ready for us again, and we moved in.'*

So the wild wood of Kenneth Grahame's story was actually what would now be called secondary woodland and not an ancient forest. Peter Ackroyd in his book *Thames: Sacred River* has suggested, however, that Grahame's inspiration came from Quarry Wood, part of the ancient Bisham Woods bordering the Thames at Cookham Dean in Berkshire, where he lived. Indeed, according to the Woodland Trust, who now own the site, it may actually have formed part of Britain's original forest. Most of the woodland consists of beech high forest and, as such, it is a southern outlier of the Chiltern beechwoods.

The declining agricultural production that was a result of the deteriorating climate must have had profound consequences. It is even possible that the raids by Picts and Scots were influenced by climatic change, since the worsening weather would have been most intensely felt by those tribes in the north and west. The Picts beyond Hadrian's Wall may have experienced conditions considerably more severe than those in the south of England, and the Scots, in Ireland, would also have had more inclement weather to deal with. The literary evidence is flimsy, but a deterioration in climate would have increased Britain's social and economic problems and made it vulnerable to attack. Certainly, this is the impression conveyed by Gildas, the sixth-century British monk and writer, who, a hundred years later, records an oral tradition of invasion, famine and social revolt.

In the year 410, after almost four centuries of Roman rule, the embattled Roman emperor Honorius apparently issued a declaration that the Britons needed to look to their own defence. This was part of a wider move in the fifth century to a post-Roman society across Europe, as the imperial influence waned. At this time there was also a movement of 'barbarians' into Roman territory. These Germanic migrants are usually called 'Anglo-Saxons' even though neither they, nor anyone else, referred to them by that name. Some did call themselves *Angelcynn* ('Angle kind'), however, because their ancestors came from *Angeln*, or Schleswig-Holstein, on the Danish frontier. The Romans had employed the Saxons from northwest Germany as mercenaries for hundreds of years, preferring to fight alongside them rather than against them.

Following the departure of the Roman army, to the west and north British kings continued to rule over large independent kingdoms, with populations wholly, or largely, descended from those of Roman Britain. It was the Anglo-Saxons, however, who brought a new approach to trees and forests. No written sources from the period provide a detailed description of the environment at this time, so any account has to be pieced together out of evidence from many sources: documentary, archaeological and ecological.

# CHAPTER 5

# *A Reliable Resource*

*Alfred rode to the stone of Egbert, in the eastern part of the wood called Selwood, which means in Latin Silva Magna, the great Wood, but in British Coit Mawr.*

Asserius Menevensis, *The Life of King Alfred*

The stone buildings constructed by the Romans were largely ignored by the Anglo-Saxons, but they often reused materials in the construction of their churches. One of the best examples of this approach is the Anglo-Saxon crypt preserved below Hexham Abbey in Northumberland, which was constructed from stones robbed from the remains of the Roman fort and town a few miles away at Corbridge. For the most part unchanged in 1,300 years, the crypt is the only part of the original church built by Bishop Wilfrid that survives intact. Stone was regarded by the Anglo-Saxons as the material of the giants of the past, in contrast to the human beings living in the present. The phrase 'work of giants' occurs several times in surviving Old English poetry; it is always used to describe ancient stone buildings, and in every case it functions as a symbol of age and durability.

While the Anglo-Saxons freely recycled the 'work of giants', their society was one in which trees were critically important. Like

114                          *Forgotten Forests*

previous cultures, they dwelt in timber houses and created a material culture using wood, which was more important than the intricate sculptures and metalwork with which we associate them today (such as the Staffordshire Hoard, the largest hoard of Anglo-Saxon gold and silver metalwork found to date). Michael Shapland, a buildings archaeologist, has suggested that the division between timber and stone buildings may represent their distinct functions, 'the one being a place for the living, whose perishable timbers shadow the lives of humans clustered beneath their rafters, whilst the other, the house of God and the temporal locus of the eternal Church, is fittingly constructed from eternal stone'.

In line with this, the archaeological evidence suggests that their timber buildings were not generally repaired or replaced. The majority either remained structurally sound until they were abandoned, or no effort was made to prolong their life. There is also remarkably little evidence that major timbers were salvaged and reused. Anglo-Saxon timber buildings may therefore have been perceived as temporary, perhaps being abandoned after the death of their inhabitants. This is fitting, considering that trees were often associated with the human body, and the human body was earthly and perishable.

Not all Anglo-Saxon churches were 'fittingly constructed from eternal stone', as described by Shapland, and at least one timber building has survived almost intact. At Greensted-juxta-Ongar in Essex, for instance, the church uniquely includes an early-eleventh-century nave made of split oak trunks. There is no evidence to indicate how common wooden churches were and therefore no way of determining the proportion of wooden to stone churches at any one time. The tradition of wooden churches is documented by the Venerable Bede, the greatest of all the Anglo-Saxon scholars, who refers to their presence at Lindisfarne and York. Likewise, William of Malmesbury, another scholarly monk, suggests that King Alfred's church at Athelney, constructed on a small island in the Somerset Levels, was also made of wood. Additionally, a wooden church is referred to in the *Memorials of St Edmunds Abbey*, edited by Thomas Arnold, whose father was headmaster of Rugby School. All of these churches were nothing like their successors. They were humble, unpretentious and purely functional, their purpose simply being to protect the altar, the priests and the congregation from the worst of the weather. There must have been thousands of them in existence by the time of the Norman Conquest. The church at Greensted illustrates the large amounts of timber needed for the walls, the structure consuming the surviving portions of thirty trees, split into sixty halves. The roofing timbers and tie beams accounted for more trees, as well as slender poles from managed woodlands.

Again, in Essex, the north doorway of St Botolph's church in Hadstock is thought to date from around 1020, the date of its consecration, which was apparently attended by King Cnut (perhaps better known as Canute, who attempted to resist the incoming tide). The door itself has been dated to around 1034–42; it consists of

*The nave of St Andrew's Church at Greensted-juxta-Ongar in Essex is said to be the oldest wooden church in the world and the oldest 'stave built' timber building in Europe.*

116                     *Forgotten Forests*

plain oak boards joined by undecorated bands of iron on the front
which are riveted through to wooden bars on the back. The oldest
door still in use in England, it was formerly covered in cowhide.
High-status doors such as those in churches were often covered with
animal hide – but in this case local folklore has it that the hide
came from a Viking who was flayed alive as a punishment for
raiding the church. Similar stories of so-called 'Daneskins' are
associated with doors at Copford, another Essex church, and
Westminster Abbey in London. The tree from which the door at
Hadstock was constructed was reasonably large, as the widest board
is 37 centimetres wide. As the boards were cut 'on the quarter', to
minimise warping, the tree must have been nearly 80 centimetres
in diameter, once allowance is made for the thickness of the bark.
There is apparently no evidence of sawpits in the Anglo-Saxon
period, so the tree must have been 'cleaved' into planks, wedges
being driven into the end so that it split along the grain.

There are also references to wooden churches in Ireland, and
although not a single one survives there is plenty of information
about their design. Some were obviously quite sizeable, as indicated
by a shocking entry in the Annals of Ulster for 850, which records
the burning to death of 260 people in a wooden church at Trevet
in County Meath. Clues can also be gleaned from paintings and
sculptures. A *dairthech*, or wooden church, was worth the equivalent
of ten heifers, but if the roof was made of shingles rather than
rushes it was twice the cost, being the equivalent of ten cows.

The Anglo-Saxons also built many other structures from timber.
In the estuaries of Essex and Suffolk, for instance, they built enormous fish traps, such as the V-shaped fish trap at Holbrook Bay
in the Stour estuary. They are the largest visible archaeological
wooden structures in Britain, and their construction is thought to
have been directed by aristocrats or monasteries.

The use of resources from the forest is referred to by King Alfred
in his preface to *St Augustine's Soliloquies*. While the topic is used to
introduce a religious philosophical discussion, the choice of a subject

which would have been very familiar to his readers underlines the fact that, to the Anglo-Saxons, forests were a reliable resource upon which they could depend for the comforts of the world:

*I then gathered for myself staves and props and tie-shafts, and handles for each of the tools that I knew how to work with, and cross-bars and beams, and for each of the structures which I knew how to build, the finest timbers I could carry. I never came away with a single load without wishing to bring home the whole of the forest, if I could have carried it all – in every tree I saw something for which I had a need at home. Accordingly, I would advise everyone who is strong and has many wagons to that same forest where I cut these props, and to fetch for himself and to load his wagons with well cut staves, so that he may weave many elegant walls and put up many splendid houses and so build a fine homestead, and there may live pleasantly and in tranquillity both in winter and summer – as I have not yet done.*

The reference to the weaving of 'many elegant walls' reflects the Anglo-Saxon practice of using wattle as infill in timber-framed buildings and to make internal screens and walls. A common technique was wattle and daub, sticks or laths that are wedged, woven, tied or nailed to form a matrix onto which is daubed a mixture of earth, straw or other reinforcing substances and, traditionally, animal dung.

Objects made from trees were recognised as having their origins in the forest, emphasising the links between the everyday wooden world of the Anglo-Saxons and the surrounding environment. As highlighted by King Alfred, the forests were regarded as a source of heat and light, food and drink, and material for the construction of buildings, tools and weapons. Archaeologists have, however, often overlooked the smaller wooden items that would have been familiar to the Anglo-Saxons in their daily lives, since they have rarely survived. Nevertheless, we still have a remarkable array of wooden artefacts from the period, including flutes, furniture, boardgames and buckets. These links to the forest affected the way in which the Anglo-Saxons expressed their relationship with the landscape, including place-names, the organisation of their settlements, and even the way in which they conducted their religion. On one of the two massive Anglo-Saxon stone crosses which dominate the cobbled market square of Sandbach, Cheshire, figures bear carved rods, or natural branches, which draw their significance from the sacred trees venerated by Pagans and Christians alike. They were originally painted, as well as carved, and are among the finest high crosses that have survived.

While our knowledge of Anglo-Saxon forestry is still sadly incomplete, we can glean some basic information from their language. The Old English vocabulary was particularly rich in this respect, with more than a hundred terms for specific tree species, as well as a range of words for forests and woods of different sizes. One of the words

*The two massive Anglo-Saxon high crosses in the marketplace at Sandbach, Cheshire.*

for a tree, for example, was *treow*, which not only meant tree but also 'trust' or 'promise'. This shared linguistic root is why the words 'tree' and 'true' are so similar, and perhaps explains the common association of trees with concepts such as reliability and steadfastness. Wold, wald and weald are all variants of the Anglo-Saxon *wudu*, though this has been described by Margaret Gelling, known for her extensive studies of English place-names, as 'probably the most colourless of Old English terms for a collection of trees'. *Sceaga*, pronounced similar to 'shaw', meant a small wood on a boundary, 'shore', which was presumably usually fairly long and narrow. 'Holt' appears to denote a wood consisting of a single species of tree, as in Asholt village in the Quantocks in Somerset, named from its position in, or near, an ash wood. There are also frequent references to timber in place-names: Borthwood (*Bordovrde, Bordwode, Bordwod*) on the Isle of Wight and the lost Tymberwood in Kent (*Tumberwod*) are probably *bord-wudu* and *timber-wudu* respectively, presumably tracts of woodland providing boards and timber. Asserius Menevensis, a Welsh monk from St Davids, Pembrokeshire, who became Bishop of Sherborne in the 890s, also refers in his *Life of King Alfred*, quoted at the beginning of this chapter, to Berroc Wood, 'where the box tree grows abundantly', as giving its name to the county of Berkshire. Indeed, the carved oak post discovered in Berkshire, described in Chapter 1, was located in the village of Boxford.

As the landscape historian Richard Jones has observed, thousands of these names survive, albeit often in changed forms. They account for the majority of town, village and hamlet names still in use today, as well as many other landscape features, and represent a storehouse of traditional ecological knowledge. Once again though traditional knowledge is often seen as a poor relation of modern scientific data. Combating the loss of memory and knowledge about the past is an ongoing struggle and Jones has shown the value of Old English place-names by using them to find the natural causes of, and solutions to, flooding.

The meanings of particular terms changed over time in response

120    *Forgotten Forests*

to transformations in the landscape. Thus, the sense of the word *lēah* altered from 'forest' or 'wood' to 'glade' or 'clearing', and later still to 'pasture' or 'meadow'. Such changes in terminology mirrored the extensive clearance of the forests undertaken by the Anglo-Saxons. Similarly, *wald* or *weald* went from referring to extensive woodland – as seen in the Weald in Sussex and Kent – to mean open high ground, as in the Cotswolds and the Yorkshire Wolds. Hundreds of Old English place-names indicate the former presence of trees, many of which have now disappeared. Over large parts of England, trees were felled and land was turned over to cereal cultivation or sheep pasture. Again, as Richard Jones has written, 'Seeing Old English place-names as traditional ecological knowledge-names brings us into better alignment with the worldviews of those who named the English landscape and who sought to make sense of it.'

What would it have been like to penetrate into a surviving forest at the start of the Anglo-Saxon period? The historian David Kirby has suggested that, as indicated by place-names, there would have been 'an infinite variety of trees and shrubs'. The overall aspect of the forest would have been very different to what we are used to today, having more in common with the forests of previous centuries. The presence of dead trees on the forest floor, in all stages of decomposition, would make passage through it very difficult, with gaps in the canopy caused by the death of individual trees enabling the temporary growth of a lush vegetation. To our modern eyes, used to seeing managed woodlands, it would look very untidy. The deeper shades of the forest provided shelter for fugitives from justice, the domain of both outlaws and wolves. The former were sometimes termed *wulfheafod*, or *caput lupinum* – literally 'wolf's head' – since they could be hunted and killed with impunity, like the wolves themselves. The association of wolf, outlaw and wilderness became even stronger in later beliefs about werewolves, a name derived from the Old English *wer-wulf*, 'man-wolf'. Wolf heads and skins were used as tributes and often requested in place of more valuable objects, their slaughter being an important aspect of Anglo-Saxon culture.

# A Reliable Resource

Wolves were feared because they were considered a threat to pastoral livelihoods, which depended on sheep and other livestock for both food and wealth. England's economic success from this period onwards relied increasingly on the wool trade, a business that depended, to some extent, on the eradication of wolves. The animals were considered an impediment to society, as expressed quite bluntly in an Anglo-Saxon proverb: 'The wolf must be in the woods, wretched and solitary; a good man should labour for glory in his native land.' The wolf's role as the adversary of civilisation is common to all literary and religious references to wolves at this time. The origin of this view is the Bible, in which wolves are presented as an allegory of spiritual danger. Such metaphors were clearly understood by the Anglo-Saxons, because predators such as the wolf presented a real danger to their sheep.

Some people have argued that the fact that an outlaw was known as a 'wolf's head', or the use of personal names such as Wulfstan, Wulfhere or Æþelwulf, does not necessarily prove that wolves still roamed England in this period. The dramatic mention of wolves in battle-poems may also be merely examples of poetic licence. The names given to features in the landscape, such as *Wulf-hlið*, 'hillside inhabited by wolves', *Wulfsēað*, 'wolf's hole' and *Wulfslǣd*, 'valley of wolves', suggest though that wolves were common. Indeed, there are two Anglo-Saxon documents that apparently refer to devices for trapping wolves. One is to a *wulf pytt*, 'wolf-pit', in a land grant of 955, while the second, from 972, refers to a *wulfhaga*, 'wolf-enclosure'. Bounties, as described in the next chapter, were also paid as rewards for killing wolves as late as the end of the thirteenth century. In the ecologist John Linnell's study of wolf attacks on people, one of the main factors he identified was the creation of highly modified environments, which severely reduce the wolves' natural prey and so force them to look further afield for food. Such an environment would have been created by agriculture altering, or destroying, woods and forests, the habitat of wolves.

Given the importance of wool, the land cleared of trees was

122          *Forgotten Forests*

increasingly devoted to sheep grazing rather than the raising of cattle, inhibiting the regeneration of the forests. Trees were also removed to provide space to grow crops, and by this time the 'scratch plough' drawn by oxen and the later 'mould-board plough' had been replaced by the 'true plough' drawn by a whole team of oxen that could work even the heavy clay soils that were previously covered by oak woodland. In an Anglo-Saxon riddle the plough is described as *har holtes feond* ('the old foe of the forest'). In general, however, documents from the time have remarkably little to say about destroying forests, perhaps because it was too common a practice to mention.

No convincing map has yet been produced of the distribution of forests in the early medieval period, the six centuries from 410 to 1066 CE formerly known as the Dark Ages. The Ordnance Survey attempted to map their extent in 1935 and 1966, and the historian Sir Frank Stenton did so again in 1971, but the results differ considerably, apart from the best-known areas. Michael Swanton also included a map covering 'areas of swamp and forest' in his translation of the Anglo-Saxon Chronicle. Additionally, in his book *Trees and Woodland in the British Landscape*, Oliver Rackham mapped settlements whose names incorporated woodland terms, producing a distribution which corresponded closely to the situation suggested by the earlier investigators. By including the Old Norse term *þveit*, which indicates a clearing produced by felling a wood, he added a concentration in Cumbria which had not been noticed earlier, though it is questionable as to what this term tells us. The extent of forests in the immediate post-Roman period remains contentious, in part because there was so much regional, or even local, variation. But, on the whole, there is little evidence for their wholesale regeneration, presumably because the demographic changes were accompanied not by the complete abandonment of land but the expansion in farming.

Together with later maps produced by other researchers, the Ordnance Survey and Stenton maps indicate that there were forests across southern and southeastern England, a second belt across

*A Reliable Resource* 123

the Midlands, from Gloucestershire through Worcestershire and the Welsh border and north into Yorkshire on the eastern side of the Pennines. A glimpse of how these forests appeared to people at the time is perhaps contained in a later twelfth-century description of Enfield Chase, Middlesex, as 'a great forest with wooded glades and lairs of wild beasts, deer both red and fallow, wild boars and bulls'. The least forested areas included the intensively cultivated lowlands of the Midlands, and the uplands of northern England, including the Pennines, the Lake District and the Cheviot Hills on the Scottish border.

As indicated by the way in which the landscape was described by the Anglo-Saxons, it seems that up until the eighth and ninth centuries the remaining forests were exploited without intensive deforestation, but this began to change between the tenth and eleventh centuries. There was thus a transition from an 'early Anglo-Saxon age', when forests were certainly exploited, but little affected by deforestation and human settlement, to a 'second Anglo-Saxon age' in which the area covered by trees began to decrease dramatically. In some areas of Essex, it is noticeable that timbers used in structures built in the sixth to eighth centuries had started to grow in the early fifth century, and, as a result, it has been argued that they were the result of forest regeneration. As described previously, a number of forests do seem to have regenerated after the departure of the Romans. The remains of Roman villas, for example, lie within a forested area at Hawling in Gloucestershire, which had apparently re-established itself by the middle of the Anglo-Saxon period.

There was a clear reduction in the age of trees used by the Romans for construction projects from the first to the third centuries. There are several possible reasons for this, but, as we have seen, the most likely candidates are intensive exploitation of the available resources by the rapidly expanding population, or industrial usage. This is not to suggest that there were no trees of any great age in England at the beginning of the Anglo-Saxon period in 410 CE. It may be that the areas of forest from which the

Romans extracted timber were not the areas exploited by the Anglo-Saxons, although trees from abandoned agricultural areas were utilised throughout the early and middle Anglo-Saxon period. It is only possible to make general observations, since many timber trees around in the year 400 were probably rotten by 500 and 600. Trees which began to grow in the first decades of the fifth century were either abandoned Roman coppices or areas of regrowth.

Over most of England during the second Anglo-Saxon age the forests were not impenetrable and rarely remote. Often, they were pastured on a seasonal basis, domestic animals being driven away from arable land and hay meadows in late spring, while in summer and early autumn the acorns and beechmast would be foraged by pigs. The use of wood-pasture, that is an area of grazing land with trees, was an important part of farming practice, and herds of pigs and cattle were kept in wooded regions across the country. One way of producing timber in areas open to grazing was to pollard them, removing the upper branches and leaving the trunk to regrow, and there is evidence of this in references to 'copped' trees in Anglo-Saxon boundary clauses. The same word also occurs in place-names such as Copdock in Suffolk (a copped oak) and Cowbeach in Sussex (a copped beech). The names Copper in Herefordshire and Copster in Lancashire may refer to whole woods of pollarded trees.

The presence of forests along tribal boundaries, often situated on areas of more 'difficult' soil, is one of the characteristic features of this period. Selwood Forest (*Sealhwudu*), for instance, situated along the borders of what are now Somerset and Wiltshire, marked the divide between the British and the Anglo-Saxons in the late sixth century. *Coit Maur*, 'the great wood', mentioned by Asserius Menevensis in the passage quoted at the beginning of this chapter, was such a barrier that Aldhelm, the early-eighth-century Bishop of Sherborne, was known as the bishop 'west of the wood'. It was named *Sealhwudu*, or 'Sallow Wood', from the willow that proliferated in its marshy vales. A dense forest of damp oakwood described by the historian Barbara Yorke as a formidable natural obstacle, the forest was in part responsible for delaying the Saxon advance on the British in the sixth century for up to 100 years, and it was the site of several important battles. The chronicles tell us that *Sealhwudu* stretched from north of Frome down to Shaftesbury and from Bruton to Warminster. Even as late as 1540 it still covered some 300 square miles (780 square kilometres), according to the antiquary John Leland.

In 878 Selwood Forest provided refuge for King Alfred and his men for two nights before the Battle of Ethandune (Edington), in which the Great Heathen Army led by the Dane Guthrum was defeated, resulting in the Treaty of Wedmore later the same year. The treaty was conditional on Guthrum being baptised, and his army leaving Wessex. Some fifteen years later the Anglo-Saxon Chronicle refers to Selwood in describing the gathering of English forces to oppose another attack in 893:

*Then Ealdorman Æthelred and Ealdorman Æthelhelm and Ealdorman Æthelnoth, and the king's thegns who were then at home at the fortifications assembled from every burh east of the Parret, and both east and west of Selwood, and also north of the Thames and west of the Severn, and also some part of the Welsh people.*

Ancient trees from Selwood Forest, dating to the medieval period, still survive in the grounds of manorial estates where they have been relatively protected. On the parkland of the Longleat Estate, well known for its safari park, there are many venerable trees, among them the 'Lion of Longleat', the estate's largest oak, which measures over eight metres in circumference. A roost for bats and barn owls, and host to fungi, rare lichens and many other species, it is typical of these old oaks. South of Longleat House is High Wood, a large, ancient, semi-natural broadleaved woodland with a predominantly 'high forest' structure consisting of large, tall mature trees with a closed canopy (unusual in southwest Britain), the major canopy tree being pedunculate oak. The lichen flora here includes species which are characteristic of ancient forests and parkland, such as lungwort,

126                    *Forgotten Forests*

which resembles the tissue inside lungs and was therefore once thought to be a remedy for lung diseases. Another area surviving from the medieval forest in Wiltshire is Picket and Clanger Wood at Yarnbrook. Unfortunately, almost two-thirds of the site has been planted with conifers, but the remaining woodland consists of oak, ash and hornbeam, with an understorey of somewhat neglected coppice.

Wyndham's Oak, sometimes known as Judge Wyndham's Oak, the Silton Oak or Stumpy Silton, is a pedunculate oak tree in Silton, Dorset. It was one of a number of oaks that historically marked the boundary between Selwood Forest and Gillingham Forest, a medieval hunting ground. It could be 1,000 years old, and its girth of 9.79 metres is one of the largest of any tree in Dorset. The current owner of the farm apparently once lost a cow, only to find it two days later stuck inside the hollow trunk. The tree was named after Judge Hugh Wyndham, who purchased the manor of Silton in 1641. He was the Justice of the Common Pleas, one of the highest officials in England, in the time of Charles II and used to sit within the tree and smoke his pipe to relax and contemplate. Towards the end of the seventeenth century, rebels convicted of participation in the failed Monmouth Rebellion of 1685, also known as the Pitchfork Rebellion, the Revolt of the West or the West Country Rebellion, were said to have been hanged from its boughs. It is interesting that, as the sanctity of trees diminished over the centuries, many became associated with famous people such as Wyndham, or William Wilberforce, who, in 1787, sat down under an oak tree at Holwood House in Kent, now known as the Wilberforce Oak, and decided to abolish the slave trade.

Other great English forests in existence during the Anglo-Saxon period included Sherwood Forest (*Scirwudu*), the Weald, noted as a *mycclan wuda* ('great wood'), and Wychwood Forest (*Hwicciwudu*). The kingdom of the Hwicce was almost completely encircled by forests, and for millennia Wychwood covered much of west Oxfordshire. Towards the end of the eleventh century, it was recorded in the Domesday Book as extending from Taynton, near

*Wyndham's Oak, in Silton, Dorset, one of a number of oaks that historically marked the boundary between Selwood and Gillingham Forests.*

Burford, in the west to Blenheim and Woodstock in the east. At that time, the forest would have covered over 470 square kilometres, and indeed, Woodstock is believed to derive its name from the Anglo-Saxon for a 'place in the woods'.

The appearance of the Wychwood, between the decline of the Roman presence in the fifth century and the arrival of the Normans at the end of the eleventh, is one of the mysteries of Oxfordshire's history. The author James Bond, writing in *Blenheim: Landscape for a Palace*, has suggested that Wychwood may have once been a frontier region like Selwood, the secondary woodland that developed here in a disputed zone eventually becoming valued in its own right for the timber it supplied and as an area for hunting. In 1792 the forest covered some 1,500 hectares and was divided into five 'walks', which were known as Patch Hill, Potter's Hill, Roger's Hill, South Lawn and the Ranger's Walk. By the beginning of the nineteenth century Wychwood and its immediate surroundings were notorious for poachers, thieves and petty criminals, and the Forest Fair, which was held in September, was thought to encourage the presence of some of the less desirable members of the public.

Today, Wychwood is still one of the largest areas of ancient semi-natural forest in Oxfordshire, but it survives only in fragments. It is mostly oak and ash woodland with an understorey of hawthorn, hazel and field maple. There is a diverse range of invertebrates, including many uncommon species that are confined to old, undisturbed woods with mature trees and decaying timber. One of the key areas of interest is the ancient deer park, known as High Park, that survives on the Blenheim Estate. Regarding the origin of the park, Bond notes that 'medieval chroniclers suggest that it was King Henry I (c. 1068–1135) who made the first enclosure of the park at Woodstock towards the beginning of the twelfth century', although direct contemporary evidence for this is lacking. A medieval deer park was a functional landscape intended to supply venison to the royal court and its supporters, to provide breeding stock for

*Nick Baimbridge, Head Forester on the Blenheim Estate, at the Queen Oak, the oldest tree in the ancient deer park known as High Park.*

# A Reliable Resource

129

the establishment of other parks as well as sporting interest and, no doubt, to supply firewood, underwood and timber. Large herds of fallow deer still roam the area, along with roe and muntjac deer.

Around 90 per cent of the woodland here consists of oak trees, including 968 veteran oaks over 400 years old, and there are even some that are said to be a thousand years old. At least sixty of the trees date back to the Middle Ages, and High Park is now regarded as the greatest collection of medieval oaks in Europe. The now ancient oaks presumably witnessed the royal hunting parties, some of them perhaps as seedlings. They have been preserved through a combination of the royal love of hunting and the landscape designer Lancelot 'Capability' Brown's respect for ancient woodlands. When he was hired in 1764 to lay out the grounds, he set aside an area to be left intact, and it is there that the old oaks persisted, undisturbed by people.

Aljos Farjon, who surveyed High Park as part of a project documenting ancient oaks for an international database, has written that 'Of all the sites with ancient oaks I have seen, High Park is the most amazing, it's like stepping back into the distant wild past of our country. No other landscape in England has greater biodiversity, especially from invertebrates, fungi and lichens.' It supports around fifty different species of beetles and sixteen butterfly and moth species. Thousands of rare forest honeybees have also been discovered here by Filipe Salbany, a bee expert now working for the Blenheim Estate, who estimates that as many as seventy colonies could exist in the woodlands, remarkably surviving throughout the winter. Some of these colonies could be up to 200 years old, and Salbany suspects that there may be colonies of wild tree-nesting bees still to be discovered in other ancient woodlands.

The newly discovered honeybees are smaller, furrier and darker than the honeybees found in managed beehives, and they are believed to be related to the indigenous wild bees that foraged in the English countryside for centuries. Until now, it was presumed all these bees had been completely wiped out by disease and competition from imported species, but Salbany is now arranging for a DNA analysis of the Blenheim Bees, as they have become known – a necessary step in assessing whether they are actually the wild heirs of the lost British honeybee. Nick Baimbridge, head of Blenheim's forestry team, said that discovering that the bees he had hardly noticed during his three decades working there were special was a big surprise. The wild colonies are small and produce swarms, of less than 5,000 bees, much more often than the foresters realised, most being high up in the canopy.

Honey from wild bees was an important sweetener in Anglo-Saxon England. There were 'Honey' brooks in Worcestershire, where the village of Beoley appears in a charter of 972 as *Beoleahe*, from *beo* meaning bee and *lea*, a clearing in a wood. A *hinig yrste*,

*A colony of wild tree-nesting bees in a cavity in an ancient oak in High Park, on the Blenheim Palace Estate. The bees have reduced the size of the original entrance hole.*

# A Reliable Resource

a 'honey wooded hillock' is mentioned as a landmark in a boundary clause in Hardenhuish in Wiltshire. Honey was important enough in ancient Ireland to have an entire law tract, the *Bechbretha* or bee-judgments, devoted to the subject. Medieval Welsh law also had a special category of damage to oak trees called *twll* (cutting into or perforation), for which the different versions assign fines of 24, 30, 40 or 60 pence (with in some cases an additional fine to the king). The damage in question was associated with the theft of honey from bee colonies in trees.

Wychwood is thought to have supplied wood for the Droitwich salt industry, which the Hwicce lords monopolised. Indeed, many Anglo-Saxon charters refer to Droitwich in northern Worcestershire as 'Saltwich'. It was the great inland salt-producing town, and enormous quantities of timber were required to fire the ovens where evaporation of the saline liquid took place. A tenth-century charter includes *sihlam izecessarium on Bradanleage ad illam prceparationem salis*, 'the woodland at Bradley necessary for the preparation of salt' and the location of places possessing salt rights. Many of these, in payment, evidently sent timber to Droitwich, suggesting that wood was obtained from a wide area, even beyond the frontiers of the Hwiccan kingdom. Manors near Droitwich, such as Bradley, routinely delivered wood by the cartload to pay for salt along trackways called *saelt straets*. According to various texts the payment rate was one cartload of wood for one 'mitt' of salt, but today it is not clear what a mitt represented, and even whether it was a measure of weight or volume.

The Weald, lying between the North and South Downs in southern England, was also originally covered by forests. It was known to the Anglo-Saxons as *Andredesweald*, meaning 'the forest of Andred', or *Andredesleah*, the second element here, *leage*, being another Old English word for woodland. According to the Anglo-Saxon Chronicle, at this time the Weald covered an area of 120 miles by 30 miles (193 × 48 kilometres), stretching from Lympne, near Romney Marsh in Kent, to the Forest of Bere and the New Forest. It was often used

132                           *Forgotten Forests*

as a place of refuge, and the Anglo-Saxon Chronicle, for instance, relates that during the conquest of Sussex the native Britons (who were called Welsh) were driven into the forest:

> *A.D. 477. This year came Ælle to Britain, with his three sons, Cymen, and Wlenking, and Cissa, in three ships; landing at a place that is called Cymenshore. There they slew many of the Welsh; and some in flight they drove into the wood that is called Andred'sley.*

The same warriors are then recorded as capturing the Roman fortress at Pevensey and killing all the inhabitants. The Weald was a well-known sanctuary and hiding place for bandits, highwaymen and outlaws until the late Middle Ages, as it was sparsely inhabited, being used mainly as a resource by people living on its fringes. Like Selwood Forest and Wychwood, the Weald also appears to have separated a number of politically distinct regions which may have had their origins in Iron Age kingdoms and Roman *civitates* that influenced the early medieval tribal districts. The core of the forest may have formed the boundary between the kingdom of Kent to the north and that of the South Saxons to the south.

Today woodlands occupy only around five per cent of the historic county of Worcestershire, one of the lowest percentages of any county in Britain. By the end of the Roman period, much of the original forest in the south and east of the county, in the Feldon and the Avon valley areas, had disappeared, but clearance was much slower on the poorer soils of Arden, which dominates the north and west of the county. The fact that Arden in the Anglo-Saxon period was forested is indisputable. Even in the Roman period, tile and pottery kilns were established here to make use of the abundant fuel. Virtually no Roman roads cross the region, and it has been suggested that this was because of the difficulty of cutting them through the area. The Forest of Arden is effectively bounded by the Fosse Way on the east side, and the Salt Road on

A Forest Glade, Arden, Warwickshire *(1845)*, *by Frederick Henry Henshaw. By Henshaw's time, ancient English woodlands were being affected, or even destroyed, by the development of industry and modern farming.*

the south. Originally, the region stretched from Stratford-upon-Avon in Warwickshire to Tamworth in Staffordshire, covering a vast area, including the current cities of Coventry and Birmingham. It was not a vast tract of largely uninterrupted forest, but nevertheless it still contained some significant areas of woodland. Much was cleared during the Middle Ages though, and by the Domesday survey only about 35 per cent of the forest remained.

Unfortunately, Arden, the part of Warwickshire that was least populated in the Anglo-Saxon period, is now overwhelmingly the most populated area of the county, and the impacts on the environment include golf courses, horse paddocks, water abstraction and non-native species escaping into the countryside. Despite these pressures, the entire area today still retains a wooded character. Everywhere there are oak trees, in small copses, in hedgerows, or marking places where hedgerows once existed. Over 500 old oaks with girths of over five metres are still standing, indicating they are around 300 years old.

William Shakespeare, born in Stratford in 1564, spent his formative years near Arden and, although it continued to decrease in size during his lifetime, the essential character of the forest remained intact. His mother's maiden name was Arden, an ancient Warwickshire surname which is presumed to be derived from the forest itself. In the State Library in New South Wales, Australia, a copy of *Mr William Shakespeare's Comedies, Histories, & Tragedies*, usually simply called the *First Folio*, is kept in an ornate casket of oak that was reputedly sourced from the Forest of Arden. While the forest is often assumed to be the location of *As You Like It*, there are two similarly named woodlands in France, and the play mentions lions and other creatures. It is, of course, a fantasy. In fact, Shakespeare's play appears to be an adaptation of an earlier story written by the English writer and dramatist Thomas Lodge that was originally set in one of the French forests.

The seventh and eighth centuries were characterised by ongoing warfare between the intruding Anglo-Saxon kingdoms of Bernicia, Northumbria and Mercia and the northern and eastern Welsh (British) kingdoms. Bernicia, the northernmost Anglo-Saxon kingdom, was part of what is now southern Scotland. In 684 there was also a raid by Anglo-Saxon forces on the Irish kingdom of Brega, roughly comparable to present-day County Meath. Additionally, there is evidence, in an archaeological dig at Copper Alley in Temple Bar West, that Anglo-Saxons occupied Dublin before the Vikings arrived in 841, but the impacts on Irish forests are unclear. One of the first recorded Viking raids in England occurred in 793, when the priory on the tidal island of Lindisfarne, also known as Holy Island, was destroyed. The raid was so devastating that some medieval writers believed that God was punishing them for their sins. But gradually the raiders began to stay, first in winter camps, then settling on land they had seized. They captured York in 867, and then besieged Nottingham. Battles also raged across southern England as the Vikings fought with the armies of Mercia and Wessex.

It is clear, however, that the Viking winter camps led to many individual takeovers of land after 876. The Anglo-Saxon Chronicle, for instance, records that on departure from their winter camp at Repton, the Viking Great Army split into two groups. One continued campaigning in southern England until forced to make peace with King Alfred after the Battle of Ethandune in 878, while the second returned north and famously 'seized the land of the Northumbrians and proceeded to plough and to support themselves'. The archaeological evidence also reveals looting and the abandonment of farmsteads, traditional market places and estates. What impact this may have had on forests and woodland is unclear. Some areas may have regenerated, but it seems that on the whole the Vikings carried on the destruction of the remaining forests. Indeed, the biologist Winifred Pennington suggested that in Cumbria many of the existing farms in the central and southern Lake District originated in the clearances made by the Vikings in the secondary forests that had not been felled during the Roman period. The Norse colonisation of northwest England may thus have resulted in one of the three major phases of agricultural expansion in the area, involving the felling of oak woodlands to make way for pasture on the uplands.

The Vikings certainly consumed large amounts of timber and destroyed many forests in the process. Iceland, for instance, has long been famous both for its rich medieval literature and for the extreme impact by humans on its vegetation, soils and landscapes since the first settlements in the ninth century. When the Vikings arrived the hills were covered with birch forests, which probably extended up to a height of at least 400 metres. Rapid deforestation closely followed the first settlements, and it has been estimated that

136                    *Forgotten Forests*

90 per cent of the forest and 40 per cent of the soil present at that time has now disappeared. As a result, nearly three-quarters of Iceland is currently affected by erosion. A passage from *Egil's Saga*, describing the settlement of the chieftain Skallagrim in south-west Iceland, noted that 'such livestock as there was grazed free in the woodland all year round', which would certainly have put paid to any regeneration.

Evidence from documents, archaeology and art all point to a significant reorganisation of Anglo-Saxon society in the tenth and eleventh centuries. Many of the developments typically associated with the Norman Conquest actually began then, Anglo-Saxon lords setting aside forests for hunting, building impressive fortified manorial centres, and establishing parishes where they erected commemorative stone sculptures such as the Sandbach crosses. Cnut was also the originator of the forest law which the later Norman invaders exploited, prohibiting hunting on royal property in addition to making land ownership a prerequisite to hunt. As mentioned in the Preface, 'forest' was a legal term, derived from the Latin *foris* ('outside'), referring to a tract of land outside the public domain, reserved for the king's pleasure and recreation. It did not mean that the whole area was covered in trees. While the Norman kings undoubtedly escalated the exclusivity associated with hunting and lordship, the origins of this behaviour are firmly rooted in the preceding period. The restrictions and practices decreed by William I therefore differed from the laws of Cnut only in degree, not in substance.

According to an eleventh-century text, the *Encomium Emmae Reginae*, Archbishop Æthelnoth refused to give his blessing to Cnut's successor Harold I (often referred to as Harold Harefoot), prompting him to turn his back on the church. When others 'entered church to hear mass', he 'surrounded the glades with dogs for the chase, or occupied himself with any other utterly paltry matters'. It is worth noting, however, that one of the pre-eminent strategies for securing your position in late Saxon society was through hunting,

# A Reliable Resource

which was used both by lords to demarcate social divisions and by lower-ranking individuals attempting to climb the social ladder. The Venerable Bede describes how the Saxons were required to hunt after the departure of the Romans left the land 'destitute', but this was a gross exaggeration.

Some regions in the late Anglo-Saxon period experienced a degree of reforestation. This is surprising given the overall pressures on land from population growth, urban development and the fragmentation of estates, but a tenth-century date has been suggested for the reforestation of Sydlings Copse in Oxfordshire. Similarly, excavations at Shakenoak Farm, also in Oxfordshire, suggest that the site reverted to woodland sometime in the eighth or ninth century. Whittlewood Forest, a former medieval hunting forest east of Silverstone in Northamptonshire, is another example of the regeneration of woodland around this time. While we know it regenerated at the end of the Roman period, the Domesday Book makes no direct reference to the forest of Whittlewood, but, nevertheless, it is clear that in 1086 the area still contained very considerable tracts of woodland. The important royal manor of Greens Norton, for example, contained a wood measuring four leagues long and three leagues wide. This is equivalent to almost 50 square kilometres, and it almost certainly extended into the heavily wooded parishes of Paulerspury, Silverstone and Whittlebury. Other parishes which lay within the boundaries of the forest, such as Passenham, Potterspury, Towcester and Wicken, also contained substantial quantities of woodland in 1086.

Reforestation can also be glimpsed in a tenth-century charter granting privileges and restoration of land in Worcestershire. This charter references a certain boundary named *ympanleage*, or the 'leah (forest) of the saplings', indicating that regeneration was occurring between two estates. The use of the Saxon term *haga* (plural *hagan*) within the charter once again reinforces the idea that woodland often formed boundaries between newly designated estates. Often translated as 'hedges', there are numerous examples where *hagan* served as boundaries between manors and parishes in forested regions. Half of the *hagan* of Worcester, for instance, occurred along the boundaries of what would become royal estates associated with the Norman Forest of Malvern. Similarly, the early-eleventh-century will of a certain Thurstan granted the use of his woodland to his servants except for the *derhage*, at Ongar in Essex. This *derhage* (or deer-haga, which can be translated as 'deer enclosure') is almost certainly the area that in the Norman period became Ongar Great Park.

The use of *haga* in the charters varies, but the term appears more frequently in regions where dense woodland was present. Whether Anglo-Saxon *hagan* were geographical boundaries, transportable enclosures, or precursors to deer parks, they indicate important issues relating to land ownership in late Saxon England. First, the charters confirm that the forests which had previously belonged to large estates were broken up, with many *hagan* serving as boundaries for woodland manors. Secondly, the concern for woodland conveyed in the charters lends weight to the idea that a degree of reforestation occurred in the face of increasing pressures on land.

The final Viking invasion of England came in 1066, when Harald Hardrada sailed up the Humber and marched to Stamford Bridge. Harold Godwinson, newly crowned king, marched north with his army and defeated Hardrada, but immediately after the battle he heard that William of Normandy had landed in Kent with yet another invading army. Marching back south to meet this new threat, the exhausted English army fought the Normans at the Battle of Hastings. As we know, the Normans won – but the irony is that William's ancestor was Rollo, a Viking, so in some ways the Norman invasion of England was yet another Viking victory.

CHAPTER 6

# Taming the Landscape

*The Welsh 'neither inhabit towns, villages nor castles but lead a solitary life in the woods'.*

Gerald of Wales

The fourteenth day of October 1066 was a disastrous day for the English army under Harold Godwinson, and indeed for Harold himself, but the Norman invasion also had a significant impact on the landscape, with the destruction of numerous forests in Britain and Ireland. The Battle of Hastings, however, was only the first stage in the Norman occupation of England. For several years afterwards, the country was torn apart by conflicts as the Normans fought to extend their rule, ending in an infamous campaign which we know today as the 'Harrying of the North'.

William's knights covered territory as far north as the River Tyne, and over the winter of 1069/70 they devastated Northumbria and Yorkshire. Entire villages were razed to the ground, their inhabitants killed, livestock slaughtered and stores of food destroyed. By depriving the region of its resources so effectively, William sought to put an end to the cycle of rebellions, ensuring that any future insurgents would lack the means to support themselves. Tens of thousands of people undoubtedly died, at a time when the total population of England was little more than two million. Afterwards Symeon, a monk in Durham Priory, wrote that no village remained inhabited between York and Durham and that the countryside was empty and uncultivated for nine years. Even when the Domesday Book was compiled in 1085, one-third of the available land in Yorkshire was still recorded as 'waste'. The areas of waste listed do not exactly align with the path of the Conqueror's army, but nevertheless it is clear that large areas of countryside in the north of England were abandoned for many years, and this probably allowed some woods and forests to expand again.

After the conquest of England, the Normans turned their attention to Wales, occupying large territories in the southeast of the country. From Chester and other strongholds, such as Rhuddlan, Shrewsbury and Hereford, the Normans set about subduing the Welsh and annexing their lands. In some areas the remaining forests were still sufficiently extensive and dense to be a formidable physical barrier to the invading forces, and were therefore of strategic importance. They also featured repeatedly as locations of battles, being used by the Welsh as both places of ambush and places of refuge and shelter. Until the publication of *Welsh Woods and Forests* by William Linnard in 1982, however, the extent and military significance of Welsh forests in the Norman conquest of Wales had never been properly considered, despite these aspects being described by Gerald of Wales, in his *Itinerarium Cambriae* of 1191 and the *Descriptio Cambriae* of 1193/94.

Together, Gerald's texts form one of the first detailed descriptions of Wales as a country. He noted that in Wales 'the battle is . . . here in forests', and pointed out the superiority of light infantry over cavalry 'when the engagement is in narrow defiles, in woods and marshes', and the advantages of a winter campaign 'when the trees are void of leaves'. For the Normans, the need to eliminate certain forests as places of ambush and shelter was highlighted by a number of events. In 1094, for example, William II's forces were defeated with 'great slaughter' in a forest known as Coedysbys in Gwynedd; the exact location of which has not yet been identified. A year later, in 1095, the Welsh 'sought a defence in their woods and wilderness' and, although intending to cut the forests down, William returned to England after an unsuccessful campaign. The Normans also retreated in 1097, 'not daring to invade the woods or the wilderness against the Britons'. In the Grwyne Fawr valley, now in the Bannau Brycheiniog / Brecon Beacons National Park, there was the 'narrow woody tract called the bad pass of Coed Grono', where the Norman marcher lord Richard de Clare, first Earl of Hereford, was ambushed and killed in 1135 by the Welsh under Iorwerth ab Owain and his brother Morgan. Similarly, in 1157, in a campaign against Owain Gwynedd, Henry II was ambushed in a place called 'the wood of Hawarden', and after severe losses he narrowly escaped 'to the open country'. The location is thought to be somewhere between Ewloe and Hawarden in north Wales, a region which was noted as containing considerable areas of woodland. Forests and woods were very dangerous places for the Normans, so they decided to remove them.

The first recorded felling of Welsh forests by invading forces since the Roman conquest occurred in 1165 when Henry II, in an effort to resolve a military stalemate, 'moved his host into the wood of Dyffryn Ceiriog' and had that wood felled. The 'Oak at the Gate of the Dead', an ancient tree at the entrance to the Ceiriog valley, below Chirk Castle, is said to be the only living witness to the Battle of Crogen, when the invading English army was ambushed by Welsh forces and a brutal battle ensued. Reputedly dating back to the reign of King Egbert in 802, the oak had a girth of 10 metres until 2010, when its trunk split in cold weather. Before the battle Owain Gwynedd is believed to have gathered his army beneath another ancient tree, the Pontfadog, or Cilcochwyn Oak, before taking on, and defeating, the English at Crogen. The Welsh forces were outnumbered, but Owain's tactics involved hiding his troops in the forests overlooking the route Henry would have to travel. To protect his army, Henry ordered 2,000 woodsmen to clear trees and widen the passage, so that his army could move quickly through the pass. Even though the woodsmen were protected by a powerful vanguard of pikemen the Welsh joined battle close to where the oak now stands, inflicting severe losses. Their ranks destroyed, the English struggled on to the Berwyn Mountains, but soon after, cut off from their supplies and beset by bad weather, they retreated. Forced to abandon the conquest of Wales, Henry returned to his court in France. Traditionally, the field on the opposite side of the road to the tree, known as the 'Gate of the Dead', is where the many English casualties are said to be buried. Rob McBride, an ancient tree enthusiast, therefore linked the two and gave the tree the name by which it is now known.

In the early hours of 18 April 2013, a storm felled the Pontfadog Oak, which at the time was the oldest tree in Wales, the third-largest in Britain and one of the oldest oaks in Europe. Looked

*The pedunculate oak known as the 'Oak at the Gate of the Dead' or the 'Crogen Oak', is reputed to be the only living witness to the Battle of Crogen in 1165. It was one of the first trees in the world to have its own Facebook page.*

after by generations of the Williams family at Cilcochwyn Farm near Chirk, the oak was another survivor of the forests which once covered so much of Wales. In 1850 two golden chisels were discovered hidden inside the trunk, which were apparently on show in 1880 but are now lost. Since gold is a relatively soft metal the chisels could not be used for woodworking but they obviously had a symbolic role for whoever placed them there. The tree lives on in the form of five cloned saplings. When the oak fell, a number of shoots about the thickness of a pencil were taken from it, and experts at Windsor Great Park used their grafting skills to create five clones. Two of these were planted in northeast Wales, close to the tree's original location, while the others were planted on the approach to the great glasshouse at the National Botanic Garden of Wales in Carmarthenshire. In 2022, the Welsh First Minister,

*The Pontfadog oak, once the oldest tree in Wales, after being felled by a storm on 18 April 2013.*

144                          *Forgotten Forests*

Mark Drakeford, and the Prince of Wales attended a ceremony to mark the next part of the oak's journey through time.

The felling of Dyffryn Ceiriog was the first act of a policy that was continued for well over a century and which had a devastating impact on Welsh forests. In 1223, for example, Henry III ordered the destruction of forests and the clearing of passes to provide free and safe passage and access to the townships of Cardigan and Carmarthen for merchants and others. A year later he also commanded all soldiers and others owning woods around Montgomery to fell them:

> *Inasmuch as you value your tenure, we order you to cut down and assart your woods which you own around our castle of Montgomery near tracks and public roads, without delay. If you do not do so, take notice that we, for the common good, shall have those woods cut down and assarted and convert them to our ownership.*

Montgomery occupied a key strategic position on the Welsh border, and extensive and repeated clearances were made in this area throughout the thirteenth century. In 1228 the Welsh forced the invading army to retreat, but not before extensive felling had taken place, probably at Ceri near Newtown. The king 'went to the said wood which was eerie large, being five leagues in length and, by reason of the thicke growthe of the wood, verse hard to be stocked (that is cleared); howbeit, the king caused the same, with great diligence and trauell, to be assarted and consumed with fire'. Five leagues is equivalent to 24 kilometres, and it is interesting that the forest is described as being 'eerie large', so it obviously stood out at this time as exceptional. Again in 1251 the king ordered an inspection of the forest passes, but if the passes were sufficiently wide, the men of Montgomery were forbidden to lay waste those forests or those of free tenants. This is one of the first regulations specifically prohibiting excessive felling of forests in Wales. In 1278, however, Bogo de Knovill was appointed:

*Taming the Landscape*      145

> *to cause to be cut down all hays and thickets in the ways in the parts*
> *of Mundgomery, Kery, and Kedewy, which give rise to danger to the*
> *passers by, homicides and robberies and other enormities committed there,*
> *and . . . to admonish . . . the lords of those lands to cut them down,*
> *and, in case of their refusal to do so, to cause it to be done at their cost.*

It is difficult to make even a rough estimate of the total area of forests permanently, or temporarily, cleared in Wales as a result of military fellings carried out by the Normans. It is clear though that the clearances were extensive and deeply resented by local people. The massive scale of the destruction is illustrated by the surviving accounts of the military campaigns of 1277, 1282–83 and 1294–95.

In the 1277 campaign, for example, Edward I's plan was to advance into Wales from a strong base, guard his workmen cutting down the forest, and then create a new base from which to repeat the process. This involved the cutting of an invasion road for over 50 kilometres between Chester and the River Conwy. The felling and building operations were carried out by large numbers of specialist workmen recruited from England. They included sawyers, woodcutters, carpenters and charcoal burners, some of the latter coming from the Forest of Dean. On one section of the road, between Flint and Rhuddlan, between 1,500 and 1,800 woodmen were engaged, and 700 to 1,000 on the section from Rhuddlan to Deganwy. The workmen were carefully guarded, for their protection and to prevent desertions, though they were always paid. It is possible to roughly estimate the maximum amount of forest felled in the construction of the road, since, whenever the width of the clearance for the road was specified, it was 'one bowshot' across. A bowshot has been estimated at between 180 and 230 metres, so, assuming that trees needed to be felled along the whole length of the route, it is possible that around 1,200 hectares of forest were felled in the space of four to five months to make this one road alone. Activities such as this marked the beginning of the fragmentation of the forest habitat in Wales, with negative effects on both plants and animals.

The main plan of campaign in 1282–83 was the same as in 1277. Once again, the clearance of forests played a vital part in the war, large numbers of woodcutters and charcoal burners being recruited. They were all carefully selected, being 'the most powerful, agile and most accustomed to the execution of these offices'. Each man had a good strong axe or hatchet suitable for felling large and small trees, and they were paid three pence a day. In December 1282 orders were given for a force of 800 woodcutters to be assembled at Chester for forest clearance operations in north Wales. This campaign was deliberately pursued through the winter in the leafless forests, as advised by Gerald of Wales. Castell y Bere, a Welsh castle near Llanfihangel-y-Pennant in Gwynedd, for example, was captured in April 1283, with 100 woodmen in the besieging forces, and more passes were cleared through the forests in that area. The Forest of Bodfari in the Vale of Clwyd was said to have been totally felled by 1,300 men in May 1283 and never recovered from the assault. This broad, fertile valley subsequently became one of the great granaries of Wales, famed for its rich corn-growing land, with only relatively small areas of woodland surviving to the present day.

Again, this war was followed by another period of systematic felling to clear passes. In 1284, for example, the burgesses of Carmarthen were granted free common in the woods of Mallaen and permitted to fell and carry away underwood, oaks for timber, and other trees, without any let or hindrance, as a matter of deliberate policy to clear dense woods where robberies and murders were said to be frequent. In 1287, 2,000 woodcutters from Shropshire and Staffordshire were ordered to fell the whole of Brecknock Forest. These fellings were one of the causes of the rising of Rhys ap Maredudd, a native lord in the Vale of Towy. In that rebellion he led the capture of most of Ystrad Tywi, the heartland of Deheubarth, including the castles at Dinefwr and

Carreg Cennen. The revolt was crushed by the autumn but broke out again in November and only ended after a ten-day siege of Rhys's final stronghold, the castle at Newcastle Emlyn. In January 1288 Rhys went into hiding, but he was eventually captured and executed for treason at York in 1292. Even in the last Welsh rising against Edward I, in 1294–95, the felling of forests still formed a vital part of military strategy, as recorded in a letter to the king from a writer 'in a wood which is called Ketthlieconhan', reputedly the strongest place in the whole of Ardudwy (an area in northwest Wales), who was 'lodged therein to cut down the wood'.

At the time of the Edwardian conquest, the Welsh, like the Irish, were still primarily a forest people, living to a large extent among, or in close proximity to, the trees. Destroying the forests was therefore also part of a deliberate attempt to destroy Welsh culture. Considered by many to be one of the greatest Welsh-language poets, Dafydd ap Gwilym was a true forest poet, gaining his inspiration there and using relevant motifs and images. Unlike his medieval contemporaries, ap Gwilym often wrote poems concerned with the events in his own life, being especially thoughtful in the exploration of the natural world. His depictions of the forests, and of creatures like the fox and the roebuck and, especially, birds, are descriptions which owe more to the poet's experience and powers of observation than to any literary convention. The vivid precision of his description of the woodcock, for instance, is far beyond anything that had come before. It was not a favourite of Dafydd's though, since for all the courtesy he shows the bird in his poem, he considered it a foolish and despicable bird of winter. Dafydd was writing his poetry in the mid-fourteenth century, but, sadly, by the end of the medieval period a century or so later, people had, for the most part, lost their awareness of the importance of the forests. As a result, their significance in Welsh poems, tales and traditions faded away, just like the trees themselves.

Apart from the immediate clearances, the other major element of military forest policy was the introduction of an organised logging industry to provide timber for the building and repair of castles. The earliest tree-ring date associated with a building in Wales, for example, is for the doors at Chepstow Castle, which were made from wood felled between 1159 and 1189. That makes them the oldest castle doors in Europe. The 'king's works in Wales' represented operations on a scale never seen before. Initially, much of the timber used for the castles was shipped from England, but, as soon as it could be organised, the Welsh forests were logged for materials. These ranged from small items such as poles, shingles and laths, to boards, and great joists and beams, some over 10 metres in length. The species used were rarely specified, but, in most places, it was undoubtedly and exclusively oak, the commonest and often the only timber tree species available. In southeast Wales, where beech is a native tree, that species was occasionally used as

*The original latticework-reinforced doors at Chepstow Castle were made from wood felled between 1159 and 1189, which makes them the oldest known castle doors in Europe.*

well as, or perhaps even in preference to, oak. At Tregrug Castle in Monmouthshire, for example, beech trees were felled, topped and squared for sawing for castle repairs in 1286–87. Castles required enormous amounts of timber, not only for the initial building but also for the regular replacement of decayed wood throughout the useful life of the fortification.

The forests in the vicinity of a castle, and especially the forests convenient for the transport of timber by water, were always logged. Because of the effort involved, lengthwise sawing was avoided except for boards, timbers generally being used in the form of a whole log roughly squared using an adze, a tool similar to an axe but with an arched blade at right angles to the handle. The larger beams were from straight standard trees, presumably growing in natural or semi-natural forest. Selecting the right tree was a skilled job, and specialists were entrusted with the job of seeking out and marking suitable timber. Large pieces were extracted by horse, or ox, teams, and floated down rivers in the form of loose logs, or as rafts, or, where possible, shipped in small coastal vessels. In 1185, for example, some 24 ships were used to transport timber from the king's woods at Chepstow to Kenfig Castle in Glamorgan, and there are many references to the shipping of wood and timber for work on castles in north Wales, including Beaumaris, Caernarfon and Harlech.

At Caernarfon, timber was first imported from Cheshire and Lancashire, but in 1295 the Conwy valley was the source of materials, and in 1321 the woods there supplied large numbers of great joists that were each recorded as being 18 feet long, one and a half feet wide and two feet thick, and also large beams 32 feet long by one and a half feet square. It is significant perhaps that this timber had to be transported some 50 kilometres to the castle and that the transport was by water, local supplies probably being exhausted. Throughout the centuries, Caernarfon Castle was maintained and repaired with timber felled in the Conwy valley and in Cheshire. Even as late as the sixteenth century, the castles in north Wales required significant amounts of wood for maintenance and

150 *Forgotten Forests*

repair. Transport, especially across land, was relatively expensive, often costing more than the value of the standing timber.

In the accounts of the Chamberlain of Chester for the period 1301–1328, submitted to the auditors appointed to scrutinise the finances of the royal possessions in Wales and the Marches, there are several references to forests in the former county of Flintshire. The English rulers wished to ensure that it was an 'appendage of Cheshire bound to it by very close bonds', so a policy was followed in Flintshire, as in other districts of Wales conquered by the English, of filling the most important towns with English people. While the county had been subdued, it was still inhabited by a 'sensitive and restless people', and the new regime was taking no chances with a further rebellion. To accelerate the approach, licences were issued to Welsh property owners, allowing them to sell their lands in towns like Rhuddlan to the English – in effect forcing them to go and live elsewhere.

The burghers of Rhuddlan were also given rights extending to the furthest limits of the commote (a division of land) in addition to those they already had. These rights included being allowed to cut wood and have grazing rights in the forest of Bach y Graig. By the mid-fourteenth century, Bach y Graig was the royal hunting forest of Edward, the Black Prince, and was important as a source of revenue, timber, game and recreation – and his interests were jealously guarded by a forester. Much of the timber went to the castle at Rhuddlan for construction works and as firewood, and no part was wasted. The foliage of elm, lime and ash was sold as fodder for cattle and the bark of the oak, with its high tannic acid content, was used for tanning leather, a process which became a major industry in later centuries. Even the honey from the wild bees was collected and sold. Edward is known to have had five hunting forests in the area, at Bach y Graig, Ewloe, Shotwick, Loidcoid and Rusty. Today only Bach y Graig survives, the 16 hectares that remain being one of Wales's oldest documented forests.

Just as Rhuddlan acquired rights in the forest of Bach y Graig,

*Taming the Landscape* 151

so Flint obtained rights to the lands stretching from Flint to Ewloe. In 1284, for example, 'with the assent of the Welsh', a grant was made to the burgesses:

> *that they may have all their necessaries both for founding lead ore and for other businesses, without sale thereof (that is for free), from the woods and underwoods and also common pasture therein, saving to the Welsh their oaks, pannage, honey and sparrowhawks in the said woods . . .*

As a result, the county of Flint became almost as wealthy as Rhuddlan, with lead being mined in Englefield and smelted using timber from the forest. The reference to sparrowhawks is interesting as one of the few references, apart from the wild bees, to the wildlife. Sparrowhawks are adapted for hunting small birds in confined spaces like forests and were regularly used in falconry at this time. While the Welsh, in this case, seem to have been allowed to keep their oaks, apart perhaps from the ones felled by the lead miners, in most cases the approach was to encourage the 'uprooting of the great forest lands of the country'. The whole of Englefield was eventually disafforested. Generally, when land was granted to the English it was made a condition that part of the area must include a portion of the neighbouring forests, cleared of trees and brought into cultivation. By such means the majority of the ancient forests of Wales were finally destroyed.

In south Wales, however, Wentwood survived, probably because it was once a hunting preserve for Chepstow Castle, and today it forms the largest area of ancient woodland in Wales. In 1584, a forest court, known as the Speech Court of the Forest of Wentwood, was established at the Foresters' Oaks, two huge trees which no longer remain. One of the oaks, a massive hollow tree, survived into the twentieth century, but navvies building the nearby reservoir sheltered inside, lighting fires to keep themselves warm, and the tree eventually went up in flames. An ancient oak tree known as the Curley Oak, one of the few remnants of a wood-pasture phase, survives but is surrounded by the conifers which sadly now dominate Wentwood. Small areas of conifers had been planted before 1760, some of the first in the United Kingdom, but two world wars saw the majority of the remaining broadleaved trees felled. The restoration of the forest though has now begun. The Woodland Trust purchased 352 hectares of Wentwood in 2006 with the aim of thinning the conifers as a commercial operation. The rest of the area is owned by Natural Resources Wales, with a small section in private ownership.

There is an ongoing debate about the main causes of the destruction of Ireland's forests. Many sources argue that most were felled during the sixteenth and seventeenth centuries, while others consider that grazing pressure, as early as the Neolithic, was the main factor. The extent of Irish forests before the Norman

*The ancient oak tree known as the Curley Oak is one of the few remnants from the wood-pasture phase of Wentwood's history.*

Conquest in 1161 is unclear, but timber was certainly used in huge quantities, and was also acquired, presumably as an investment, by the Vikings. The Danish kingdom of Dublin, Dyfflynarskiri, for example, is recorded as exporting substantial amounts of timber, even as far as Iceland and the Faroes, as there was considerable trading with both countries. In addition, the cities of Ireland – Dublin, Cork, Waterford and Limerick – had timber buildings, as well as the traditional wattle and clay houses, which consumed large amounts of coppice products.

It is clear that after the Norman Conquest there was extensive deforestation in Ireland, along the lines of that imposed on Wales. Once again, this formed part of a colonial narrative focused on subjugating the native population through destroying the landscape on which they depended. Even in the early seventeenth century James Neales, estate manager for the Earls of Ormond in County Tipperary, noted in his accounts that there were 'English cattle' and 'Irish cattle' on the estate. The historian Victoria McAlister has argued that importing cattle from England into a place where contemporary accounts complained of too many cows meant that they must have been seen as an important part of the colonisation process. Tudor and Stuart governments were aiming to 'civilise' Gaelic Ireland through the imposition of breeds they considered superior, an approach that unfortunately still influences farming practices in Ireland today. In a talk to the Animal History Society, McAlister highlighted that the invaders' emphasis on the raising of livestock was a defining factor in labelling the Gaelic Irish as primitive. Irish cattle, having more freedom to graze in the forests and other areas, were perhaps seen as wilder. Communal ownership gave way to feudalism, a system under which the Irish could be more easily controlled. The domestication of the landscape brought about the domestication of the people, turning them from semi-nomadic pastoralists to peasants tied to their local landscape. Many of the native Gaelic-speaking Irish were expelled from the east and southeast of the country and replaced with English peasants and

154                *Forgotten Forests*

labourers, just as the Welsh inhabitants of towns like Rhuddlan were forced to go and live elsewhere.

The forests that have survived in Ireland therefore belonged mostly to English and Anglo-Irish nobles who kept their estate grounds wooded for both beauty and hunting. Muckross House and Gardens, for example, form the gateway to the Killarney National Park in County Kerry. The park contains the largest and most important surviving fragments of oak forest on the whole island. Indeed, it is said to be one of the very few places left that have been continuously covered by forests since the end of the last glaciation, some 10,000 years ago. Alongside the trees can be found the last indigenous herd of red deer. This is predominantly a species of open deciduous and mixed woodland, but hybridisation with introduced sika deer now poses a significant threat to their genetic integrity. In the Wicklow Mountains, for example, the populations are composed almost entirely of red–sika hybrids.

One of the oldest oak trees remaining in Ireland is undoubtedly the King Oak, a pedunculate oak in the grounds of Charleville Forest, on the outskirts of Tullamore, in the centre of the island. The Gothic Revival castle, built between 1800 and 1812 and now being restored by a trust, was named Charleville Forest, rather than merely Charleville Castle, in deference to the numerous ancient oaks that dominated the estate. The King Oak is at least 400 years old, and possibly up to 800 years old, being mentioned as a very old tree in seventeenth-century records. Determining the exact age is difficult because the tree has been heavily pollarded, the main stem being cut off to encourage lateral growth. There is a superstition attached to the King Oak which states that if one of its branches falls a member of the Bury family, the owners of the Charleville Estate, will die. The death in 1963 of Charles Howard-Bury has been considered as confirmation of this belief, since he died shortly after lightning split its main trunk. The Charleville Estate covers some 170 hectares, and together with the smaller woods at Abbeyleix, County Laois, which extend to some

120 hectares on either side of the River Nore, they are the finest surviving examples of what the naturalist David Cabot describes as 'ash–pedunculate oak–hazel woodland'.

Other ancient survivors include the Belvoir Oak in Belvoir Park, Belfast, which has been dated by dendrochronology to around 1650 and is probably the oldest oak in Northern Ireland. During its lifetime, Belfast has grown from a small settlement to the large city it is today. In December 2020 the *Irish News* reported that the tree, sometimes known as 'Grandad', had produced six acorns, which were going to be planted by schoolchildren. Trees dramatically reduce the number of acorns they produce as they age, and Grandad has barely enough branches, let alone twigs, to produce acorns – but it is clearly still viable. Belvoir Park, which forms part of the Lagan Valley Regional Park, is another estate that has retained a significant number of veteran trees. Some 270 trees there have a girth of three metres or more, and nearly half of these are oaks. Analysis of their genetics has shown them to be similar to native oaks in other areas of old forest, such as Breen in County Down, suggesting that they are of native stock, rather

The King Oak, Charleville Forest, Tullamore, County Offaly. This is one of the most impressive oaks in Ireland, thought to be between 400 and 800 years old.

than being introduced. Breen Forest itself, which covers 600 hectares, is designated as a National Nature Reserve and is one of the last fragments of the extensive oak forests that covered much of northeast County Antrim. The word *breen* means 'fairy palace' in Irish and may have referred to an earth fort, or rath, which once stood there. Since it was considered unlucky to disturb land associated with the fairies, this is probably the reason for the survival of the forest through the centuries. Ancient gnarled and stunted oak trees form most of the canopy here, along with downy birch, hazel and holly.

The oldest oak in the whole of Ireland is said to be the Brian Boru Oak, which is over 1,000 years old. This famous tree has long been associated with the last High King of Ireland, who was born nearby around 941. It stands in one of the last surviving parts of

*The ancient oak in Belvoir Park Forest is almost 400 years old.*

the Forest of Aughty, which once stretched from Derrybrien near Gort, County Galway, across to Tulla and down to Tuamgraney in County Clare. Given its importance, the National Monuments Service has listed the tree as a Ritual Site/Holy Tree. The Tree Council of Ireland carried out surgery on the oak tree in the 1980s 'to prolong its life', but it would almost certainly have survived without such drastic intervention. Battered, but unbowed, it still bears acorns – and thousands have been planted throughout the country.

Dependent for the most part on fishing, gathering, hunting and keeping cattle, the Gaelic civilisation before the Conquest was automatically considered inferior by the Normans, who mainly depended on agriculture. Gerald of Wales, for instance, whose father was a Norman knight, travelled to Ireland in 1183 'partly to join the Norman Conquest, partly to see and explore the country', and considered the lack of interest in farming and husbandry a sign of barbarity:

*The Brian Boru Oak, which is reputed to be the oldest oak in the whole of Ireland.*

> *The Irish are a rude people, subsisting on the produce of their cattle only, and living themselves like beasts – a people that has not yet departed from the primitive habits of pastoral life . . . their pastures are short of herbage; cultivation is very rare, and there is scarcely any land sown . . . The whole habits of the people are contrary to agricultural pursuits.*

The Irish were also described as a 'salvage nation', an obsolete term for 'savage' and a derivative of *silva*, Latin for wood, which again links the native people with their forested landscape in a negative way.

When England's Tudor armies began their conquest of Ireland in the sixteenth century there were still extensive forests, the local forces taking advantage of the cover to plan their attacks. Indeed, throughout the sixteenth century the opposition to the Tudor conquest increased the role of forests as strongholds for the Irish. As in Wales, they were secure rallying areas for the natives, but for the English colonists they were places of fearful ambush, and this remained an important strategic issue until the following century. Gerald of Wales observed that the Irish were accustomed to improve the impregnable character of a forest by cutting down trees on both sides of a passage through it, casting some in the way, forming breastwork with others, and plashing or interlacing the lower branches of standing trees with the undergrowth. When the English were marching to the siege of Dunboy in 1602 they were forced to detour around dense forests in the region of Kinsale and Timoleague. As a result, Elizabeth I ordered their destruction in order to deprive the Irish of shelter, and improve England's supply of timber. The Irish did not give in easily though, and it was not until 1603 that the entire country finally came under the nominal control of James I. This left the way clear for extensive areas of land to be confiscated by English, Scottish and Welsh colonists, culminating in the Plantation of Ulster. The surviving forests provided the only available shelter for the dispossessed Irish, who were known as 'woodkerne', a reference to Irish foot-soldiers called *ceithearnaigh*, or 'kerne'.

There was an interest by American authorities in the English activities in Ireland, as they colonised the country and the eastern seaboard of North America at the same time, in similar ways, with comparable attitudes towards the existing inhabitants. The writer James Doan has pointed out that there is, in fact, a whole body of literature comparing the 'Wild Irish' to Native Americans. The English were advised that 'no less cautions were to be observed' by those engaged in the Plantation of Ulster 'than if these new colonies were to be led to inhabit among the barbarous Indians'. Thomas Blennerhasset (1550–1625) became one of these planters or 'undertakers'. In his book *A Direction for the Plantation in Ulster* (1610) he argued for the removal of the Irish, as the best means for the 'securing of that wilde countrye to the crowne of England', and urged careful attention to fortifications and military preparedness in an area where great hostility and resistance from the displaced Irish could reasonably be expected. Describing both the wolf and the woodkerne as the most serious dangers to the Ulster colonists, he recommended periodic manhunts to track down the human wolves to their lairs in the forests. 'No doubt,' he observed, 'it will be a pleasant hunt and much prey will fall to the followers . . .'

Wolves and woodkerne were usually considered together, as they represented a common threat to the settlers, and there were rewards for their destruction. Sir Richard Boyle, Earl of Cork, writing in 1632 about the forests that once diverted the English before the siege of Dunboy noted, for instance, that:

> *The place where the Bandon Bridge is situated is upon a great district of the country and was within the last twenty-four years a mere waste bog and wood serving a retreat to woodkernes, rebels, thieves and wolves and yet now (God be praised) as civil a plantation as most in England.*

Ireland was often referred to as 'wolf-land'. In Shakespeare's *As You Like It*, for instance, Rosalind compares lovers' complaints to the 'howling of Irish wolves against the moon'. Later in the seventeenth century, letters from Richard Boyle, the first Earl of Cork, mention wolves in the Bandon area, while over a hundred years later they were still present, the settlement of Gougane Barra being referred to in 1720 as a 'Howling Wilderness of Wolves'. It was a third invasion of Ireland in 1649, by Oliver Cromwell with his New Model Army, that seriously reduced the Irish wolf population. Cromwell made an order on 27 April 1652 to prevent the export of wolfhounds from Ireland, as they were getting rare and the wolves were considered to be too numerous. Because of their great size, wolfhounds were in high demand in Rome at this time to protect the estates of nobles. Cromwell also issued a declaration which placed a bounty on the wolf:

> . . . *for every bitch wolfe, six pounds; for every dogg wolfe, five pounds; for every cubb which prayeth for himself, forty shillings; for every suckling cubb, ten shillings; and no woolfe after the last of September until the 10th of January be accounted a young woolfe, and the commissioners of the revenue shall cause the same equallie assessed within their precincts.*

Five or six pounds was literally a fortune in the 1650s, equating to around £1,000 pounds today, so there was a considerable incentive to kill wolves, wherever they occurred. Despite this persecution, wolves survived as a key species in the Irish fauna until the end of the eighteenth century. The last wolf is said to have been killed in 1786, but there are many 'last wolves' in the records and the exact date and place of their extinction will never be known for certain. They were perhaps luckier than the people. Four years after Cromwell's arrival a quarter of the Irish population was dead and many thousands had been sold into slavery abroad. Like the forests it once inhabited, the memory of the wolf lives on in Irish place-names. An old Irish name for a wolf is *faol* or *faolchú*, and it can be found, for example, in Feltrim (Faoldroim) Hill in County Dublin. A popular boy's name, even today, is Faolán, which means 'little wolf'.

After the Tudors, deforestation continued apace, and in less than

*Taming the Landscape* 161

a hundred years the environmental effects of deforestation were clearly visible, with native species such as wolves, eagles and wildcats declining as a result of losing their natural habitat. In 1643 Sir Charles Vavasour, an English soldier who fought against the Irish Rebellion of 1641, found the Gap, properly known as Barnakill, County Waterford, to be full of oak, ash and birch. Nearby at Clonegar, on the southern banks of the River Suir, Arthur Young over a hundred years later referred to 'a natural wilderness of tall venerable oaks . . . the whole wood rises boldly from the bottom, tree upon tree to a vast height, of large oak'. At the end of the eighteenth century both areas were barren, but as early as 1715 many of the London guilds and companies that had acquired land in Ireland were already examining their leases to clarify their position in relation to the decline in timber resources. The Irish Society, which had been formed to exploit the newly conquered colony, like the East India Company a century or so later, decided in 1720 that the timber allowance to their tenants should be reduced. In a period when timber was such a vital part of everyday activity this was a savage restriction, especially as the situation had been brought about by the landlords themselves. By 1781 the problem had become so severe that a number of Parliamentary Acts were introduced to try and conserve the existing timber and encourage planting, but they had little effect.

Research by Mike Baillie has, in fact, found that 'modern oaks' in Ireland – that is, those originating after 1700 – are not Irish but were imported. The oldest modern oak investigated so far dates back to 1640. One clue was that from 5200 BCE to 1700 CE the mean width of an annual growth ring was one millimetre, but after 1700 the mean increased to two millimetres. Most of the surviving Irish oaks in the eighteenth century were on private estates, whereas outside these areas few trees survived. The doubling of the human population, from about four million in 1740 to eight million in 1840, resulted in an increased demand for timber.

Once the Irish had been subdued, their forests, like those in

England and Wales, were governed under the Norman legal system, which has been described as 'a perfect instrument for the monopolisation of natural resources in the interests of the rulers of feudal England'. Compared to England, relatively few Irish documents from the seventeenth century have survived. They were lost through various mishaps over the centuries, not least through the siege of the Four Courts in the Irish Civil War. The siege ended on 30 June 1922, with a catastrophic explosion that destroyed the Public Record Office and hundreds of years of documented Irish history. The Virtual Record Treasury of Ireland, launched in June 2022, is a digital archive which has thankfully recovered many of the lost documents, and this will enable further research, although it seems that there will never now be a reliable account of Irish forests during the medieval period.

Since forests were legally defined areas rather than having a particular physical form, there are sometimes few archaeological traces. The documents that have survived have therefore proved crucial in identifying them, some of which, such as Cratloe Woods in County Clare, or Glencree in County Wicklow, are still large areas of woodland or unfarmed open land. Much of the original oak forest at Cratloe has been replaced with coniferous softwoods but small pockets of the original forest survive, notably Garranon Wood. The roof beams of the Palace of Westminster in London and the Royal Palace in Amsterdam are said to have been made from ancient oaks felled when Cratloe was cleared. In May 1290, 100 pounds in silver was issued to William de Mones to pay for timber from Glencree to be sent to Wales, where Queen Eleanor was constructing a castle at Haverfordwest. This evidently took some time, as it was July before the wages were paid to the various carpenters and other workmen involved.

The majority of the surviving records relate to the forests held by the king. Most were located close to the major centres in Dublin, Waterford, Wexford, Limerick and Tipperary. Where their function is recorded, it is notable that once again most references relate to timber, although the forests still had an important role in providing venues for hunting parties. But with high levels of absenteeism by the lords and only very rare royal visits to Ireland, this was not their main function. Instead, their main value lay in the power to control access to venison and timber that could be used as gifts, and to provide opportunities for giving lucrative positions to favoured subjects and so bind them closer to the crown.

The Normans never ventured far into Scotland and, as the land was both a long way from London and considered to be fairly poor, they eventually gave up the idea of conquering the country. Some English nobles sought sanctuary at the court of Malcolm III, including Edgar Ætheling, a member of the house of Wessex and therefore the last English claimant to the throne of England. Faced with a hostile Scotland in alliance with disaffected English lords, including Ætheling, in 1072 William rode north and signed the Treaty of Abernethy. Although the specific details of the treaty are lost to history, it is known that in return for swearing allegiance to William, Malcolm was given estates in Cumbria and Edgar Ætheling was banned from the Scottish court. The direct effects of the Norman invasion therefore remained confined to England and, despite political changes, Scottish forests were spared the extensive destruction that occurred in Ireland and Wales.

From the thirteenth century onwards, many maps and detailed surveys, especially in England, make it possible to follow the histories of individual forests and woods, their management, and even the products that came from them. The historical geographer John Langton has described forests in Britain and Ireland as part of a common resource that existed before land was privatised for the pursuit of financial profit by individual owners. Even today the rights and access of indigenous peoples and communities to forests across the world are under increasing threat from land acquisitions and other pressures associated with global trade and investment. The next chapter therefore examines how people in the medieval period living in and around the surviving forests used this resource.

CHAPTER 7

# The Forest Economy

*In fact, both the forest economy and the peasant economy of forest regions
at this date were more complex than has sometimes been supposed.*

Jean Birrell

Forests, especially those in medieval England, have been described as landscapes of 'oppression, for hunting, avarice and selfish indulgence' where kings and nobles hunted and the local people were restricted by forest laws. Certainly, in the eleventh and twelfth centuries the administration of the law was very severe, with mutilation and even death for some offences. In 1215, however, several clauses of the Magna Carta provided relief from the most oppressive legislation. After King John's death in 1216, a version of the charter was also issued for Ireland in the name of his son, Henry III. More importantly perhaps for our story, in 1217, all of the rules in the Magna Carta that related to the forest were put into a separate charter, the Charter of the Forest (*Carta Forestae*). Essentially, this re-established the rights of access to the forest for free men that had been severely reduced by William the Conqueror and his heirs. The final version of the charter, following some minor changes, was produced in 1225. An extraordinary document, it is regarded by many authorities as one of the world's first pieces of environmental legislation. In 2017, to mark 800 years since the charter was first created, over fifty organisations in the UK, led by the Woodland Trust, launched a Charter for Trees, Woods and People to recognise their current value to society. According to the Trust, the new charter 'sets out the modern-day relationship between people and trees and the vision for a future'.

The original charter radically changed rights relating to the royal forests. In particular, it significantly diminished the power of the king, improved the system of forest courts, converted some forests into commons, returned other parts to private owners, and served to mediate conflicts. Importantly, the first chapter protected common pasture in the forest for all those 'accustomed to it', and chapter nine provided for 'every man to agist [take cattle to graze] his wood in the forest as he wishes'.

*A copy of the final version of the Charter of the Forest, produced in 1225, held in the British Library.*

166 *Forgotten Forests*

Especially in England, with its high population, land was a relatively scarce resource, and demand for arable fields, necessary to feed around five million people or more, was high. Sometimes, in the rush to clear additional land for the plough, even manorial and parish boundaries were ignored. The remaining forests were therefore often the only common land on which animals could be grazed. Due to the demands on pasture, farmers, landlords and peasants all paid fees to put their horses, cattle and pigs in the forests. Sheep and goats competed for food with deer and so were normally excluded. The king or lord could also use the forest for their own grazing animals. For example, in 1211–1212 the king's steward put 173 cows into the forest of Trim on the banks of the River Boyne in Ireland. It should of course be noted that in the later medieval period the term 'forest' could include woodland, heath, farmland and even villages, together with lands that were held by the king, or by his subjects, for hunting.

Despite the restrictions, reduced as they may have been, for most people at this time forests offered a life of independence and opportunity. Records suggest that people living there enjoyed a more varied and less constrained life than those living in the deforested and planned 'champion' countryside – from the French *champ*, meaning field. The historian Christopher Dyer has noted that 'their mentality tended to individualism and nonconformity; they turned more readily than the solid champion peasants to rebellion and crime'. This seems an unfair characterisation but, owing to their position, forest people certainly had more autonomy than those in deforested areas, and generally took advantage of the freedom. Indeed, it is arguable that, despite the restrictions placed on them by the various laws, the peasant communities in Britain and Ireland at this period in history were the last people to have a really close, and continuous, relationship with the forest.

Most people still lived, like their ancestors, in a wooden world. Perhaps most importantly, until the nineteenth century, and plentiful supplies of coal, people relied on a supply of firewood in order to survive the winter. Forests and woodlands were therefore indispensable to every community. In addition to fuel, they yielded timber for the construction and repair of buildings, agricultural implements, fences, grazing for livestock, and beech nuts and acorns for fattening pigs in the autumn. Licences were also issued to carpenters and turners enabling them to work for specified periods in the forest, where they made wooden items such as furniture, barrels, casks, buckets, bowls and dishes, for sale.

Thefts of timber could be a problem, and for this reason permission for its extraction was usually granted on the basis that it was cut under the supervision of a forester. Foresters were responsible for managing the woodlands on a lord's property, and for this reason they were sometimes known as 'woodwards'. The rules were often quite detailed. In the charter of William de Breos to the English and Welsh of the Gower peninsula, wood could be taken under the watch of the forester, but if the forester was not present, the applicant had to blow a horn three times or, if he had no horn, strike a tree three times with an axe and await the forester's arrival. If he did not appear within a suitable time, then the wood could be taken without his approval. Cases were not always straightforward. In 1305 a carpenter, Thomas de Sandeby, was accused of stealing timber and wood from Glencree in the Wicklow Mountains in Ireland and kept imprisoned in irons for three weeks. He was eventually acquitted but complained that the king's forester, John Matheu, who had originally arrested him, was subsequently the chairman of the jury that freed him. There was clearly some history of disagreement between them, which was not recorded in the court documents, and the case provides an insight into the way that relationships between individuals in small communities could shape the administration of the forests.

Petitions concerning disputes were numerous, and in 1270 a dispute between Llywelyn Vychan, a Welsh baron, and the king's men of Oswestry over the felling of timber even resulted in bloodshed. In 1309 the burgesses of Overton in Flintshire complained about the destruction of 500 acres of woodland, and in 1386 there were complaints about the felling of 3,000 oaks in Coydrath and Rodewode in Pembrokeshire. Indeed, these disputes were so frequent that medieval lawyers often had a model complaint to hand, ready to be used when the issue arose. Despite remarkably complex arrangements governing the way the forests of these islands were managed, primarily to facilitate hunting, they were essentially open to all. Branches removed from trees felled for timber, trees and branches blown down by the wind, small branches that could be pulled down by hand, twigs and other dead wood that had fallen from trees and bushes, tree bark and bushes cut by foresters to feed deer – all were put to good use.

Traditional wood-gathering rights are still exercised today in Grovely Forest, one of the largest woodlands in Wiltshire. The proceedings of a court held in the forest on 15 March 1603 recorded the long-held right to gather 'all kinde of deade snapping woode Boughs and Stickes' for firewood, the boughs to be 'drawen by strength of people'. Hand carts can be used but horse-drawn carts

*The villagers of Great Wishford with their banner outside Salisbury Cathedral on Oak Apple Day in 2013.*

are not allowed, nor any other powered vehicle. When bicycles were invented, there was some debate about them but finally it was decided that, since human strength is necessary to move them, they could be permitted. Perhaps there needs to be another discussion now that electric bikes are available! This right to gather wood is renewed every year on 29 May, Oak Apple Day, by the villagers of Great Wishford wearing oak leaves or oak-apples, the galls found on many species of oak, and shouting 'Grovely, Grovely, Grovely, and All Grovely' at the high altar in Salisbury Cathedral. At one time those taking part in the custom are said to have danced the whole 10 kilometres between the village and the city. The banner that they now carry repeats the words of their claim but also the phrase 'Unity is Strength'.

One of the theories surrounding the origin of the Abbots Bromley Horn Dance, a unique dance performed with reindeer antlers in

*The Abbots Bromley Horn Dancers around 1900, as illustrated in* Sir Benjamin Stone's Pictures: Festivals, Ceremonies and Customs.

the Staffordshire village and surrounding district on Wakes Monday, is that it dates to the reign of Henry I, following the granting of hunting rights in Needwood Forest. There is no evidence that any such privileges were given at this time, but it does appear that five men were given grazing rights in the forest in 1125. Although now performed in September, in the early seventeenth century it was one of the entertainments of the Christmas season, the date being changed when the dance was revived, after a lapse of nearly a hundred years, in the early part of the eighteenth century. The antlers have been carbon-dated to around 1065, so it could be argued that they are roughly contemporary with the gift of grazing rights, but it now seems that the tradition began with a midwinter hobby-horse custom and the antlers were added as an 'exotic extra'. As the folklorist Ronald Hutton has said, 'It is an Abbots Bromley original and all the more worthy of respect for that.'

Even as late as the sixteenth century Needwood was certainly

*A sketch of Needwood Forest before it was felled, showing the ancient trees and deer, from* English Pictures Drawn with Pen and Pencil *by Samuel Gosnell Green and Samuel Manning (1889).*

well stocked with deer, John Leland, an English poet and antiquary, observing that 'The Forest of Neede Woode by Tuttebrri . . . is mervelussy plenished with dere.' Unlike many of the English medieval forests, Needwood was originally well wooded and was noted for its especially fine oaks, but by the end of the nineteenth century it had been destroyed, following an Act of Parliament in 1803 which allowed the forestry commissioners to enclose it and fell the trees. Luckily its past glory was captured in a book by Samuel Gosnell Green and Samuel Manning, which was published in 1889.

Much of the basic information on forests and woods in England in the medieval period comes from the Domesday Book. One of the questions asked by the Domesday commissioners was 'How much wood?' Unfortunately, the form of the answers varied in different areas and often did not reveal as much as we would like. Occasionally it was stated merely that there was enough wood for fuel, or for repairing houses. Sometimes the amount of woodland was indicated by the number of pigs that fed on the acorns or beechmast, a very unsatisfactory measure. Despite this, the book provides information on around 7,800 woods, which means that about half of the places recorded had their own woods, while in areas such as the Midlands, the Fens, Breckland and east and northwest Yorkshire there were large tracts of land with little tree cover. The largest single wood covered around 9,600 hectares and later formed part of Cannock Chase in Staffordshire. Most woods were much smaller, many being only two hectares, or even less.

Indeed, the survey revealed that by this time the majority of settlements in England had little or no woodland within their boundaries, but many had the right to take timber and graze their animals in woods, which were sometimes some distance away. In Shropshire, for example, much of the area around the Severn Gorge was still forested, and it was here that many of the agricultural communities in the north of the county had their rights. Indeed, by the eleventh century, a single large wood was often shared among several communities, perhaps being physically divided by 'trenches', that is cleared strips along the boundaries. Eyton upon the Weald Moors and Preston upon the Weald Moors (their names describing one of Shropshire's largest wetland landscapes) both had rights in Hortonwood, near Wellington, in the early medieval period and 'intercommoned' there. In fact, both communities' animals jointly grazed there until 1238, when the northern part of the wood was physically divided between them. Many examples of detached woodland rights exist. Most communities on the coastal plain of Kent and Sussex had rights on the Weald to the north, while in Oxfordshire villages situated as far away as 16 kilometres from Wychwood had rights there.

Almost all medieval woodland management was based around the principle of cutting trees in such a way that natural regrowth was ensured and encouraged – unconsciously mimicking, perhaps, the tree-smashing elephants of the previous interglacial. A large number of straight, quick-growing, poles were the result, usually cropped when they were between four and eight years old and perhaps six metres high. Wood-pasture was a less intensive form of land use. Scattered across what was often a very rough tract of grazing land were mature trees such as oak and beech, which were either left as standards or pollarded. An important feature in the wood-pasture landscape was clumps of thorn bushes, for it was within these, as described earlier, that future standard trees were able to grow safely for the first few years of their life.

Surnames signifying the practice of various woodland crafts occur frequently in most of the surviving forest documents. The names Carpenter, Cooper, Fletcher, Bowyer and Turner, for instance, appear in a document of 1296 covering villages in the Weald. Wheelers, Coopers and Carpenters are also noted as living in villages in Worcestershire in 1280, and in the Forest of Dean in 1282. The Bowyers and Fletchers frequently mentioned in forest documents were making bows and arrows for sale. All these people also worked for part of their time in agriculture. Crafts indicated by these surnames, whether carried out at home or in the forest, were probably a task for the winter months, when less time was needed on the land. In Ireland the status of woodworkers in the early medieval period was defined by their skills and knowledge, and craftsmen who could build a timber church, together with millwrights, were considered minor nobles. The ability to build a timber bridge added two cows to the 'honour-price' of a master woodwright.

Another important forest industry, as we will see in a later chapter, was the production of charcoal. This was also work which could be carried out in the winter months when people were not fully occupied on their land. People with the surname Askebrunner, or Ashburner, were concerned with the manufacture of potash, which was used in various processes, including the manufacture of glass. There is evidence for glassmaking at Bromley Hurst in Needwood Forest by the end of the thirteenth century, and Abbots Bromley had two taxpayers with the surname Le Glasmon in 1327. They were probably skilled immigrant craftsmen, as glassmaking skills were not widespread and the market for glass at this time was still small. A more typical forest occupation was ropemaking, using tree bark. In Needwood bark from lime trees was used to make what were called 'bastonropes', and an early-fourteenth-century tenant was called Thomas the Roper. In general, forest craftspeople were reasonably well off by the standards of the time and this is indicated by their appearance on tax lists.

Trees were removed from the forests in various forms, as tree trunks, rough dressed timber, semi-manufactured timber, or a range of wooden goods. Complete records of the numbers of trees felled do not, of course, exist for any thirteenth-century forest, but some indication of the scale of exploitation can be gained from records from the Forest of Dean. Edward I used the timber from this forest for various purposes, particularly for the repair of royal buildings, but also to raise money by cash sales and as gifts. Consequently, large numbers of trees were felled every year. In 1252, for example, 90 oaks and 60,000 shingles were sent from the forest to Gloucester Castle and between 1275 and 1277, 935 oaks were cut and sold.

*Oaks in the remnant of wood-pasture near the Speech House in the Forest of Dean, where the Verderer's Court meets.*

In the end, by 1282 forest officials had documented the stumps of 7,497 oaks, 34 chestnuts and 4,585 beeches. In view of these figures, it is unsurprising that woodcutters in the forest were so numerous that the king could demand the services of a hundred at a time to clear passes for the army in Wales. A similar level of exploitation took place in many thirteenth-century forests as private wood owners cut timber for their own use and for sale.

By far the most common tree in the medieval forest was oak. Its wood is strong and durable, but pliable and workable for months or years after felling. It then hardens, becoming difficult to saw or chop across the grain, but a skilled woodworker can easily split it into structural timbers, roof shingles or fuel. Trees in open areas may have a canopy 25 metres across, with massive branches sprouting from the trunk just above head height. In contrast, close-growing forest trees, or flitterns, tend to be tall and straight and largely branchless for the first 9–12 metres. It was trees like this, often up to a hundred years old, that were most in demand for buildings, carpenters often constructing the frames within the forest where the timber had been felled. Crucks, those great paired and curved timbers which formed the uprights in some of the simpler houses, were obtained from trees which were naturally bent. Trees like this were most often found on steep, exposed sites, which might explain why cruck buildings are more common in the rugged landscapes of the west and north of Britain.

Elm, which grows at around twice the rate of oak, was the second most widely used timber, being especially favoured in situations where unusually long or thick timbers were needed. While it can be 'treacherous', rotting quickly from the centre outwards, it lasts better than other timbers when permanently wet. It was therefore often used for weather-boarding, conduits, piles, coffins and the keels of ships. Ash, often found with oak, was rarely used in buildings as it is too flexible and susceptible to attack by beetles. The poorer members of society, of course, did not always have the luxury of choosing the best timber, and when Thomas of Merdene in Buckinghamshire died and his son moved into the parental home he gave his mother two and a half marks and three ash trees 'of the better sort' with which to build herself a house.

There was a continual demand for huge trees at this time. In the thirteenth century windmills began to be built across the countryside and each had, at its centre, a massive post which supported it and around which it revolved to catch the wind. Such posts were around 12 metres long and 60 centimetres thick and weighed up to four tonnes. Since post-mills were inherently unstable, it was essential that the post was securely fixed. The usual solution was to set it in a massive pair of cross-beams (the cross-tree), which were themselves sunk in deep trenches. These tower mills were one of the greatest scientific triumphs of the medieval period and an important source of power for nearly 600 years. In England alone, an estimated 4,000 windmills had been built by 1300, and like other timber buildings they needed constant maintenance. The massive gothic cathedrals demanded even bigger timbers, which today would be almost unobtainable – and indeed even then they were often only found after an extensive search. This was the case in 1328 when oak posts 19 metres high and 800 millimetres in diameter at the top were needed for the lantern of Ely Cathedral. Similarly, the 52 huge trees needed in 1395 for the double hammer-beam roof in Westminster Hall had to be fetched from near Farnham in Surrey, over 60 kilometres away. Each timber required two carts and sixteen horses to transport it.

In Scotland, logging flourished in the construction boom encouraged by David I in the twelfth century. As the journalist John Fowler has written, 'Woods, and especially oakwoods, resounded to the thud of the axe, the crash of great trees falling and the clangour of heavy teams of horses and oxen engaged in the extraction of timber.' In the mid-thirteenth century, oak from the west side of Loch Lomond was in great demand for the construction of the newly founded religious houses, and in 1291 forty trees from the great oakwood at Darnaway in Moray were ordered for the roof of Dornoch Cathedral. Darnaway was heavily exploited for timber in this period, and today only a line of huge oak trees remains alongside the River Findhorn. At the same time the Bishop of St Andrews reserved sixty oak trees in a forest near Selkirk for a similar purpose, and forty oaks were cut down for Arbroath Abbey, famously associated with the Declaration of Arbroath of 1320, which asserted Scotland's independence from England.

While the grander buildings needed to be solidly constructed, the common people often had to make do with much smaller pieces of timber to construct their houses. In Scotland the walls of the houses were often made of wattle, a woven basketwork plastered with turf, while the windows were also wattled. Indeed, in the Highlands, the whole house was often constructed almost entirely of wattle, the roofs being thatched with straw, bracken or heather. These were known as creel houses, creel being the Scottish word for a basket. Essentially, people were living underneath a large

## The Forest Economy

177

upturned basket. Archibald Menzies, the inspector for the commission administering the forfeited Jacobite estates after the unsuccessful rising in 1745, reported that:

*in all Highland estates they have nothing excepting creel houses which are formed of basket work covered with fale (turf). They make use of the most pliant plants for that purpose which are generally young trees.*

These fragile buildings only lasted a few years, which meant that there was a constant demand for young trees. The pressure on the remaining forests and woods must have been immense. Some years later a report of 1767, referring to Lochaber, noted that:

*It may be supposed that a small house erected in that manner will destroy two thousand of the straightest and best of the young wood as the old does not answer to the purpose.*

In 2022 the National Trust for Scotland built a replica creel house next to the Glencoe Visitor Centre. A frame of Scots pine and birch supports an internal framework, woven from freshly cut green wood, and there are thick external walls built from blocks of turf. Today these creel houses have completely disappeared from the landscape, but until the nineteenth century they would have been the main buildings in the Highlands.

No Welsh timber-framed houses can be securely dated to before 1400, but the Welsh poets often provide good descriptions of houses from the fourteenth century onwards when praising their patrons. Iolo Goch's vivid description of Owain Glyndŵr's manor house at Sycharth mentions that the house was constructed with timber 'cruck' framing and had a slate roof. Glyndŵr was the last native-born Welshman to hold the title Prince of Wales, and his house was burnt to the ground in May 1403 by a force led by Prince Hal, Henry IV's eldest son. Similar houses are concentrated particularly in the historic counties of Montgomeryshire and Denbighshire, mainly in areas which lack good building stone but have an abundance of timber for construction. The earliest are hall houses, which were single-storeyed buildings, the main room of which was heated by a fire on an open hearth with the smoke escaping through a vent in the roof. In many houses the hall would have consisted of just a single bay. These smaller buildings are rarely recognised now, and, where they survive, the single bay is likely to form part of the structure of a larger house with more recent additions.

The clearing of forests to create land on which to grow crops and graze animals, and their exploitation for construction materials and fuel, as described in this chapter, is now recognised by scientists as the most important human impact on the natural environment before the Industrial Revolution. Over the centuries Britain and Ireland experienced successive cycles of deforestation, abandonment and regrowth. Probably the most dramatic of these events was the desertion of land in the middle of the fourteenth century as a result of the greatest pandemic in human history, which caused the deaths of up to 200 million people.

# CHAPTER 8

# *Death, Recovery and Dissolution*

*. . . the Pestilence which was so great and so hideous among the English lieges, and not among the Irish . . . that the land and the lieges are so enfeebled by the said enemies that they can nowhere be defended nor protected, as formerly, save by the presence of your said justiciar.*

Petition to King Edward III of England from the Dublin Parliament in 1360

The period covered by this chapter was a time of change even greater than that which went before. As a result, although we know the overall picture, at the beginning we have only a few pieces of the jigsaw and even those do not always fit together properly. But, if we search hard enough, we can find sufficient fragments to carry the story of the forests forward. During the early years though the chroniclers were fixated on death rather than forests – the Black Death.

The Great Pestilence, as it was known at the time, arrived in England with a sailor who had landed at Weymouth, from Gascony, in June 1348. By that autumn, the plague had reached London, and by the following summer it covered the entire country. It is now thought that it may have killed around 45 per cent of the population of England within a year. In 1361–62 the plague returned once again, devastating the survivors. It has proved extremely difficult to determine the death toll with any degree of certainty, as contemporary accounts are greatly overestimated. By the time of the poll tax of 1377, though, England's population, at around 2.75 million, was only about half of its pre-plague level.

The verderers, foresters who managed crown land, were among those who died. In the 52 years between 1346 and 1398, of the 190 verderers recorded in the Close Rolls, a medieval administrative record, 103 died during the pandemic. From the beginning, therefore, it became easy for people to ignore the formerly oppressive rules. In 1348, for instance, when the Black Death arrived in Frome, Somerset, we are told that the villagers of Marston, Nunney and Trudoxhill fled to Selwood Forest, sustaining themselves there, and did not return until the outbreak had passed.

*A detail from the Millennium Plinth, a mosaic featuring over 2,000 years of local history, near the ancient Monnow Bridge in Monmouth, illustrating the effects of the Black Death in the area.*

## Death, Recovery and Dissolution

181

The Scots were quick to take advantage of the situation. Believing that the English were overwhelmed by the 'terrible vengeance of God', their troops gathered in the Forest of Selkirk before raiding Durham in 1349. Whether they caught the plague as a result of this action, or whether it found its way north by other means, it was certainly devastating Scotland by 1350. According to some accounts, a third of the population died. Wales, due to its relative isolation, is frequently regarded as having largely escaped, but it was certainly not immune and the plague eventually killed around a quarter of the population. Welsh monasteries were particularly badly affected, as they were the only institutions that could provide aid. As a result, many monks died and there were few people left to record the terrible events.

The Black Death, and its subsequent outbreaks, had a significant and lasting effect in Ireland as well. In 2001 the historian Maria Kelly published a history of the Black Death in Ireland, noting, as indeed did contemporary chroniclers, the uneven distribution of the plague. While it certainly affected the north of the island, the deaths there seemed few and far between and it was much less virulent than further south. The English colonists suffered much more severely than either the Irish or the Scots in Ulster. Gerald of Wales, who observed health differences in Ireland about 150 years before the Black Death, stated in regard to the west of Ireland that 'anyone born here, who has never left its healthy soil and air, if he be of the native people, never suffers from any of the three kinds of fevers'. Raymond Ruhaak at Liverpool University has suggested that the varied response was caused, in part, by the overall health of the landscape in the different areas, notably the presence, or absence, of forests. The northeast of Ireland had retained its forests, while the midlands were increasingly marked by clearances, deforestation and cash-cropping. These very signifi-cant regional differences were in contrast to what was happening two and a half centuries earlier. At that time trees and large shrubs, including oak, ash, hazel and holly, were protected by the *Bretha*

*Comaithchesa*, the 'judgments of neighbourhood', and were expanding again all over Ireland, with the west and the midlands seeing the greatest growth.

Although, as covered in a previous chapter, the traditional agricultural system in Ireland involved an extensive semi-nomadic production of meat and dairy products and a certain element of transhumance (the seasonal movement of livestock), the Anglo-Norman approach depended much more on raising cattle in fields, alongside poultry and corn-fed pigs. In the intensively farmed areas that were heavily stocked with non-native cattle, Ruhaak argues there were better conditions for the Black Death to spread. Alongside human-induced changes in the structure of ecological systems, and the interactions of people within these, malnutrition and previous ill-health contributed to the colonists' vulnerability. The simplification of ecosystems that occurs as a result of deforestation, clearance and cultivation diminishes biodiversity as a whole, while providing opportunities for generalist species, including pathogens, to spread. The villagers that escaped to Selwood Forest in 1348 to avoid the plague were instinctively doing the right thing.

The economic, social and political effects of the drastic reduction in human numbers were significant, and these are the aspects most commented on today. High death rates, for example, enabled the survivors to acquire the land, jobs and positions of those who had died. But the effects on the natural world would have been just as marked. The impact of successive epidemics must have greatly eased the pressure on the countryside, as the survivors retreated to the more easily cultivated land. Relieved of human influences, we can only speculate on how nature rebounded – but it undoubtedly did, and we have some tantalising glimpses from our own experience during the recent COVID-19 pandemic. Erik Stokstad described what many scientists are now calling the 'anthropause', the reduction in human activity on land and sea during the pandemic. It has been estimated that in April 2020 over half of the people on Earth were confined to their homes to prevent the spread of the virus.

One of the experiences Stokstad quoted was that of ecologist Francesca Cagnacci. During the first week of Italy's strict lockdown, Cagnacci obtained special permission to visit the forests around Trentino, in the heart of the Italian Alps, where she was tracking deer and other animals with radio collars and camera traps. The forests are usually subject to all sorts of disturbances from mountain bikers, hunters and vehicles. Then all of a sudden there was silence. As she installed additional automated cameras, Cagnacci saw something very unusual: many animals that were not usually seen during daylight were wandering around freely. This was an experience she says she will never forget as long as she lives. Closer to home, in Wales a herd of Kashmiri goats, which usually live on the Great Orme, started roaming the streets of Llandudno, and fallow deer from Dagenham Park took over a housing estate near Romford in London. This all happened when the anthropause had only just started, and it lasted a very short time, but the effects of the Black Death were still evident centuries later. The human population of western Europe did not reach its pre-1348 level again until 1500.

While the animals of the forest would have quickly responded to the reduction in human disturbance, what about the forests themselves? Once the marginal land was abandoned it seems obvious that the trees would have gradually returned. Mike Baillie of Queen's University Belfast, an expert in dendrochronology, has shown that it is the trees themselves that provide the missing jigsaw piece. After searching extensively for fourteenth- and fifteenth-century oak timbers suitable for dating in the north of Ireland, Baillie found that no buildings with timbers survived from before 1600. Many seventeenth-century buildings, however, did have oak timbers, and a consistent pattern started to emerge. The oldest of these oaks, which had been felled in the seventeenth century, had all started life in the last decades of the fourteenth century. Until these studies it had always been assumed that woodlands present in the north of Ireland in the seventeenth century were the remnants of the original primeval forests. The evidence from tree rings showed that this assumption was incorrect. If these timbers were from ancient forests, why could none be found that showed a timescale longer than 280 years, when oaks regularly reach ages of 400–500 years in natural conditions? The forests that existed in the seventeenth century had to be the result of regeneration in the late fourteenth century, when, because of the Black Death, land was abandoned. This is also consistent with the findings from a number of oak timbers from medieval and Tudor buildings in southern England.

Some people have suggested that the ancient yew forest in Kingley Vale, West Sussex, spread onto open land during the Black Death, when there were not enough people to stop the trees encroaching onto previously farmed land. Today, although most of the trees on the steep slopes are less than 200 years old, there is a group of yews in the valley bottom that are said to be among the oldest living things in Britain. It is a remarkable survival, since most yews in

*Kingley Vale National Nature Reserve in West Sussex contains one of the finest yew forests in western Europe. It has been suggested that the forest here expanded during the Black Death.*

## Death, Recovery and Dissolution

Europe were felled after the fourteenth century to make longbows, decimating the forests. During the Black Death though forests regrew on abandoned farmland across Europe, and there is abundant evidence of this, including pollen recovered from the infill of an oxbow lake of the River Roer in the Netherlands. Studies here show that a reduction in pollen from cultivated plants was mirrored by an increase in tree pollen between the years 1350 and 1440.

In Wales, the Owain Glyndŵr rebellion, which started in 1400 and continued for over a decade, also took pressure off the forests at this time. In fact, the war seems to have had a bigger effect on the Welsh landscape than the Black Death. Around 200 years later, the results in the Conwy valley, Caernarfonshire, were vividly described by Sir John Wynn of Gwydir, who recorded that:

> . . . all the whole countrey then was but a forrest, rough and spacious as it is still, but then wast of inhabitants, and all over growen with woods, for Owen Glyndwrs warres . . . brought such a desolacion, that greene grasse grewe one the market place in llanroost . . .

This respite, whether from the Black Death or from war, unfortunately did not last forever, and further changes to the English and Welsh forests resulted not from the terrible vengeance of God but from the vengeance, and greed, of a king. The dissolution of the monasteries began in 1539, when Henry VIII wanted to divorce his first wife, Catherine of Aragon. When the Pope refused, Henry created the Church of England. The monasteries were an unwelcome reminder of Rome and the wealthiest institutions in the country – and Henry needed money to support his lifestyle and the war with France. After the Pilgrimage of Grace, a popular rebellion against the dissolution, the king sought to destroy them totally. Scotland's monasteries, meanwhile, continued undisturbed until the rejection of papal authority there in 1560.

Although, once again, the available evidence is sadly fragmentary and incomplete, the destruction of over 800 monastic estates had a major influence on the forests. The various monastic orders had originally been pioneers in husbandry, felling forests, draining marshes and cultivating the 'waste' places. Before the dissolution they owned over a quarter of all the cultivated land in England. Depending on their religious order, the monks sought places in the 'wilderness' near forests, or on floodplains. They cleared areas to create cultivated land and established field systems: they shaped landscapes. Among all the orders, it was probably the Cistercian abbeys that were the most important in relation to the forests, although other religious houses, even relatively small ones, often cleared trees and owned and managed areas of woodland. The Cistercians became noted for their active clearance of the forests, and their accounts often refer to 'assarting', that is forest clearance for agriculture.

Derived from the Old French word *essarter*, meaning 'to weed', assarting was an expensive and labour-intensive undertaking. It involved felling all the trees and undergrowth using axes, removing all the useful timber, burning the remaining debris, and extracting and burning the stumps and roots. Surprisingly, perhaps, even clear-felling a forest will not remove it completely from the landscape, since all our native tree species will regrow, if not cut too low, and there are always plenty of tree seedlings waiting for a gap in the canopy. But grubbing out the stumps and roots means the end. Even seedlings cannot withstand the plough. As a result of assarting, therefore, whole forests simply disappeared, and, despite the effort needed, vast areas were cleared.

Much of the assarting in England was driven by the growing population, which is thought to have at least doubled, and possibly tripled, between 1086 and 1300. As a result, in many areas, the area for growing crops proved inadequate, and the amount of land under cultivation increased dramatically. In the Chilterns and the Sussex Weald, for example, 180,000 hectares of forest were cleared in about 260 years. Extensive clearances also took place in the forested areas of Warwickshire, Worcestershire, Surrey, Berkshire,

## Death, Recovery and Dissolution

Northamptonshire, Derbyshire, Staffordshire, Yorkshire, Somerset, Dorset and Suffolk. A second form of forest clearance became common towards the end of the thirteenth century, when the abbots were ordered to fell and bring into cultivation the thick forests where robberies and murders and other offences against the king's peace had been committed. The area of forest felled as a result of this order seems to have been relatively limited, compared with assarting to provide areas for cultivation, and there are few contemporary records.

There are many examples to be found of unlawful felling and the abuse of forests by monastic orders. Adjoining the lands of Abbey Dore in Herefordshire, for instance, was the Royal Forest of Treville, which the abbot had coveted for many years. After bribing various people, in 1198 he told King Richard that some 300 acres (120 hectares) of the royal domain adjoining the abbey lands, 'wild and rough', were 'a peril to the neighbourhood, inaccessible to all save Welshmen and robbers, to whom they offered a secure refuge'. For 300 marks, roughly equivalent to £325,000 at today's prices, the abbey got a splendid tract of fertile land, with excellent timber, which, when cut down and sold in Hereford for building purposes, resulted in a profit three times the original purchase price. Gerald of Wales reported that the monks had 'changed an oak wood into a wheat field'. If his description is correct, what the monks destroyed was apparently one of the finest surviving areas of natural high oak forest, with tall straight stems free of branches and small compact crowns.

Descriptions of the structure of a medieval forest like this are comparatively rare, but the assarting Gerald described is typical of numerous other examples across England and Wales. The abbot did not get all his own way, however, since when King Richard died, King John, who had often hunted in this very spot and knew the value of the land, at once stripped the abbey of its new possession. As a result, significant areas of woodland survived, mainly on the higher ground. Treville Forest, once celebrated for its 'champion' sessile oaks and small-leaved limes, can still be visited, though there were few estates in England untouched by the nineteenth-century interest in exotic trees.

At Holme Cultram Abbey in Cumbria, a Cistercian monastery, the monks were in a continuous legal dispute with the king's representatives over their use of Inglewood Forest, which once stretched from the walls of Carlisle to Penrith and the Cumbrian fells. Successive kings were keen to keep the forest intact, since it served as an important buffer zone between England and Scotland. It is said that the 'last gnarled and knotted' oak in the forest 'fell from sheer old age' on 13 June 1823. It was remarkable, 'not only for the beauty of the wood, which was marked in a similar manner to satin-wood', but as a boundary marker between the manors of the Duke of Devonshire and the Dean and Chapter of Carlisle.

*A pencil drawing by Lady Dunne of the 'last gnarled and knotted' oak in Inglewood Forest, which 'fell from sheer old age' on 13 June 1823.*

## Death, Recovery and Dissolution

A pencil drawing of this tree by Lady Dunne, wife of Sir John Dunne, chief constable of Cumberland and Westmorland, is now in the Jackson Collection of the County Library in Carlisle. Her obituary in the *Westmorland Herald* noted that she was 'in her youth an amateur artist and in later years devoted much time and attention to the study of bee-culture, upon which she was a recognised authority' – although they were probably not the wild bees described in a previous chapter. While the old oaks have gone, the remnants of Inglewood Forest can be found in Wreay Woods along the course of the River Petteril near Carlisle, where a deep gorge has been cut through the land exposing the underlying red sandstone.

According to the fifteenth-century *Orygynale Cronykil of Scotland* by Andrew of Wyntoun, Robin Hood belongs to Inglewood and not Sherwood Forest. There is some doubt though as to whether either Inglewood or Sherwood was actually the location of his exploits. The original Robin Hood ballads, from the fifteenth century, located events in the medieval forest of Barnsdale in Yorkshire. In this area, John Leland, who made a journey through England during the reign of Henry VIII, observed:

*Along on the lift hond a iii miles of betwixt Milburne and Feribridge I saw the woodi and famous Forest of Barnesdale wher they say that Robyn Hudde lyvid like an outlaw.*

Originally Barnsdale Forest would have covered large parts of South Yorkshire, just as Sherwood Forest once covered most of Nottinghamshire. Indeed, the town of Barnsley probably got its name from a clearing in the forest. All that now remains of this once-great woodland habitat are small groups of trees to the north-west of Doncaster, beside the A1 at Barnsdale Bar and in Brodsworth Community Woodland.

Of all the ancient forests, Inglewood seems to have held a special fascination for the early bards. Many poems first written down in the fifteenth century, for instance, describe the legendary King Arthur hunting there. In three tales which begin with a hunt and end in adventure, *Sir Gawain and the Carle of Carlisle*, *The Awntyrs off Arthure* and *The Avowyng of Arthur*, the hunts awaken various supernatural elements but the omens are eventually derailed, supposedly demonstrating the uncontrollability of the forest space. These poems belong to what is known by scholars as the Northern Gawain Group, 'a cluster of distinctly popular, predominately northern, late-medieval romances' in which the Arthurian knight Gawain plays a central role. They are almost invariably located in the area around Carlisle and Inglewood Forest, with which Gawain seems to have been traditionally associated.

The anonymous poet who described Sir Gawain's search for the Green Knight provides a picture of a forest in winter that would have been familiar to many people in the past. Considered to be one of the masterpieces of Middle English literature, the poem was composed in the West Midlands at the end of the fourteenth century. Translated into modern English, one passage reads:

> *Into a wondrously wild wood in a valley,*
> *With huge hills on each side overpeering a forest*
> *Of huge heavy oaks, a hundred together*
> *The hazel and the hawthorn were intertwined,*
> *And all was overgrown with hoar-frosted moss,*
> *And on the bleak branches, birds in misery*
> *Piteously piped away, pinched with cold.*

It is hard not to feel sorry for the miserably cold birds, but the unexpected can always be found within forests. For example, lying between Derby and Nottingham are the sparse ruins of Dale Abbey. Its story begins when a Derby baker had a dream in which the Virgin Mary appeared and told him to go to Depedale, as the area was known then, to live a life of solitude and prayer in the forest. After his death there were three attempts to establish an abbey on the site, but all failed due to the isolation of the area and the dense vegetation. Finally, around 1199, the abbey was established and, following the acquisition of additional land and other property, it survived for the next 340 years. During this time the surrounding forest was destroyed, and all that remains today is Hermit's Wood, in which is a cave said to be hewn out of the sandstone cliff by the baker as a place to live. As in Treville Forest, one of the trees to be found in Hermit's Wood is the small-leaved lime, whose leaves are renowned for supporting a number of moth caterpillars, including the lime hawk moth, peppered moth and vapourer moth. Considered an indicator species of ancient woodland, small-leaved lime is probably our best indication that Hermit's Wood is indeed a relic of the original forest in this part of the Midlands.

Small-leaved lime can also be found in what are known as 'assart hedges', which were often left behind as field boundaries when the

*The hermit's cave in Hermit's Wood between Derby and Nottingham, a remnant of the ancient forest of Depedale.*

land was cleared. Because of their origins they often contain a number of forest species, which, in addition to lime, include wild service tree and hazel. At Hatfield Broad Oak in Essex, which lies to the south of the remaining area of the ancient Hatfield Forest, the present-day hedges still follow the boundaries of an area of ancient forest which was cleared by assarting. Adjacent to the village church is the site of a Benedictine priory, which was probably responsible for the destruction of the forest. Interestingly, around 1230 a fire destroyed part of the priory church and Henry III granted ten oaks from each of the forests of Hatfield and Wristle for its repairs. This suggests, perhaps, that by this date there were few suitable trees in the immediate vicinity.

Similarly, a study focused on the parish of Highley, between Bridgnorth in Shropshire and Bewdley in Worcestershire, revealed that it was originally one of a number of clearings in a northern extension of the Wyre Forest. Once again, the assart hedgerows here typically contain species found today in the local woodlands, such as hazel, dogwood and field maple, whereas the later enclosure hedges tend to contain mainly common hawthorn or, less commonly, suckering elm, as these were freely available for transplanting. Many of the pastures in the parish also probably originated from assarting. For example, the Wulstan's Wood estate, alongside the River Severn, originated from a grant of woodland but by 1332 it included pasture with a farmstead. It would not be surprising if some of the assarts were originally used for arable cultivation. Fields sometimes reflect their origin in assarts through names such as 'Stocks', 'Stubbings', 'Stubs', 'Sart' or 'Ridding', and most obviously 'Assart'. Examples of the latter include Assart Close in Farnsfield, Nottinghamshire.

While the Cistercians were noted for their vigorous clearance of forests over very considerable areas, they were also the leading exponents of forest management at the time, at least on the areas they left standing. Surveys of some Cistercian woodlands around the time of the dissolution provide evidence of careful management for at least a century. Gilbert's Hill, a monastic wood to the east of Abbey Dore in Herefordshire, contained '120 acres, whereof 13 acres be of 50 years growing, and the residue of a hundred years growing and above'. There were also attempts to restock areas with trees, and the earliest record we have of a forest nursery is that of William Blair, cellarer to the Cistercian Abbey of Coupar Angus in Scotland, who raised trees to grow in the Highland Forest of Ferter, now part of Glentrool Forest, South Ayrshire, as early as 1460.

On the dissolution of the monasteries all this changed. The land the monasteries owned was transferred to the crown and subsequently sold. Those able to buy monastic land could, if they wished, make an immediate profit from the sale of timber, or they could continue to manage the land as before. Most was sold off in the few decades following the dissolution to quickly raise funds for the war with France. Such was the scale of these land sales that by the accession of Elizabeth I in 1558 less than a quarter of the former monastic land remained in the hands of the crown. Much of the land was sold to 'sundry and divers persons upon sundry bargains concluded and agreed'. The real beneficiary of the dissolution, however, was not royalty, but the new class of commercial farmers, the gentry in England and Scotland, who bought the land. Abbey Dore fell into disrepair following the dissolution, but was later restored for worship by the Viscount John Scudamore (1601–1671). His generosity, which followed family tragedies, is thought to have been driven by guilt about his living on the proceeds of earlier monastic lands.

The disposal of Welsh monastic land occurred at the same time as the passage of the Acts of Union with Wales (1535–1542), making the period immediately following the dissolution a time of great change for Wales in more ways than one. Wales also had a monastic history all of its own, influenced by Welsh history and custom. As a result, some medieval processes continued without significant disruption and, in many places, long leases kept families on their land for hundreds of years. There was therefore a continuity of land management which was not always evident in England. In Ireland the subsequent distribution of property served to consolidate the positions of the gentry just as it had done in England, but there seems to have been less stability.

By 1543 there was increasing concern about the possibility of useful timber becoming scarce, particularly in England. This resulted in the Statute of Woods or Act for the Preservation of Woods, which begins with the following words:

> *The King our Sovereign Lord perceiving and right well knowing the great Decay of Timber and Woods universally within this his Realm of England to be such, that unless speedy Remedy in that Behalf be provided, there is great and manifest Likelihood of Scarcity and Lack, as well of Timber for building, making, repairing and maintaining of Houses and Ships, and also for Fewel and Fire-wood, for the necessary Relief of the whole Commonalty of this his said Realm.*

Indeed, timber for the 'building, making, repairing and maintaining of . . . ships' was becoming increasingly important in the late sixteenth century, as England's rise as a seafaring nation affected forests across the world, especially in Britain and Ireland. As we have seen, the Black Death resulted in an increase in forest cover, followed by extensive felling as the population rebounded, and the activities of the monasteries generally intensified this decline, but there was more to come.

# CHAPTER 9

# *The Floating Forest*

*The Lords and Commons in Parliament assembled . . . being informed of the great and pressing wants of Tymber for the supply and use of his Majesties Navy Royall, without which there can be no Fleete put to Sea for the defence of the Kingdome.*

Acts and Ordinances of the Interregnum 1642–1660

In 1489 five English ships sailed up the Firth of Forth and attacked the town of Leith, Edinburgh's main port. Scotland was still an independent country at the time, and King James IV and his councillors, outraged, issued Letters of Marque (effectively a commission to act on behalf of the government) to Andrew Wood, a sea captain, who confronted and overpowered the English ships off Dunbar with his two merchant vessels. Henry VII also sent three men-of-war, but Wood beat those off, too. This success encouraged the Scottish king, who, considering 'the great and unnumerable riches that is tinte in fault of schippes', decided to create a Scottish fleet. All burghs and towns near the coast were therefore ordered to build, if they were able to, ships of more than twenty tons. This sudden increase in shipbuilding created demands that the existing forests were unable to meet. Supplies were therefore purchased from Norway and France, and in 1503 an Act of

196                                    *Forgotten Forests*

Parliament was passed commanding every Scottish estate to plant an acre (0.4 hectares) of woodland. Additional timber was also procured from France in 1506, on the understanding that the Scottish navy would be at King Louis XII's disposal.

There was also a shortage of shipbuilders, so craftsmen were hired from the continent, starting in 1502 when the shipwright John Lorens came from France. Others, from Spain and Portugal, followed shortly afterwards. The largest ship built by James as part of his policy of building a strong Scottish navy was the *Saint Michael*, popularly known as the *Great Michael* because of its size. When it was launched it was the largest ship afloat, with twice the displacement of her English contemporary, the *Mary Rose*, completed in 1510. Timber to construct this massive ship, which is said to have been 240 feet (73 metres) long and 36 feet (11 metres) at its widest point, came from forests far and wide. The chronicler Lindsay of Pitscottie wrote that the ship 'took sae meikle timber that she waistit all the woods of Fife, except Falkland, besides the timber that cam out of Norroway'. Whether what was left of Fife's forests was destroyed by the construction of the *Michael* is uncertain, since only a proportion of the oaks would have been suitable for ship's timbers, so the description should not be taken too literally. A warship of this size was costly to maintain, particularly for a relatively small country like Scotland, and after James IV and many of his nobility were killed at the Battle of Flodden in September 1513 *Michael* was sold to France. It has been suggested that she may have taken part in the Battle of the Solent in 1545, the French attack on England that led to the sinking of the *Mary Rose*, but, in the end, her new owners allowed her to rot at Brest.

Henry VII of England, who reigned from 1485 until 1509, had also started to think of forests in terms of timber and ships rather than areas for hunting. In fact, the increasing expense of maintaining forests led both Tudor and Stuart monarchs and nobles to sell, or disafforest, their lands to reduce costs. Administration of the land and maintaining herds of deer for the exclusive use of a privileged few had become expensive, and areas reserved for hunting began to be viewed as anachronistic and unprofitable, and better cultivated for timber.

When he succeeded his father, Henry VIII became an enthusiastic shipbuilder, whose pride in his 'army by sea' saw his fleet grow from five ships at the start of his reign to 58 by the time of his death in 1547. Not to be outdone by the Scots, he ordered the building of the 1,000-ton *Henry Grace à Dieu*, later known as *Great Harry*, which was even larger than the *Michael*. While he had many ships, though, it is the *Mary Rose* that is remembered as his favourite. The remains of this vessel were raised from the Solent in 1982, and are now on display in Portsmouth, along with thousands of the original objects recovered alongside her, providing a unique insight into life in Tudor England.

Constructing warships of the size of the *Michael* and the *Mary Rose* was a major undertaking, requiring vast quantities of material. It is difficult to determine the total amount of timber needed for the construction of the *Mary Rose*, since only about one-third of the ship has survived. One fairly reliable estimate though is that around 600 trees were used to construct her, mostly large oaks

*The remains of the* Mary Rose *in Portsmouth Historic Dockyard.*

representing about 16 hectares of woodland. The huge trees, which had been common in Europe in previous centuries, were by the sixteenth century quite rare, which meant that timbers had to be brought in from all over southern England. The largest timbers were roughly the same size as those used in the roofs of the biggest cathedrals in the medieval period. An unworked hull plank would have weighed over 300 kilograms, and it is estimated that one of the main-deck beams would have weighed nearly three-quarters of a tonne. Attempts have been made to reconstruct the Tudor treescape near to the dockyards, from the evidence provided by the timbers used to build the ship. They seem to have been derived from parkland, hedgerows, closely stocked coppice woodland and isolated trees in fields, not from any surviving forest. All these can still be found in the vicinity of Portsmouth, and near Chatham on the River Medway in Kent, although the largest and tallest oaks are now scarce. A study of the sequences of tree rings in the frame timber and deck planking also revealed evidence of pollarding or shredding, practices in which the branches of a large tree are repeatedly cut for various uses before the main stem is eventually harvested for timber.

Trees were being felled in large numbers. During the reign of Elizabeth I, for example, the felling of timber in Duffield Frith near Derby was excessive, and a survey of the trees in the forest, carried out in 1560, showed that there were at that time 59,412 large oaks, 32,820 small oaks and 19,736 'dottards', that is trees considered to be fit only for firewood. 'Frith' was one of the old names for a forest, which still survives in the county in the settlement of Chapel-en-le-Frith ('chapel in the forest') in the Peak District. There is no other known forest return of the sixteenth century which provides such details. It was printed in full, together with later surveys, in the Derbyshire Archaeological Society's journal for 1903, and it is an important source for this period. The large trees were entirely oak, and the underwood included hawthorn, blackthorn, hazel, holly, maple, crab-tree and alder, as well as birch. The contrast between this survey of 1560 and another undertaken in 1587 is extraordinary. By then, the number of trees had been reduced to such an extent that there were only 2,764 large oaks and 3,032 small oaks left. Thus, in 27 years, 56,648 large oaks had been removed from the forest, an average of 2,098 per year. More trees were taken by 'trespassers', one offender being charged by the forest court for taking so many 'bigis Anglia sleydfulls' of timber.

In Scotland there had, for centuries, been concerns that the country would run out of usable timber, and the magnificent Cadzow Oaks in the Clyde Valley Woodlands National Nature Reserve near Hamilton, probably the best example of oak woodland with pasture in Scotland, were almost certainly planted at a time when the country was said to be running out of timber, as there is a broad rig cultivation system underneath them. 'Rigs' were long strips of arable land, often separated by 'runs' of uncultivated land, hence run-rig. The trees date from the mid to late

*The Cadzow Oaks, in the Clyde Valley Woodlands National Nature Reserve near Hamilton, were planted in the fifteenth century at a time when Scotland was said to be running out of timber. They are the oldest scientifically dated living oaks in Scotland.*

200                          *Forgotten Forests*

fifteenth century, and as such are reputed to be the oldest scientifically dated living oaks in Scotland.

Concerns about the deforestation of the English countryside reached a peak in the seventeenth century, when the requirements of the Royal Navy had already grown so large that Sweden purchased control of the straits separating it from Denmark to ease access to its main customer for timber and reap the benefits of associated duties, taxes and shipping fees. In *The Commons Complaint*, first published in 1611, Arthur Standish urged English landowners to plant trees, describing, as he saw them, the consequences of ignoring his advice. A writer on agriculture, he blamed a 'disgraceful scarcity' of firewood for driving people to burn straw, which he said would have been better fed to cattle, and cow dung, which should have been used to fertilise fields. Standish maintained that burning these materials depleted the strength of livestock and soils and increased the danger of fires. He describes an alarming scenario of 'a dearth of corne', starvation, and fire:

> *The want of wood causeth too many great losses by fire, that commeth by the burning of straw, and so it may be conceiued, no wood no Kingdome.*

This little book was one of the first of many practical treatises on forestry published in England during the seventeenth century. They fall into two main groups, manuals of husbandry that concentrated on detailed techniques of silviculture and arboriculture, and political tracts, like Standish's, arguing the need for government action. Motivated by the Midland Revolt of 1607, an unsuccessful uprising against the enclosure of the commons, and concerned about the poverty that caused the revolt, Standish travelled around England searching for ways to prevent further rebellions. Only 12 per cent of England remained wooded at this time, and it became clear to him that a regular supply of timber was essential both for the defence of the realm and for social stability.

The 1613 edition of Standish's book, under the title *New Directions of Experience to the Commons Complaint*, was endorsed by James I of England, who praised Standish for highlighting the problem of 'increasing of Woods, the decay whereof in this Realme is universally complained of'. In 1615 Standish published a sequel entitled *New Directions of Experience for the increasing of Timber and Firewood*, in which he proposed planting trees on 240,000 acres (97,000 hectares) of 'waste' land, and endeavoured to prove that 'there may be as much timber raised as will maintaine the kingdome for all uses for ever'. As a result, James I issued proclamations instructing his subjects to heed forest law, expressing disappointment at the lack of respect showed to him by poachers, and threatening swift action if the laws were disregarded.

The fact that monarchs like James I, and before him Elizabeth I, took a personal interest in such matters, rather than delegating them, indicates a remarkable attempt to control the forests of the kingdom and their subjects within them. Even if they were not always riding with a pack of hounds, monarchs in general applied forest law to protect their privileges and assert control over the aristocracy. During Elizabeth I's reign, for example, authorities in the Forest of Dean imposed fines virtually every six weeks for longbow hunting, cutting down large branches, digging up trees and collecting acorns. The long history of this forest, like many others, is indeed one of constant negotiation between the various factions, suggesting that, despite forest law, the forests were essentially ungovernable. Economic and social changes though proved to be a greater danger than poachers, even if they were severely punished.

The disintegration of the forests accelerated in the years leading up to the English Civil War and, indeed, during the war itself. Daniel Beaver of Pennsylvania State University has pointed out that the politics of English forests were even one of the causes of the revolution in the 1640s, which led to the creation of the republic, or 'commonwealth', in 1649. The constant balancing act between claims to the forest by the monarchy and the legitimate rights of the commoners, such as the villagers of Great Wishford, broke

202                           *Forgotten Forests*

down dramatically in the late spring and summer of 1642. People sought to redress long-held grievances in a radical, and often violent, campaign that defied existing forest law to restore the principle of common wealth. The result was a series of attacks on forests, deer parks and chases across the country. Local coalitions of both gentlemen and commoners killed thousands of deer and cut down hundreds of trees in many forests, showing a willingness to attack and even destroy the traditional approach to their management, justifying their actions during this summer of extreme violence as a defence of high principles.

Among many other reports in 1642, the House of Lords received information, for example, from the officers of Waltham Forest in Essex that a 'riotous assembly' had taken place under the leadership of John Browne, who was apparently an old offender against the forest laws. Browne and his companions using 'guns, bills, pitchforks, and clubs' as well as 'a mastiff dog' to 'kill diverse of the king's deer in the forest'. When asked for an explanation they responded defiantly that 'they came for venison and venison they would have', and that 'there was no law settled at this time'. Their words evoked the long histories of communities within, or on the margins of, the forests.

The politics of the forest remained an important feature of the political landscape and had an enduring impact on both royalists and parliamentarians. The wonderfully named 'Committee for Compounding with Delinquents' allowed royalists whose estates had been confiscated to pay a fine and recover them, as long as they pledged not to take up arms against parliament again. The size of the fine they had to pay depended on the worth of the estate and how great their support for the royalist cause had been. They often paid their fines in trees. Peter Pett, and Henry Goddard, 'Master Shipwrights to his Majesties Navy Royall', for example, had permission to enter into 'certaine Copses, woods, and springs in the Counties of Kent and Essex'. In April 1644 there was 'An Ordinance for felling of Tymber Trees in the Woods of severall

*The Floating Forest* 203

Delinquents for the use of his Majesties Navy Royall', which lists the number of trees to be cut down on different estates:

*In the Woods of Sir John Lucas Knight, lying in Greensteed and Mile-End, within the Liberty of Colchester in the County of Essex, foure hundred Trees of Oake . . . In the Woods of Sir Henry Audley Knight, lying in the Parish of Beare-Church, and Lady Delahay, neere Colchester in the County of Essex, three hundred Trees of Oake . . . In the Woods belonging to the Earle of Worcester, the Lord Lumley, Master Poynes, Master Cotton and Sir Edward Ployden Knight, Scituate and lying upon the confines of the County of Sussex and Hampshire neere Portsmouth, the number of one thousand Trees of Oake, Ashe, and Elme for supply of his Majesties Navy Royall.*

And the list goes on. In total, just under 3,000 mature trees were requestioned by the ordinance. It is interesting though that the parliamentary authorities still referred to 'His Majesties Navy Royall'.

The seventeenth century was indeed a particularly difficult time for British forests. Whole areas were reserved for naval shipyards, and even the ancient trees of Sherwood Forest were not spared. Within eighty years the number of oaks was reduced from 23,000 to 1,300, William Camden, the antiquary, noting at the time that:

*the forest is sadly altered now only a few of its olden glories survive . . . at Bilhaugh are oaks which cannot be less than six or seven centuries old.*

The area known today as Birklands and Bilhaugh is the only major surviving fragment of the original Sherwood Forest, which covered over 50,000 hectares of Nottinghamshire in the eleventh century. Until 1485 Sherwood was reputed for being so thickly overgrown with trees, and branches intermingled with each other, that it was difficult to travel through. While less than 2 per cent of the original Sherwood Forest now remains, the 800 hectares at Birklands and Bilhaugh support

204 *Forgotten Forests*

one of the largest surviving populations of ancient trees, with at least 2,386 specimens recorded. In fact, Sherwood has the finest collection of ancient oaks in western Europe – that is, trees over 400 years old. The harvesting of timber, illegal felling, unrestrained grazing, ornamental landscaping, the planting of conifers, military training and mineral extraction have all taken their toll over the centuries, but even today the past glories of the forest can still be glimpsed.

Amongst the remaining trees is probably the most famous and most visited ancient tree in England, the Major Oak, over 600,000 people coming to see it every year. Consistently voted Britain's favourite tree, the Major Oak is named, not for its size, but after Major Hayman Rooke, a soldier and a passionate antiquarian, who, in his retirement in 1799, published a pamphlet called *A Sketch of the Ancient and Present State of Sherwood Forest*. This inspired tourists to visit and see the old oak tree, and it came to be known as the Major Oak in his honour. Before this, it was called the Cockpen Oak, owing to people keeping fowls inside the hollow tree for cockfighting. A pedunculate oak, which only survived the fellings because it was a landmark, it is often said to be over 1,000 years old. These estimated dates need to be treated with caution, however, since, in a study of the trees here, Mike Baillie found no examples that dated earlier than 1425. It is also not clear whether the Major Oak is one tree, or several saplings that have fused together. There are large grooves visible on the exterior, and the hollow interior consists of several open chambers combined together, which suggests that this is a possibility. The hollow interior is caused by fungi, the most invasive of which is the beefsteak or ox tongue fungus, a bracket fungus whose fruiting bodies are sometimes seen growing on the bark of the tree during the autumn. The soil is also relatively poor and acidic, so the oak has grown slowly, over a long period, before reaching its current size. Additionally, it seems to have grown in a clearing for most of its life, which has enabled it to grow outwards without having to compete with other trees. Indeed, it is still growing, adding just over a centimetre to its girth every year. Trees become

*The Floating Forest*

*The Major Oak in Sherwood Forest is the most famous, and most visited, ancient tree in England: a survivor from hundreds of years of deforestation.*

shorter and squatter as they age, which means they can cope better with high winds. The decaying wood also produces additional nutrients, which the tree often reabsorbs.

In most cases, any intervention, even propping branches or felling encroaching birch trees to provide these old oaks with more sunlight and nutrients, can change the delicate ecology which has given them such stupendous lifespans. The Major Oak though is a memorial to a more brutal approach. In 1904, for example, steel collars and hawsers were attached to the tree to support it, and later it was repaired with concrete and fibreglass. It is a tough old tree though and is still thriving, producing as many as 150,000 acorns in a good year. But the Major Oak, despite the care and attention it receives, will not last forever.

At the heart of Birklands there was once an equally famous tree, known as Robin Hood's Larder. An 1874 guidebook to the region mentions the tree and states that it was used formerly by a thief named Hooton to hang the carcasses of stolen sheep. It has also been known as the Butcher's Oak, the Slaughter Tree and the Shambles Oak ('shambles' being an old name for an area where butchers and abattoirs were located). Towards the end of the nineteenth century the tree was badly burned in a fire when a group of schoolgirls boiled a kettle within the hollow trunk. The novelist Robert Murray Gilchrist commented in 1913 that there 'is something pathetic in the valiant greenness of its scanty leaves. It is like an old, old man who will be brave to the end.' The foliage was indeed sparse but the tree's upper branches remained alive until at least 1938, when the trunk measured over seven metres in circumference. Sadly, in 1961 it was blown down in a storm and no trace of it remains today. The emphasis now in Sherwood is on developing the next generation of ancient oaks by allowing existing oaks around 150–200 years of age to develop naturally, without the interventions of previous centuries.

Shipbuilders laid the keel of HMS *Victory*, which became Horatio Nelson's flagship, in July 1759 at Chatham. The *Victory*, a 'tripledecker' equipped with 104 guns and manned by 875 sailors, was finally launched in May 1765 at a total cost of about £63,000 – approximately £7.8 million in today's prices. A large ship for the period, it is estimated that its construction consumed 6,000 trees, 90 per cent of which were oak. Some of those trees were over 400 years old, producing timbers more than half a metre thick. Throughout the eighteenth century, England spent quite a number of years at war, which led to constant demands for timber. The *Victory* was well built, but in other cases shortages often led to malpractices, the major one being that vessels were often built with unseasoned wood owing to the urgency of the situation. This resulted in many vessels beginning to rot before they were even launched. By 1800 the life expectancy of a wooden vessel had fallen to eight years, and in 1815 a naval officer is said to have observed that 'There is no duration.' Dry rot pulverised whole fleets, and the problem remained unsolved to the end. Large quantities of timber were also lost by the policy of having three years' supply of timber stacked in the shipyards. While this seemed a good idea, in practice it resulted in excessive waste as a result of decay.

During its lifetime *Victory* was involved in many battles and underwent numerous repairs and refits, consuming even more trees, before it was retired from seagoing service at the end of the Napoleonic Wars in 1815. By the later stages of its life, a ship often had to be renovated piece by piece and, in some cases, it seems that hardly any original timbers were left. To keep a vessel in service, constant repair and replacement were needed, and most were in a state of permanent reconstruction. Tree planting therefore became an especially important patriotic gesture in the years

*HMS* Victory, *Lord Nelson's flagship at the Battle of Trafalgar in Portsmouth Historic Dockyard.*

208 *Forgotten Forests*

between 1793 and 1815, when Britain was locked in a protracted struggle against France – but there was more felling than planting.

John Evelyn's *Sylva*, or, to give its full title, *A Discourse of Forest-Trees, and the Propagation of Timber in his Majesty's Dominions*, was first presented in 1662 as a paper to the Royal Society, and was published two years later, urging landowners to plant more trees. It was a huge success, and remained popular until the early nineteenth century. In what is now recognised as one of the most influential texts on forestry ever published, Evelyn warned that the continued growth of glassworks and iron industries would have dramatic consequences for British timber resources. In particular, he received a lot of attention for his assertion that careless deforestation would cause the downfall of the British fleet. The oaks in the Forest of Dean, for instance, were a valuable source of timber for the navy, and Evelyn records that the commanders of the Spanish Armada were ordered:

> *That if when they landed they should not be able to subdue our nation and make good their conquest they should yet be sure not to leave a tree standing in the Forest of Dean.*

The 'Forest Poetess' of Cinderford, Catherine Drew, a farm labourer, published a book of poems on her native area in 1841. One of these, *The Forest of Dean in times past, contrasted with the present*, presents a detailed history of the forest which recognises its role in supporting the navy:

> *Strippers and fallers, now have work'd their will,*
> *All did combine this noble oak to kill;*
> *A century back thee'st been a noble shade,*
> *To cattle, when the heat did them invade,*
> *But for the Navy, now thou are design'd,*
> *Thy native forest thou will leave behind;*
> *Freighted with hearts of oak thou'lt plough the deep,*
> *And in sweet peace, our free-born Britons keep.*

'Oak for the Royal Navy': the frontispiece to The Modern Druid by James Wheeler, published in 1747.

The Forest of Dean is linked to the Ceremony of Quit Rents, which usually takes place between St Michael's Day (11 October) and St Martin's Day (11 November) in the Royal Courts of Justice in London. One of the duties of the ancient judicial post known as the King's Remembrancer is to oversee the planting of trees in the Forest of Dean to ensure an adequate supply of oak for the navy. Like the payment of rents, this duty is now only ceremonial.

The frontispiece to James Wheeler's *The Modern Druid*, published in 1747, features an oak tree loaded with acorns, alongside naval ships and Britannia holding an oak seedling. A Latin inscription across the top of the illustration can be translated as 'The glory and protection of Britain', emphasising the link between a good supply of oak and the defence of the kingdom. The Royal Navy needed so much timber though that wood had to be purchased from Scandinavia, the Baltics, Germany, Russia, even New England.

As a result, the demands had significant impacts on ecosystems around the world and trade was maintained even through politically difficult times. By the late eighteenth century, the Royal Navy needed 50,000 loads of oak a year to keep its shipyards operating – almost a quarter of the country's total requirements. Later, from 1803 to 1815, the Napoleonic Wars generated further requirements for shipbuilding timber.

As mentioned in the Preface, one of the forests allegedly felled to provide timber for the navy at this time was the ancient Jed Forest. It was also said to have been hewn down in 1316 to deprive the Earl of Douglas – who took part in numerous military excursions into England during the Scottish wars for independence – of his hiding place. No doubt both parties were to blame, but it seems that Jed Forest survived, in all likelihood reduced in size, until the early nineteenth century and the final felling.

The New Forest, which was even more important to the Royal Navy than the Forest of Dean, had long been a valued source of

*The Capon Tree near Jedburgh, like its namesake in Brampton, was once known as 'The Hanging Tree', and it is said that it survived the destruction of the forest which once surrounded it because its branches served as gallows.*

timber. Because of the increased demand, parts of the forest were 'inclosed', an area being fenced off to prevent browsing by deer and ponies while young trees became established. Because the navy also required straight trees, an Act of Parliament was passed in 1698 making it illegal to pollard trees in the forest. Surveys of all the crown forests and woodlands were carried out between 1604 and 1612. The survey for the New Forest in 1608 records the area just before the navy arrived, including 123,927 'timber trees' and enough 'fyrewood and decayed trees' to yield 118,072 loads, equivalent to around 79,000 trees. A 'load' was 50 cubic feet (1.42 cubic metres) and an average oak of suitable size contained about one load of timber and made up nearly a ton of shipping weight. The trees were 'for most part oake, and some small quantetyes of beech and ash' and 'all the said trees are very old and in great decaye'. The 'fyrewood and decayed trees' probably represented a generation which arose in the late twelfth century, while a few of the youngest trees present in 1608 may be among the most ancient oaks still standing today.

A destructive extratropical cyclone that struck central and southern England on 26 November 1703, known as The Great Storm, is reported to have uprooted 4,000 oaks in the New Forest, and this together with increased felling for shipbuilding radically changed the landscape. The hurricane-force winds also sank dozens of ships in the English Channel and the North Sea, including a number of Royal Navy warships. Some vessels that did survive were driven hundreds of miles north and west before the sailors could regain control of their vessels. As a result of the fellings and damage from the storm, a survey of the forest in 1707 found only 12,476 trees suitable for shipbuilding where there had been almost 124,000 in 1608. The forest received regular visits from the naval surveyors, who left the King's Mark, in the form of an arrow, on trees that were considered fit for shipbuilding. Even today the mark can be seen on a few of the older trees in the forest.

John Hassell's aquatint *Oak Felling for Ship Timber: a View in the New Forest, Hants* was published in July 1798, just before one of Nelson's most significant victories against France, the Battle of the Nile. The scene is set in the New Forest and the tree being felled by two men is a mature oak, with a thick trunk, one that would be sure to provide the curved and angular pieces needed for the construction of a wooden warship. In the background, a tree that has already been felled is shown being carried away on a horse-drawn timber-wain. Hassell produced a number of aquatints of agricultural and industrial processes in the countryside. His subjects include lime kilns, clay pits, copper works and slate quarries, pictorial evidence of a flourishing and productive land at a time of war. The location depicted in John Hassell's picture also inspired William Gilpin's *Remarks on Forest Scenery and Other Woodland Views*, which was published seven years earlier in 1791. Gilpin alerted his readers to the changes that 'the vast quantities of timber, which are felled, every year, for the navy, and regularly assigned for various other purposes' made to the New Forest scenery he so lovingly described. Although he found the felling of timber beautiful, along with the timber-wain, 'an object of the most picturesque kind, especially when drawn by oxen'.

Oak Felling for Ship Timber: a View in the New Forest, *published in 1798 by John Hassell.*

*The Floating Forest* 213

The main effect of more than two centuries of periodic exploitation was to alter the species composition of the New Forest, with the result that there was more beech than oak. The disturbance was not sufficient to eliminate the old-forest lichens and insects dependent on dead wood, presumably because the scale of exploitation at any one time was small in relation to the size of the individual woods that make up the forest. But, as the author of the Collins New Naturalist on the New Forest, Colin Tubbs, noted, 'how much richer they must have been, and how much more complete their flora and fauna, before the navy purveyors found them'. A pioneering study of the genetics of the barbastelle bat has suggested that populations in Britain have declined by 99 per cent over the past 500 years, mainly due to the felling of oaks for the navy. Led by Orly Razgour of the Bat Conservation Trust, the study looked at the barbastelle's genome, its unique collection of DNA sequences, and from this it was possible to reconstruct changes in the population over time. A decrease in the number of bats results in more inbreeding and therefore less genetic diversity. The reduction seems to have started around 550 years ago, in the mid-fifteenth century, when the demand for oak for shipbuilding began to have a marked impact on the remaining forests. Barbastelles require relatively tall trees, usually oak or beech, for roosting, the same trees favoured by the navy's suppliers, and this, inevitably, had an impact on the species. Losses continued throughout the seventeenth and eighteenth centuries and the research again links this decline to the ongoing clearance of oak woodland.

By the late eighteenth century, the Royal Navy had almost exhausted the supplies of large trees located within easy reach of the dockyards, but demands were constantly growing. In 1796 William Marshall, an agricultural writer, estimated that a standard 74-gun ship needed 2,000 large well-grown timber trees for its construction, representing the produce of 23 hectares of land. At this time the navy's main fleet consisted of some 300 vessels, which would have required at least 1.2 million oaks. As warships grew in

214 *Forgotten Forests*

size, it took about 4,000 oak trees, or up to 40 hectares of forest, to build a single 100-gun ship of the line, which, on average, was only in service for a maximum of 12 years before it was decommissioned.

In 1926 the American historian Robert G. Albion's dissertation, *Forests and Sea Power: the Timber Problem of the Royal Navy, 1652–1862*, was published. In it, he suggested that the navy's voracious demand for timber to build and repair wooden ships stripped the landscape of trees. He called it 'the timber problem'. Albion became the first professor of oceanic history at Harvard, and his work inspired two generations of maritime historians. Based on his findings, many people considered that eighteenth- and nineteenth-century English shipbuilding was a major cause of deforestation. But Oliver Rackham, in his analysis of the historical impacts on woodlands in Britain, disagreed with Albion, considering it implausible that shipbuilding had been responsible for the destruction of woods, commenting that 'only very rarely did a wood consist wholly or largely of suitable trees' and that 'there is no evidence that this ever happened'. While he admitted that 'the dockyard had a wide, but by no means universal, impact on woodland', Rackham considered that the regenerative nature of trees and the way in which British woodlands were managed meant that they survived.

The truth probably lies between these two positions. Patrick Melby, writing in 2012 in a paper titled 'Insatiable shipyards', felt though that Rackham's findings were at best inconclusive, and asserted that his claims 'have been taken too far'. In particular Melby highlighted that the surveys that Rackham relied on were usually incomplete and he had overestimated the trees' regeneration rates, almost doubling the figures. There may not have been a universal wood shortage, as Albion suggested, but the continual demand from shipyards certainly removed trees more quickly than they regenerated, resulting in a decline in the quality and quantity of available timber. and, as mentioned earlier, an increasing reliance on imports. Even well before the shipbuilding boom of the eighteenth and nineteenth centuries, Admiral William Monson

## The Floating Forest 215

(1569–1643) considered that English forests and woods were 'utterly decayed', and that Ireland was in the same position.

Ireland seems to have been the only significant forested country in western Europe where widespread exploitation of woodlands was the key policy. Timber there was extensively felled for ship-building, the navy selecting great tracts of the forests growing near waterways, or within 10 miles (16 kilometres) of them, as timber was still too costly and difficult to transport by land. They had first refusal on the best specimens of timber available and, as well as building ships locally, also exported timber to England for ship-building there. From looking at old maps, Oliver Rackham calculated that by the early seventeenth century only 2 per cent of Ireland was covered in forests. Jonathan Swift, the Anglo-Irish author and clergyman, noted, in his *Drapier's Letters* of 1724/25, that nowhere had 'such a prodigious quantity of excellent timber' been cut 'with so little advantage to the country either in shipping or building'. Likewise, fifty years later the renowned English agri-culturalist and writer, Arthur Young recorded that:

> *Throughout every part of Ireland, in which I have been, one hundred contiguous acres are not to be found without evident signs that they were once wood, or at least very well wooded . . . The greatest part of the kingdom exhibits a naked, bleak, dreary view for want of wood, which has been destroyed for a century past, with the most thoughtless prodigality.*

Ironically, the Republic of Ireland is still one of the largest exporters of wood to the United Kingdom, though it is now softwood from commercial conifer plantations that are exported, rather than oak.

Wooden merchant ships also consumed large quantities of timber, but in due course the Industrial Revolution meant that shipbuilders could build bigger ships using iron, and these new vessels did not need such extensive maintenance to keep them seaworthy. When the first iron ships were built at the beginning of the nineteenth century, they were small and experimental, and it

216 *Forgotten Forests*

was not until 1837 that one of them, *Sirius*, proved to be commercially successful. A few years later, in 1843, when Brunel's *Great Britain* was launched in Bristol, she was not only the first major iron ship to be built but, at that time, was the biggest ship in the world. When HMS *Warrior* was built in 1860 the use of iron was still a rarity, despite the increasing scarcity of suitable timber. In fact, the same year the navy spent nearly £750,000 on buying timber for shipbuilding and almost £1 million the following year, just over £83 million at current prices. For a while, it was felt that iron would never entirely supersede timber in ship construction, but early in 1862 an event occurred which changed the whole situation, virtually overnight.

That year there was a major naval battle during the American Civil War, the Battle of Hampton Roads, near the mouth of the James River in Virginia. This was the first time ironclad warships, the USS *Monitor* and CSS *Virginia*, were used in war. On the first day of the battle the Confederates were opposed by several conventional wooden-hulled ships of the Union Navy. The CSS *Virginia* easily destroyed two of them, the USS *Congress* and USS *Cumberland*, one being rammed and sunk and the other blown up, their guns being ineffective against the ironclad.

When news of the battle reached England, it signalled the end of wooden ships in the Royal Navy, and it was realised that, unless the navy was provided with ironclads Britain's role as a great sea power had ended. There was an immediate, and widespread, effect on the machinery for providing the navy with timber. The future of the forests that had been planted with oak for the navy was called into question, the purchase of timber was drastically curtailed, and the people concerned with the transport of timber to the dockyards quickly realised that their services were no longer required. Many of the smaller shipbuilding yards faced ruin. In Ireland the effects were less dramatic, for the simple reason that there was now almost no timber, much less oak suitable for shipbuilding.

For 300 years writers had appealed to the patriotism of landowners and urged them to plant oak, in the hope that it would grow to the size which the dockyards required. While numerous treatises, pamphlets and books on forestry had been published in England and Scotland during the seventeenth century, it was not until much later, in the mid-eighteenth century, that publications on forest trees by Welsh authors appeared. The first of these was *A Treatise on Forest-Trees* by William Watkins, curate of Hay on Wye in Powys, published in 1753. Like the many writers before him, Watkins urged landowners to promote planting as a 'public and private economy, to ensure naval defence, the creation of a strategic reserve of timber, and as a benefit to posterity'.

Some, like Admiral Cuthbert Collingwood, a partner with Lord Nelson in several British victories in the Napoleonic Wars, had responded to the call. When he was home on leave Collingwood could often be seen wandering around his estate in the College Valley in Northumberland with his dog, Bounce, and a pocket full of acorns, which he scattered in suitable locations. Collingwood had ambitious plans for his estate, but died at sea in 1810 on his

*The Collingwood Oaks in the College Valley in Northumberland, planted by Admiral Cuthbert Collingwood's widow in 1815 to provide timber for future warships.*

way back to England. He was buried in St Paul's Cathedral close to Nelson. His widow, Sarah, made sure that her husband's wish to provide timber for future warships came true, for in 1815 she oversaw the planting of 200 oak trees, known as the Collingwood Oaks. One for every ship in the Royal Navy, it was said. The Collingwood Oaks feature in the third verse of G. K. Chesterton's 'The song of the oak', published in 1915, and there is even a Scottish country dance named after them.

*Great Collingwood walked down the glade*
*And flung the acorns free,*
*That oaks might still be in the grove*
*As oaken as the beams above,*
*When the great Lover sailors love*
*Was kissed by Death at sea.*
*But though for him the oak-trees fell*
*To build the oaken ships,*
*The woodman worshipped what he smote*
*And honoured even the chips.*

All this came to an abrupt end within a few decades, well before Chesterton wrote these lines. Since there was no longer a need to grow oak to build ships for the Royal Navy, especially in the forests owned by the crown, the sense of urgency quickly evaporated. John Nisbet remarked in his book *The Forester*, published in 1905, that:

*All the former concern to the national importance of British woodlands appears to have been completely forgotten; it seems to have passed abso-lutely and entirely from the recollection of the public, and of their representatives in Parliament.*

Eventually, the situation was accepted, but the Royal Navy had not yet finished with the forests. Their products were still needed for the production of iron, as we will see in the following chapter.

# CHAPTER 10

## *Industry and Animals*

*The Surrey hills glow like the clinkers of the furnace: Lambeth's Vale*
*Where Jerusalem's foundations began: where they were laid in ruins*
*Where they were laid in ruins from every Nation & Oak Groves rooted*
*Dark gleams before the Furnace-mouth, a heap of burning ashes.*
William Blake, *Milton* (1811)

By the nineteenth century, iron for ships and other purposes was one of the most basic requirements of the British economy, and once more timber, in the form of charcoal, played a key role. As described in previous chapters, the demand for iron went back centuries, but the massive increase at this time meant that the consumption of charcoal was on a much greater scale than ever before. The word coal, or cole, originally referred to charcoal, the verb 'to charke' meaning to char or coke. In the middle of the sixteenth century what we now refer to simply as 'coal' was known as sea-coal or pit-coal, being named after either its method of transportation or the fact that it was dug from a pit. This was in order to distinguish it from char-coal. Originally 'colliers', or 'wood colliers', were people engaged in charcoal burning and not those working in coal mines.

As early as 1558 an English law prohibited the felling of wood

220          *Forgotten Forests*

for charcoal, quoting the quantities of smoke produced by hundreds of charcoal burners, and the fears of scarcity, since as we have seen in previous chapter wood was also essential for the construction of ships. Since the supplies of wood were insufficient and England needed iron, this law seems to have been mostly ignored, and the forests diminished further. By 1600 the manufacture of iron with charcoal had so exhausted suitable forests in England that various Acts of Parliament created new laws for their protection. In 1609 the Scottish Parliament also passed a similar Act that tried to prevent 'some personis' taking advantage of the situation, who:

*wald erect yrne milnis in the same pairtis, to the vtter wasting and consumeing of the saidis wodis.*

People like Sir George Hay, first Earl of Kinnoull, however, had already made serious inroads into the forests. In 1607, for example, he signed a contract with Kenneth Mackenzie, Laird of Kintail, which enabled him to have all the oak, pine, ash, elm and aspen along the shores of Loch Maree, but only half the birch, hazel and holly, for his blast furnace there. Sir George did agree though to leave enough pine for Mackenzie to build his seagoing galleys, and to only cut the oak once. For his part, Mackenzie sold all the rights to the iron ore and other ores, except for gold and silver. The iron that was produced here was good enough to sell to the Master of Works at Edinburgh Castle in 1617. By 1624, however, the furnace at Loch Maree was 'blown out' and the stock of raw materials exhausted, the remnants of the forest being described as 'sick'.

In some areas, by contrast, the ironworks assisted the preservation of the woods, as they needed a ready and relatively nearby supply of timber suitable for charcoal. The best charcoal was ideally made from oak and many areas were coppiced to ensure a relatively stable supply, although this approach inevitably changed the structure of the forests. The eradication of 'inferior' wood, such as birch and hazel, and the planting up of gaps with acorns, alongside the exclusion of grazing animals, inevitably produced more uniform oakwoods. Generally, an acre (0.4 hectares) of coppice produced enough fuel to make a tonne of iron every 25 years.

The real losses in Scotland occurred after the Jacobite Rising of 1715, the unsuccessful attempt by James Stuart to regain the thrones of England, Ireland and Scotland. After the Rising the Highlands were placed under military regulation, and this provided an opening for English entrepreneurs. This time there were no scruples about the waste of timber, and Scottish forests were extensively used for the conversion of English ore. The ore, being heavy and compact, was more easily transported to the wood than the timber to the ore.

Equally, in Ireland – except in Wicklow, which had a strong history of forestry – the life of an ironworks was limited by the supply of readily available timber. The Great Forest of Aughty was only one of many forests to be destroyed by the need for huge quantities of charcoal as fuel. In England, coppicing provided regular charcoal supplies, while conserving the original rootstocks, but this approach was rarely adopted in Ireland. Not only did the Irish people lose the plants and animals of the forest but they also lost the traditions and skills associated with its management. The only remnants of the Great Forest today are Cahermurphy and Raheen oakwoods. The Raheen oakwood covers a mere 16 hectares but consists of trees ranging from 400 to 600 years old, providing a glimpse of how most of Ireland would have looked when it was still covered by forests. Cahermurphy is even smaller, with only 12 hectares remaining, and it is in a worse condition with no understorey vegetation and little or no regeneration, possibly due to overgrazing. Instead of coppicing, the ironworks were moved from place to place as supplies became exhausted. James McParlan, a medical doctor, in his *Statistical Survey of the County Mayo* published in 1802 for the Dublin Society, noted that the Drumshambo ironworks in 1717 were ringed with heaps of charcoal 'as big as three

Dublin houses', and that it took approximately two tons of charcoal to make one ton of iron bar.

In Wales, three poems written in the sixteenth century all lament the felling of local woods to make charcoal for ironworks: at Coed Marchan in Denbighshire, and at Coed Glyn Cynon and Coed Mwstwr in Glamorgan. The poems list the numerous traditional forest products and services lost to the local communities as a result. The poem about Coed Marchan was written around the year 1580 by an itinerant Welsh poet called Robin Clidro 'on behalf of the squirrels who went down to London to file and make an affidavit on the bill for the cutting down of Coed Marchan near Rhuthun'. Importantly, it provides a picture of the forest providing browse for goats, acorns for pigs, hazel nuts for squirrels and people, timber for joinery, kindling, firewood and charcoal. The other poems refer to the loss of game, in the form of red and roe deer, shelter for wild birds, lovers' trysting places, and finally clean spring water.

*Members of ProSilva Ireland, which promotes continuous-cover forestry, visiting the sessile oaks in Raheen Forest in October 2016.*

## Industry and Animals

The mention of goats is significant, as they used to be so numerous in Wales that Shakespeare could include, as a snub for Pistol to give to the Welshman Fluellen in *Henry V* the line 'Not for Cadwallader and all his goats!' Goats have a severe impact on the growth of young trees and would have been another factor in the deforestation of the area. Coed Marchan was classed as 'reserved woodland' during the medieval period and referred to as 'Parke Coed Marchan' in a document of 1655, dilapidated, mortared limestone walls running through part of the area possibly being a rebuilding of the deer-park wall described at that time. Narrow spinneys and linear strips of deciduous woodland on the limestone crags, such as Eyarth House Wood, Coppice Wood, Coed y Parc, Coed Pen-y-graig, Hirglust Wood and Graig-ddyrys Wood are fragments of the once-extensive forest. Part of the area was still referred to as 'Forest Eyarth' in 1603.

Hazel nuts may have been an important part of the Mesolithic diet, but the practice of collecting them continues to this day. In the past though it was resented by landowners, as they thought it damaged woodland boundaries and shrubs. In 1809 the Pegges of Beauchief near Sheffield went so far as to post warning notices around their estate which read as follows:

*Whereas, The Woods and Wood-Fences, in the Lordship of Beauchieff, Have for several Years past suffered great Damage about this Season of the Year, from a set of idle People who style themselves NUTTERS: THIS IS TO GIVE NOTICE, That if any Person or Persons are caught Nutting, or pretending so to do in the above-mentioned Woods, or Premises, they will be prosecuted as the Law directs. Beauchieff, August 1809*

It is not clear why people would pretend to be 'nutters', unless they just wanted to annoy the landowner, but needless to say the notices had little effect and the 'idle' people continued to gather hazel nuts as they had always done, the event being a social occasion. The excavation of the Norman castle at Quatford, on the banks of the River Severn in Shropshire, in December 1830 and January and February the following year found a 'nuthook', an 'implement to reach down the hazle boughs on Quatford Witches and the Forest Morfe while their fruit was gathered and collected for the dissert of the count's table'. Nutting in this case would have been a 'labour service' for the lord of the manor.

The complaints by Robin Clidro and other people were intensified by the fact that Welsh forests were being acquired and felled by ironmasters from England. A large charcoal-burning industry, based on iron and lead smelting, developed in many areas of Wales and, while oak and beech created the best charcoal, in practice any available timber was used. Production was typically intermittent. For example, at Clydach, near Swansea, in 1704 the furnace was worked from September to January, the rest of the year being used to lay in stocks of charcoal. At Merthyr, where the first furnace was built in 1765, the agreement was that the furnace was operated for three days a week, with the other three working days devoted to wood-cutting, 'which the men enjoyed immensely, especially as they combined it with snaring game and shooting blackcock'.

William Blake, the English poet, artist and printmaker, witnessed at first hand the loss of old-growth oaks on the Surrey Hills south of his home in London. The trees were burned by colliers to supply ironworks with charcoal during the extended war with France. In his prophetic poem *Milton*, Blake combines his experience of seeing the glow of the charcoal kilns with a vision of global revolution catalysed by fiery forces, as quoted at the beginning of this chapter. Charcoal burning could be a dangerous occupation, as the colliers had to live close to their slowly burning stacks in small, temporary, huts that must have been highly combustible. It was important that the stack of wood, covered by turves, burned steadily and did not burn through the covering. For this reason, the collier had to be in constant attendance, protecting his charge from sudden wind changes with wooden hurdles and sacking, and closing any gaps in the stack with bracken, turf and soil.

In Ecclesall Woods, an area of ancient woodland in Sheffield, there is a unique memorial to a wood collier, George Yardley, who was burnt to death in his cabin on 11 October 1786. His grave lies amongst the trees, marked by a stone and surrounded by a wrought-iron fence. Colliers' families often joined them in the woods during the burning season between April and November, and this relieved the stresses on the collier and allowed him to sleep more. The wood collier's memorial suggests that George Yardley was working alone when he died. His friends who paid for the stone — William Brooke, salesman, David Glossop, gamekeeper, Thomas Smith, besom maker, and Sampson Brookshaw, innkeeper of the nearby Rising Sun Inn — may have visited him in the evening and he apparently slept too well after their visit to respond to the start of the fire. It is interesting that two of the four names listed

*The grave of the wood collier, George Yardley, who died in a fire in his cabin in Ecclesall Woods, Sheffield, on 11 October 1786.*

on the stone were a gamekeeper and a besom maker (broom maker), people who also worked in the woods. Ecclesall Woods contains more than 300 charcoal hearths, but they are not always easy to spot. They can be identified though from the small pieces of charcoal in the top layer of soil.

William Ogden, the last known charcoal burner in the Sheffield region, also died while attending a burn in Lincolnshire. It is said that while he was sleeping in the hut near his stacks the wind changed direction and he was overcome by fumes. The chemistry of wood is complex, but it is basically cellulose with other substances, such as resins and turpenes, some of which burn during the preparation of charcoal. The best charcoal is produced by burning at low temperatures, so not all of these materials are lost. A good collier therefore could get a layer of tar under the turves in the clamp. On opening the clamp, once it was cool, this could be torn away in sheets. In the Anglo-Saxon period this had been an important source of ship tar, used to waterproof their boats.

Some relief to the devastation of the woodlands came during the eighteenth century, when Abraham Darby developed an efficient technique for using coke from coal to replace charcoal in his blast furnaces in Coalbrookdale in Shropshire in 1709. By 1779, when his grandson Abraham Darby III erected the first iron bridge, in the settlement now known simply as Ironbridge, two-thirds of the furnaces in England were fired by coke.

Alongside charcoal production, however, there was another woodland industry also producing fuel for smelting ore. This time the ore was lead and the fuel was called whitecoal. No one today has ever seen any whitecoal, as it has not been produced for well over 200 years. Small lengths of wood were dried in a kiln until all the moisture was driven out, and so it differed from charcoal, which is carbonised wood. William Linnard says that charcoal and whitecoal were mixed together in lead smelting because 'charcoal made too violent a fire and wood alone was too gentle'. Whitecoal was produced in distinctive circular pits with a spout which always faced downhill, known as Q-pits. They are frequently found in the woods of South Yorkshire and other lead-mining areas, although it is still not clear what the whitecoal kilns looked like when complete, or exactly how they worked.

The iron and lead industries were only two of the factors which determined the fate of the oak woods and forests. The other, which actually had a much wider and longer impact, was the tanning industry. Tanning is the process of transforming animal hides into leather using solutions of tannic acids, which are soaked out of oak bark in cold water. 'Tanbark' was for centuries a small-scale business, with people cutting bark generally within a short distance of their homes. When the demand for leather increased and bark was in short supply it naturally increased in value. In fact, it was

*Tanbark stripping illustrated on the Millenium Plinth in Monmouth, Wales.*

228 *Forgotten Forests*

the movements in price that determined the strength of outsiders' interest, particularly that of the Irish, whose oak forests had been devastated. The tanners in Ireland in the late seventeenth and early eighteenth centuries condemned the fact that 'the planting of trees [and] the enclosing and fencing up of copses . . . for many years had been greatly neglected' in their country and, as a result, they had become entirely dependent on imports of bark. Their main sources were the oakwoods of Wales and the west of England. Indeed, communities like Troutbeck in the Lake District came to depend on their purchases. Supplies would be obtained from trees around 25–30 years old, the bark being peeled off during the spring when the rising sap made the process easier, and stored in special bark barns to dry. The tanbark workforce consisting largely of women and children who peeled the trees after the men had felled them. The main price boom was fuelled by a combination of the French Revolutionary Wars after 1793, which halted imports, and rapid industrialisation.

The new factories all demanded leather belts to drive engines and machinery on an unprecedented scale, and an ever-increasing supply of black cattle driven down from the Highlands provided the hides. The rapid increase in the price of cattle encouraged farmers to put more and more animals on the hills, to the detriment of the existing forests. This was the great era of the drove roads, with 60,000 animals sold at the Falkirk Tryst, once the most significant cattle market in Scotland, in 1794. At its height the Tryst was a sensational sight, with cattle, sheep and horses arriving in great streams from all corners of Scotland and settling in the fields with the drovers, their ponies and dogs. The major constraint in the production of leather though remained the supply of bark. At the conclusion of the Napoleonic Wars in 1815, supplies of bark increased again and it was said, on good authority, that 10,000 tonnes of foreign bark was being imported into Ireland each year, a similar amount in Scotland and around twice that in England. Prices therefore fell rapidly and the oak woodlands became progressively neglected.

The climate, particularly in the seventeenth century, was less favourable than it had been in the Middle Ages, and this also affected the remaining forests. The records kept by Scottish church courts provide a rich, and generally unknown, source of information on weather patterns, especially severe weather events that caused disruption to court meetings. The accounts indicate that there was a marked change in conditions around 1600, with heavy and persistent rains during summer and autumn, with harvests rotting in the fields. Indeed, the sixteenth and seventeenth centuries were characterised by the Little Ice Age, when temperatures fell, precipitation increased and small glaciers are thought to have appeared again in the high Cairngorms. With the accelerated formation of peat, especially in the west, forests could simply have failed to regenerate, collapsed and disappeared – as they had done in earlier periods of climatic deterioration.

In 1651, for example, Sir George Mackenzie, the future Earl of Cromartie (nephew of the Mackenzie of Kintail mentioned earlier), was travelling between Little Loch Broom and Loch Broom in Wester Ross when he encountered a small inland plain with 'a firm standing Wood; which was so very Old, that not only the Trees had no green Leaves, but the Bark was totally thrown off'. The local people told him that 'this was the universal manner in which Firr Woods did terminate' and that within twenty or thirty years the trees would blow over and they would carry them off. Fifteen years later he returned and there was no trace of the trees, only 'a plain green ground, covered with a plain green Moss', into which the wood had disappeared without being touched by people until the trees fell. The death of this wood appears therefore to have been entirely natural, and the manner of its disappearance completely familiar.

While the weather affected tree growth, a large number of seedlings were now also at risk of being grazed by domestic animals. As we have seen, grazing was a natural component of the forest ecosystem, red and roe deer and domestic animals

230 *Forgotten Forests*

replacing the vanished megafauna, but the numbers of animals in the Highlands were probably limited by the presence of wolves. According to Hector Boece (1465–1536), author of an important history of Scotland, 'wolffis' were considered as being 'rycht noysum to the tame bestiall in all parts of Scotland'. The dense forests provided a refuge in which it was extremely difficult to hunt them, and indeed, the relative lack of grazing pressure must have allowed the remaining forests to survive in reasonably good condition. Wolves, rare in the northern Highlands after 1600, were eventually exterminated, possibly before 1700, but certainly before 1750. The absence of predators removed the constraints on the number of livestock that could be kept, particularly sheep and goats, and the latter became so numerous that they were checked by improving landlords concerned at the damage they were doing to the trees.

Many pinewoods were also turned into deer forests and, as the income from rents was high, the numbers of deer were increased, sometimes by winter feeding. John Henderson, writing about Sutherland in 1812, gave the fullest account of the situation and its consequences. He recorded the 'remains of a shrubbery of birch, hazel, aller [alder], willow and some oak bushes, in the straths of the several rivers and burns in the country' that was 'not of so great extent as formerly, and is rapidly decaying in some places'. There was little doubt about the grazing pressure, Henderson himself observing that 'from the constant browsing of black cattle, it is not surprising that the oak is nearly gone'. He also described how, until recent years, every farmer had a flock of twenty to eighty goats.

The grazing pressure was also preventing large expanses of woodland from reaching maturity. There are some interesting, and significant, examples in the Highlands, where, in the absence of any attempt to protect the woods and forests, the quality of the land appeared to be deteriorating so much that it affected the viability of the holdings. In a situation where the animals were always outwintered, the woods were diminishing, pasture deteriorating and watercourses being eroded, as there was nothing to regulate the flow during periods of heavy rain. As a result, by the end of the eighteenth century the remaining forests in Scotland were under considerable pressure, many of them eventually disappearing completely. Sir John Sinclair spoke of the 'natural birch woods' as 'much in decline' and likely to disappear within a generation or two, which would be a 'melancholy situation' for the people.

In the eighteenth century a keen natural historian and professor at Edinburgh University, the Reverend John Walker, observed that the Highlands contained the remains of numerous forests, and:

*the forest trees are still to be seen vegetating from large old roots; but what they shoot forth in summer is eaten down and destroyed by the cattle in winter.*

He lists the species to be found: oak, ash, elm, birch, alder, holly, yew, rowan, hazel, whitebeam, goat willow, apple-leaved willow, grey willow, crack willow, bay-leaved willow, hagberry (bird cherry), water elder (guelder rose), blackthorn and whitethorn – all indicative of a rich and vibrant ecosystem that was almost certainly at the end of its life. Yet, providing the pressure was not too intense, the system may have been sustainable, providing farm animals with some sustenance at a time when the grass had withered. It may have fulfilled a similar function to 'leaf hay' in Norway and Sweden, where the winters were too cold for animals to be left outside in the Scottish way. Such a system would have been finely balanced: if there were too many animals the 'large old roots' would almost certainly die.

It is important to realise that the situation being described was not due to the extensive sheep farming that took over these lands in the following century, but the result of a farming system still based on the small black Kyloe, or West Highland cattle, which were able to survive in more exposed conditions than the larger

Highland cattle. Until the second half of the eighteenth century the flocks were mixed and consisted of cattle, the Old Scottish Shortwool, the *seana chaorich cheaga* (little old sheep), goats and a few horses. The sheep, usually housed at night, were valued mainly for their milk, which was made into cheese. The arrival of novel breeds of sheep continued, however, and intensified a process that was already under way. In the following decades, once the problem of keeping them on the hills over the winter had been solved by feeding turnips, sheep became the dominant grazing animal.

The replacement of cattle by sheep on the hills was condemned by a number of writers for their effect on native woodland. Sheep rearing on a large scale had a distinct effect upon the Highland forests. They ceased their natural expansion, the young seedlings all being eaten, while the herbage got so rough that there was not a suitable bed for the seed to fall in. On the other hand, black cattle, if there were not too many of them, could be favourable to the production of forests, as they kept the herbage down and trampled the seed into the ground, the result being that wherever they fed in the proximity of a forest an abundant crop of young trees invariably appeared.

The introduction of commercial sheep farming was inextricably linked with the Highland Clearances, the eviction of many thousands of tenants in the eighteenth and nineteenth centuries and their forced removal to the coastal margins. All so that the interior could be used as a relatively small number of sheep estates. Sutherland was the last county to be affected, and the changes here were said to have caused particular bitterness, the incoming sheep being described as a 'white tide' sweeping over the hills. The issue was therefore not the introduction of sheep, but rather the appearance of large flocks managed on a completely commercial basis. At first, with good shepherding, and estates that valued their forests and woods, the new flocks were actually compatible with heathy trees. By the 1830s, for instance, the forests in Sutherland, at Assynt and Strathnaver, were 'rising rapidly' and 'now an object

*Industry and Animals* 233

worthy of attention'. But elsewhere, as profit margins were squeezed and the number of shepherds reduced, they suffered badly. At Tarbat in Easter Ross, for example, only 70 acres (28 hectares) were left of the old pines 'which had once occupied the whole area', the sheep having 'destroyed the natural growth of fir which was springing up as the wood got thinner'. Sometimes forests were even burnt to extend the sheep pastures, or converted to arable land in districts where it was profitable to plant turnips in order to provide winter feed.

The Clearances, and the introduction of intensive sheep farming, also had other, perhaps less well-known effects. In particular, they broke a connection between rivers and the remaining trees, as well as the connection between people and the land, and both forests and rivers have suffered ever since. In fact, throughout Britain and Ireland, we have almost lost an entire forest ecosystem due to the natural vegetation cover of floodplains being cleared for agriculture and urban development, with inevitable consequences in the form of erosion and flooding. Most native woodlands associated with watercourses now mainly contain alders and willows and are of limited height. Remnants of natural floodplain forests survive though in a few locations, notably along the small rivers in the New Forest and along the lower Spey in Scotland.

Some authorities have compared the structure of this lost habitat to that of tropical forests. In the parts of Europe where they still exist these natural floodplain forests form a very varied and complex structure and, if they were restored, they would be tall forests containing oak, ash, willow, suckering elms, alder, birch and lime. Specialist floodplain trees that are currently rare and localised, such as black poplar, would have been much commoner on the extensive floodplains of the past. There is still a significant population of black poplars in the Usk valley in south Wales, and it includes some of the best examples of these trees in Britain. The largest black poplar in Britain, with a girth of 6.5 metres and a height of 33.5 metres, is located on the banks of the river at Christ

College in Brecon. In Ireland black poplar is largely confined to the floodplains of the Shannon, Suir and Liffey, while the most extensive forest remnants can be found along the Shannon and its tributaries and the lower and middle reaches of the Suir, Barrow, Nore, Slaney and Bann. Restoring this ecosystem is inevitably linked to the relationship between forests and water, and modelling exercises investigating the effect of floodplain regeneration have been carried out on rivers in Somerset, Yorkshire and mid-Wales. These studies showed that the restoration of floodplain forests would decrease the flow rate of water within the planted area, raising the water level, and delay peak discharges as well as staggering the flood peaks from adjacent tributaries.

Deforestation, along with overfishing and salmon farming, has also contributed towards the extinction, or near extinction, of Atlantic salmon in many river catchments in Britain and Ireland. Riverside trees have a role in providing healthy breeding grounds for salmon while the fish return the favour by supplying the trees with marine nutrients. Forests have been known to play a key role in controlling water since the time of Pliny the Elder, and in France a decree in 1219 recognised the relationship, but it was the Water and Forest decree of 1669, proclaimed by Louis XIV, that unified and improved the legislation. Their importance for fish has also long been recognised. *Hortus Sanitatis* ('The Garden of Health'), published in 1491 by Jacob Meydenbach in Mainz, Germany, the first natural history encyclopaedia, makes a visual link between trees and salmon. One of the woodcuts in the book depicts a salmon swimming beneath a tree, whose roots are in the water. In Japan, fish-breeding forests, *uotsukirin*, existed in the tenth century, and logging was restricted in designated areas upstream to protect the habitat for fish. Upstream forests were therefore intimately linked with the coastal ecosystem. The main purpose of *uotsukirin* was to support sardine fishing, because sardines were an important resource. Huge numbers of sardines, herrings, and even sometimes whales, were transported inland as fertiliser to support large-scale

## Industry and Animals

*In this illustration, copied from the fifteenth-century* Hortus Sanitatis *for an exhibition in the Royal Botanic Gardens in Edinburgh by Cooking Sections, a fish swims beneath a tree that has its roots in the water.*

agriculture in the Edo period (1603–1867). In 1623, in the southern part of present-day Oita Prefecture, for instance, the First Lord of the Fief proclaimed:

> *I have heard that sardines do not come near the coast if the trees are not dense in the mountains along the seashore. To promote sardine fishing, therefore, I firmly forbid the felling of trees in small islands and the slash-and-burning in the mountains near the creek.*

It was also in Japan that the first detailed research on the relationship between inland forests and the sea was carried out. Endo Kichizaburo, a professor at Sapporo Agricultural College who researched seaweed, identified in 1903 that the cause of *isoyake* (rocky-shore denudation) was the devastation of inland watershed

236 *Forgotten Forests*

forests. In 1951 Inukai Tetsuo, professor of zoology at Hokkaido University, observed that forests all over Japan used to be *uotsukirin*. Today, fishermen are actively replanting forests to help conserve fish stocks. Similarly, a study in Nigeria has shown that the density of forest cover around rivers is positively, and significantly, correlated with the number of freshwater fish consumed in nearby villages.

Scotland has had legislation designed to conserve the Atlantic salmon since at least the twelfth century, and this medieval legislation continues to influence attitudes towards salmon conservation to the present day. A distinction was made between 'white fish' and 'fish of the salmon kind', with the right to fish for salmon on particular stretches of rivers being reserved for particular people. Salmon exhibit two characteristics that enable them to influence the forests surrounding the streams and rivers they live in: first, they return to the headwaters where they hatched, sometimes in large numbers; and, second, they often die after they spawn. This transport of nutrients derived from the sea, to generally nutrient-poor headwaters, has a substantial impact on the terrestrial ecosystem. A study of forests in the Pacific Northwest of America, for example, showed that about 18 per cent of the nitrogen in the foliage is of marine origin and directly attributable to salmon. The presence of Pacific salmon in rivers allows the trees to grow faster than their counterparts in watercourses that lack salmon. Black and grizzly bears along the coast of British Columbia also move large numbers of salmon carcasses from the rivers into forests, and these nutrients are then incorporated into a variety of plants and animals. Winter wrens, commonly found there in evergreen forests along salmon breeding streams, carry a distinctive molecular signature in their tissues that is characteristic of nutrients derived from the sea. Unfortunately, we no longer have bears in Britain and Ireland, or rivers that support huge runs of spawning salmon, but nutrient flows could still be taking place between fish and forests.

We know for certain that river sediments in Britain and Ireland contain traces of the ocean transported by Atlantic salmon, but until recently trees had never been analysed to see if they also absorbed the nutrients. In 2022 therefore Chris Ellis from the Royal Botanical Gardens in Edinburgh, Peter Crittenden from the University of Nottingham and ecologist Ali McKnight, in conjunction with Cooking Sections, an art collective who use food as a tool to observe landscapes in transformation, sampled 35 trees in the Cairngorms National Park to see if the transport of marine nitrogen, via salmon, into headwater catchments in Scotland could be detected. The samples were sent to a specialist laboratory in Austria, as this is one of the very few that can analyse the relevant nitrogen isotopes in wood. While some of the preliminary results are inconclusive, two clear trends have emerged. At one site on the River Luineag there are higher nitrogen values in the trees closer to the river than in those further away, which is consistent with the enrichment of nitrogen by salmon. On the River Nethy the levels of nitrogen in riverside trees are higher the further back in time you go, and this could be consistent with declining salmon populations in recent decades. Overall, the results are therefore consistent with the suggestion that salmon and forests in Scotland are interlinked, but the laboratory is going to rerun some of the wood samples in the hope that these early results can be verified, or further refined over time.

Burning, to improve the ground for sheep, deer and grouse, was the other great enemy of the forests, clearing out large areas covered with birch, willow and regenerating oak. By the nineteenth century the association of red deer with a forested landscape had been broken, and while the owners of some deer forests might have seen the need for trees to shelter their animals during the winter, stalking took place on the open moors, which provided a clear line of sight for the hunter's rifle. As the price of charcoal and tanbark plummeted, and cheap timber came in from abroad, there was little point in excluding stock from previously enclosed woods either, unless the woods were reserved for game shooting.

238                    *Forgotten Forests*

Many of the areas where the trees survived are former royal forests, of which Glen Finglas is the prime example. James II, James IV and Mary Queen of Scots all hunted here. The estate, at the heart of Loch Lomond and the Trossachs National Park, was acquired by the Woodland Trust in 1996 and is now open to the public. It is known for its upland wood-pasture, consisting of old-growth trees growing on open pasture land, grazed by a herd of Luing cattle, a hardy breed suitable for the conditions. In areas such as Glen Finglas trees were given priority over stock for longer, since their owners assumed that the deer they hunted needed woods and forests to survive. Indeed, in 1707 the Earl of Moray's factor, or property manager, is reputed to have said 'no woods, no deir', impressing on his owner the need to prevent poaching and protect the trees against domestic stock.

There was also the new forestry. Increasingly a high proportion of Scottish forests and woods were plantations, either on new ground, or existing sites. In 1750 the proportion of planted trees was still very small, despite the long history of legislation to encourage planting and efforts by noblemen in the seventeenth and eighteenth centuries to plant for ornament and profit. Afterwards the fashion for planting gained momentum, and by the end of the nineteenth century the Scots were synonymous with forestry in Britain. A vast number of new trees were introduced by the Victorians, many of the most important species originating from the explorer and plant collector David Douglas, once on the gardening staff at Scone Palace.

Scots pine was planted in very large quantities in the nineteenth century, the activities of the Grant chiefs on their vast estates at Seafield being typical, though on an unusually large scale. The Seafield Estate divided its Speyside holdings into three great divisional forests, Duthil, Grantown and Abernethy, with a twelve-acre (five-hectare) nursery at Abernethy supplying all three areas. In 1884 the nursery grew 'over two million plants preparing for transference to the hillsides'. Yet Abernethy National Nature Reserve, the majority of which is now managed by RSPB Scotland, is now considered to represent one of the largest remnants of Caledonian pinewood. The planting would not have seriously disturbed the forest, as nineteenth-century forestry was unable to cope with deep peats or high, rocky, hillsides. The trees were planted by two foresters, using garden spades, assisted by a woman who carried the saplings.

It has never been easy to determine whether a pinewood is genuinely native, that is, descended from one generation to another by natural means, because it is also known from the *Black Book of Taymouth*, which has been used as an authority in the Highlands for many years, that Scots pine was also planted on a large scale before 1600. Later, in a letter dated 1775, James Farquharson, owner of the Invercauld Estate which is now in the heart of the Cairngorms National Park, said that he planted Scots pine in such a way that they appeared natural. Similarly, a plantation near Grantown-on-Spey was created at the beginning of the eighteenth century with plants raised from seed in Abernethy Forest, while Balnagown Wood at Nethybridge

*Scots pines, like these in Abernethy Forest, were, surprisingly, planted on a large scale before 1600.*

240 *Forgotten Forests*

regenerated naturally at the beginning of the twentieth century from a plantation that was almost certainly grown from Abernethy seed. Such areas are best considered as semi-natural, because while they almost certainly occupy sites that were previously native pinewoods, and the trees have been grown from native seed, most of the trees have been planted. Scots pine tends to regenerate freely, however, in the open or under a very light tree canopy, particularly when the soil is exposed and not covered by vegetation. Its ability in this respect is illustrated by a remark made at the end of the eighteenth century during a legal dispute relating to Ballochbuie Forest near Braemar: 'These highland fir woods shift their stances.' The pine forests were then much more extensive than they are today, and Ballochbuie once extended along the north-facing slopes as far as Abergeldie. Indeed, there is a seventeenth-century record of 'firs of immense size' covering the slopes here.

Like many pine forests in Scotland, Abernethy had previously been exploited for timber. In 1773, for example, it was sold to 'certain Englishmen' for nineteen years, who paid £1,000 a year for the right to cut 12,000 trees annually – a low price because the timber was small, only one tree being noted as large. These external enterprises were usually distinguished by their inefficiency and short-lived character, although they often removed the largest trees. Felling in a pine forest mimics the effects of fire or windthrow, and if the regeneration was not affected by grazing, then the forest would have returned of its own accord.

As discussed in the first chapter, the Highland pinewoods were not originally single-species forests. When James Robertson, an Edinburgh botanist, was exploring Rothiemurchus near Aviemore in 1771 he described the forest as mixed fir and birch, with a good deal of aspen and hazel, not a description that would be recognised today. Similarly, in 1760 the factor on the Lochiel Estates explained that 'the firr woods are so interspersed with the other woods that they cannot conveniently be cut seperatly'. Although birch is ecologically an integral component of pine forests, nineteenth- and

*Industry and Animals* 241

twentieth-century foresters considered it as the 'weed of the forest'. When Caroline Stuart, the last Countess of Seafield, took a carriage ride through Abernethy she always complained to the forester if she saw a birch amongst the pines.

Active forestry was abandoned at Abernethy in 1878, and the area became a deer forest following the clearance in the previous decade of over 104 people from twenty crofts, five employees being enough to support the sporting interest. Thirty-six years later, however, with the outbreak of the First World War, forests would once again be considered a national priority.

# CHAPTER 11

# *World Wars and Conifers*

*The old wood, look, is growing again,*
*On every side life is flooding back*
*Though it's been felled, cut down to feed inferno*
*In the trenches of France for four black years.*
Waldo Williams, *Yr hen allt* (translation by Tony Conran)

Waldo Williams (1904–1971), widely regarded as one of the finest Welsh-language poets who has ever lived, wrote his poem *Yr hen allt* ('The ancient wood') about the recovery of a local site after the First World War. It is unclear how many trees eventually grew back from the cut stumps, but the war changed many things in Britain and Ireland, including our woodlands and forests. In August 1914 there was a potential crisis in timber supplies, as Britain at the time depended on foreign imports for around 90 per cent of its requirements. At the outbreak of war, there had been little anxiety about timber supplies, but there was soon a shortage due to imports from overseas being affected by German submarine attacks. The Royal Navy was in particular trouble, as it required huge quantities of coal to power the fleet. It was therefore critical to expand production from the existing coal mines. As the mining galleries were enlarged, increasing numbers of timber pit props were required to support the roofs. Without timber, coal could not be extracted, and without coal, ships would have to remain in port. Much of industry was also fuelled by coal. While the government had originally been complacent, it was soon decided that action would be necessary to stave off the escalating crisis. As David Lloyd George, Prime Minister from 1916 to 1922, remarked, Britain came closer to losing the war through lack of timber than want of food.

In order to conserve supplies the French government agreed to supply the British Army with timber from their forests for the Western Front, massive amounts of wood being needed to build defences, to shelter and warm troops, and to repair transport systems. As increasing numbers of ships were sunk it was also decided that maximum use should be made of Britain's own resources. To address the issue, the Home-Grown Timber Committee was created under the directorship of John Sutherland, who had previously been in charge of the Forestry Department of the Board of Agriculture for Scotland. Indeed, in many respects Scotland led the way. Two Scottish landowners who would later chair the Forestry Commission – Simon Fraser, the fourteenth Lord Lovat, and Sir John Stirling Maxwell – had advocated the creation of a national forestry body for many years. Today, the fact that two private landowners were arguing for public intervention in land management might seem strange, but they were certainly not unique in their thinking.

Across Britain, and especially in Scotland, there was growing opinion amongst interested parties that land that could have been utilised for forestry was being allocated for less useful purposes. More radical thinkers, such as John McEwen, a future president of the Royal Scottish Forestry Society, and Tom Johnston, later another chairman of the Forestry Commission in Scotland, also had plans for a state role in forestry in the UK, though they planned a programme of nationalisation regardless of the interests of the landowners. Ironically, it was to Germany, as well as France, that

244    *Forgotten Forests*

many people looked for guidance on how the state could take a greater role in forest management. Many Scottish forestry managers in the Victorian and Edwardian periods had received training in Germany, where the idea of 'scientific forestry' had a longer history than in Britain.

These discussions had to be put aside for more practical considerations. With imports increasingly at risk and unable to meet demand, timber stocks running low, and the lack of experience and indeed suitable equipment, Britain faced a potential crisis if action was not taken. As described in the previous chapter, Edwardian forestry had been dominated by wealthy landowners more interested in growing woodlands in which to rear pheasants for shooting than in timber production. It was in these circumstances that the Colonial Secretary, Andrew Bonar Law, telegrammed the Governor-General of Canada in February 1916 to explain that:

> *Owing to the very serious shortage of freight for munitions, food, forage and other essentials, which is a matter of the gravest concern to H.M. Government, it is impossible to continue to import Canadian timber on a sufficiently large scale to meet War requirements . . . (Request) that a Battalion of Lumbermen might be formed of specially enlisted men to undertake exploitation of forests of this country.*

There was a swift response, and around 10,000 lumbermen arrived to work in Britain during the course of the war, one-third of them based permanently in Scotland. Besides Canada, they came from Finland and Portugal, and even German prisoners of war worked in the forests. There were also opportunities for women to become practically involved in forestry for the first time. The Women's Forestry Service was set up under the Board of Trade, and worked closely with the Women's Land Army. There were 182 government-run sawmills by the end of 1917, supplemented by a further 40 mills run by groups such as the Canadian Forestry Corps and Women's

Forestry Corps. By 1918, 182,000 hectares of woodland had been felled, an area larger than Greater London.

In Scotland, Speyside was, unsurprisingly, a focus of activity since it was one of the most densely forested areas of the country. Large areas of the surviving Scots pines in the Abernethy, Glenmore and Rothiemurchus forests between Nethybridge and Aviemore were cleared from October 1917 until the end of the war, producing over 56,000 cubic metres of timber. The Black Wood of Rannoch, on the southern shore of Loch Rannoch, which contains some of the largest areas of ancient pine forest in Scotland, was also threatened by plans to clear it completely, but the end of the war saved it. This was not the first time that the Black Wood had been under threat, for there are also records of exploitation during the seventeenth century, the pine being converted into 'deals' at sawmills, and it was stated in 1683 that 176,000 deals had been produced. The forest was further damaged in the eighteenth century by indiscriminate felling. A report in 1757 by Ensign James Small, factor to the estates of Robertson of Struan, and George Sandeman, a joiner in Perth, stated that:

*The whole wood has been so mangled and destroyed in the cutting, by felling trees every year in so many different places, which not only destroys a good deal of what is too small to be cut, by the fall of the trees when cut down, but entirely prevents the growth of any seedlings . . .*

At the beginning of the nineteenth century a great part of the Black Wood was again felled, but the enterprise ultimately failed because of the difficulties of transporting the timber. Canals were dug in the wood, with locks and basins in which logs were floated and collected, and the larger trees were slid down a mile-long sluice to the loch, where they were bound into rafts and floated down the Rivers Tummel and Tay. It is recorded that some of the timber was accidentally carried out to sea and eventually stranded on the shores of the Netherlands.

*The Black Wood of Rannoch was threatened by felling during the First World War, but the end of hostilities saved it.*

In total, around 47 per cent of the Canadian Forestry Corps' total timber production in the First World War was sourced in Scotland. Given that Scotland was one of the least afforested areas of Europe at this time, this felling had a dramatic impact on the landscape. A census of woodlands in 1924 showed Scotland to have around a million acres (405,000 hectares) of woodland at the end of the war, of which some 21 per cent was classed as 'felled', or 'devastated'. As the area of productive woodland accounted for only a further 40 per cent, around one-third of potential timber had been felled over the course of the war. John Stirling Maxwell, a Scottish landowner, politician and philanthropist, went so far as to estimate that had the war continued for another year or two, Scotland's forests and woods would have been 'largely swept away'.

Proportionally, many more trees were felled in Wales during the First World War than in England or Scotland. The result was a very large increase in the areas classified as 'unproductive'. The 1924 Census of Woodlands recorded that 24.5 per cent of all

Welsh woodland was classed as 'felled or devastated', as against only 11.9 per cent in England and 20.6 per cent in Scotland. West Wales, Waldo Williams's home area, was particularly badly affected, and in Pembrokeshire the felled area was 43.8 per cent, while in the adjacent county of Cardiganshire over 50 per cent of woods were destroyed. Also felled were the survivors of the larch woods created by Thomas Johnes at Hafod in Cardiganshire, which had been described in 1833 as the most extensive coniferous plantations in south Wales. Due to his enthusiasm, Johnes obtained the Royal Society of Arts medal five times for planting trees. Only Monmouthshire, traditionally subject to strong English influences, and even considered as effectively part of England, was an exception to the general picture of destruction. A stronghold of natural beech forests, it had, over the centuries, retained an area of woodland practically double that of any other Welsh county and had the largest number of people employed in forestry. But it was relatively untouched, with only 10 per cent of its woodland area being classed as 'felled or devastated'. It was not until the Local Government Act of 1972, which came into effect in April 1974, that the county was finally confirmed as part of Wales.

On 1 September 1919, the Forestry Act became law in the UK. This created the Forestry Commission, which had a remit to plant new forests, create a supply of home-grown timber and provide jobs for demobilised servicemen. With the war having devastated timber stocks on many private estates, some landowners recognised the financial and practical difficulties of taking on such a long-term project as the planting and maintenance of forests and woods and decided to sell, or in some cases donate, land to the Commission. With the end of price controls for agriculture in 1921, forestry became a significant employer in rural areas and was considered to be of assistance in reducing the migration of workers to cities. As Mark Louden Anderson remarked in his book on the history of Scottish forestry, however, the Act was not 'a true forestry policy but a policy of afforestation'. Almost all of the trees planted were non-native conifers, and this substantially changed the landscape in many areas. After the war the Commission also embarked on a controversial policy in the New Forest of steadily replacing the broadleaved trees with faster-growing conifers. In 1923 the partial felling of Burley Old Inclosure, an area of old-growth forest, created such a public outcry that the Commission temporarily halted their activities here. As a result, in 1927 a consultative forum was set up to discuss the management of the forest, and this remained in place until the Second World War, thankfully slowing the destruction.

As a result of this approach, forests in Wales were perceived as becoming more 'industrial' than 'natural', and the rapid afforestation became politically contentious. It was drawn into the cultural debate when the great Welsh-language poet David James Jones, better known by his bardic name Gwenallt, suggested in his poem *Rhydcymerau* that the saplings planted in Welsh landscapes would grow to become the 'trees of the third war'. This war, inspired by the planting of Brechfa Forest near Carmarthen, was perceived not as a military one, but

*Brechfa Forest in Carmarthenshire is today dominated by conifers. Many small hill farms were lost when the trees were planted.*

rather as a cultural struggle against the erosion of a deep-rooted traditional way of life in rural Wales. His poem described how, instead of a vibrant community, there was now nothing but trees whose 'arrogant roots' were 'sucking dry the old soil'.

Brechfa Forest, which covers some 6,500 hectares, is the modern name for the ancient Glyn Cothi Forest, greatly extended by the Commission with the fast-growing conifers. In 1935, a camp was set up just north of Brechfa to house a labour force, drawn from the unemployed of the south Wales coalfield and elsewhere, to work on the new plantation. The men worked for three months at a time and, while they were not paid, refusing to take part would have meant they lost their unemployment benefits, so they had little choice but to comply. Conditions were extremely harsh, and trade unions campaigned against what they termed the 'slave camps', while the men living and working there frequently went on strike.

Many small hill farms were swallowed up by the new planting, some of which were of great significance, both historically and culturally. The remains of some of these can still be seen to this day, their low moss-covered walls engulfed by the conifers. Some farms were completely obliterated, dynamited out of existence to make way for the planting of hundreds of thousands of saplings. The result of this process, which took place over a number of years, was the depopulation of an area which had been intensely Welsh in nature. Gwenallt's poem combines the realism of the expansion of Brechfa Forest, near the village of Rhydcymerau, which gave his poem its title, with the symbolism of its lost culture and way of life. Recently, great holes have been punched in the conifers in the southern part of the forest to accommodate wind turbines and the associated roads, further industrialising the area. The wind farm here consists of 28 turbines with a maximum tip height of 145 metres. Although the plans were opposed from the beginning by local activists, they were approved by the UK government and Carmarthenshire Council, the site becoming operational in 2018.

Like Brechfa, much of the land bought by the Forestry

Commission in its early years was intensively planted with conifers, including Kielder Forest. Originally the land here was mainly open moorland, managed for grouse shooting and sheep grazing, with remnants of the original forest, such as the Kielderhead Pines, along stream sides and in isolated rocky areas. This was the wild moorland, England's empty quarter, divided into the huge sheep farms described in the books of the hunter-naturalist Abel Chapman (1851–1929). Since the 1920s, the area has experienced massive amounts of tree planting, creating one of the largest man-made forests in western Europe. Dominated by Sitka spruce, it now covers an area of more than 60,000 hectares in Northumberland and Cumbria. One benefit of the extensive areas of conifer is that Kielder supports around half of England's red squirrel population and is a key stronghold for the species. Sources of food in these forests tend to be limited to small pine cones, which red squirrels are better at exploiting than the more generalist grey squirrel.

Throughout the 1920s and 1930s the Forestry Commission's estate continued to grow, and by 1934 it owned just over 360,000 hectares of land. The low cost of land and the need to increase timber production meant that by 1939 the Commission was the largest landowner in Britain. The Second World War arrived though before the modest plantations of the 1920s and 1930s had matured. At the outbreak of war, the Commission was split into the Forest Management Department, to continue with the Commission's duties, and the Timber Supply Department, whose role was to produce timber for the war effort. This division lasted until 1941, when the Timber Supply Department was absorbed by the Ministry of Supply.

During the conflict Ireland remained neutral, but the experience of what was known as 'The Emergency', during which timber was in scarce supply, increased the importance given to the state afforest-ation programme. As in Wales, the new coniferous forests destroyed many rural communities, most of the older forestry plantations being in upland areas following a state-led drive for planting. The Slieve Felim Mountains in Counties Tipperary and Limerick, for

*World Wars and Conifers*      251

example, were planted with Sitka spruce and lodgepole pine, completely changing the landscape.

In Scotland, Binning Wood had been planted on the sandy coastal dunes near Dunbar by the energetic Earl of Haddington in the early 1700s and was carefully conserved by successive generations of the family. By the 1940s the magnificent oak and beech trees, in particular, were extremely large. The area was then taken over under emergency powers and the loggers moved in. In total 4,500 oaks, 2,300 beech, 690 sycamores and around 1,000 conifers, including a fine stand of 300 Scots pine, were felled, along with many other trees. In the end nothing was left of the Earl of Haddington's fine wood but 10,000 stumps. It may have been some consolation to his descendants that the best beech was used to make Mosquito aircraft, which were unusual in that their frames were constructed mainly of wood.

Binning Wood was not an isolated case, and the war devastated some of the best forests and woodlands in Britain, even more severely than during the First World War. On Deeside the great Glen Tanar Estate, which contains one of the most important areas of Caledonian pine forest in the Grampian region, suffered serious losses, and Rothiemurchus on Speyside was affected again. The Black Wood of Rannoch, spared at the eleventh hour in 1918, finally succumbed when 8,000 trees, representing most of the best specimens, were taken out by the Canadian Forestry Corps. But it survived and is now one of the most extensive areas of relict native pinewood remaining in Perthshire, supporting the largest number of rare insects of any Scottish site, apart from Speyside, as well as important communities of lichens and fungi characteristic of old pinewoods. Wildfires also affected forests because of the amount of waste material on the ground, and outbreaks were not uncommon. Commandos on a training exercise north of the Great Glen, for example, were blamed for starting a fire that burnt through over 400 hectares of old pinewood around Loch Arkaig. At the end of the war brushwood from heavy fellings in the native pinewoods at Dulnain in Strathspey was set alight, probably by sparks from a railway locomotive, and the fire burned through the forest for a week.

In Wales the first responsibility was, once again, to ensure a continuous supply of pitwood for the coal mines, and during the war not one colliery was ever 'on stop' due to the lack of suitable pit props. Pitwood consumption changed, in a matter of months, from around 95 per cent imported timber to 100 per cent home-produced. The devastation was immense, and in six momentous years well over a million cubic metres of timber came off the hills and valleys, converting 81 square kilometres of forest into a barren waste. Previously the valley slopes were clad, to within a short distance of the mountain ridges, with oak and birch interspersed here and there by rowan. Carefully tended and cut on proper rotation for the production of charcoal and tanbark, they had previously supported red squirrels, badgers, foxes, polecats and probably pine martens.

In the First World War, foresters had been allowed to volunteer for military service, but this mistake was not repeated, and they were now exempted, becoming part of the Forestry Corps. But it was not enough, and far more women were recruited than before, first by the Forestry Commission itself and then by a new organisation, the Women's Timber Corps. Despite the experience of the previous war, the idea of women wielding axes and saws was still sometimes treated as a joke. Forester James Tait informed readers of the *Scottish Forestry* journal that, when he chanced to walk along a country lane, he 'espied thinning operations in progress entirely carried out by a squad of women without even the supervision of a man'. When he moved closer though he had to admit that he was impressed by their skill.

Much of the timber supplied for the war from England came from the New Forest and the Forest of Dean, because they were the most mature of the remaining forests. In the Forest of Dean George Aston, a forestry worker, recorded the impact of the war in his memoir *Forest Folk*. In it he describes the 'wholesale slaughter', that resulted from the Royal Engineers felling mature and semi-mature oaks across the forest. The poet Leonard Clark also knew the area well, having grown up in Cinderford, but he left to become a trainee teacher. He regularly returned home though and always looked out for Chestnuts Wood, his favourite area, which consisted of a mixture of sweet chestnut coppice and oak trees planted during the Napoleonic Wars:

> *I heard terrible whispers that the Chestnuts Wood might have to be felled . . . In the summer of 1945, I went home again. I was determined to find out the worst for myself. And so, I stood once again on my childhood heights and looked around me . . . Yes, it was all there as it had always been. And then I turned my eyes to the left of the familiar landscape. There, to my horror, I saw a bald hill with just a thin ring of trees on top. My eyes flooded with tears . . . Seventy acres of forest had gone and, with it, I felt that my roots had been pulled up. I cannot begin to calculate how much of my life went with the destruction of those trees.*

Some idea of the contribution which was made by forests and woodlands during the Second World War can be gathered from the following figures. Around 12,000 hectares of forests were felled and some 196,000 hectares of private woodlands were recorded as either 'felled since September 1939' or as 'devastated', meaning that 'all the worthwhile timber had been cut'. Shortly after the war Frank Fraser Darling was moved to declare that 'our land is so devastated that we might as well have been the battlefield'. But by the summer of 1945, with Germany defeated, the Forestry Corps and the Women's Timber Corps had been disbanded and most of the scarred forests and woods were left to recover. The fellings did not entirely stop with the cessation of hostilities, however, and areas continued to be felled because of restrictions that had been placed on the importation of timber from abroad.

After the war it was decided that, as any future conflicts would be nuclear ones, there was no point in maintaining a strategic reserve of timber. The Forestry Commission was instead required to deliver forestry at the lowest possible cost. Any increases in forest cover therefore continued to be achieved by planting non-native conifers. The 'forest year' which ended on 30 September 1953 was notable for the fact that during the course of the last twelve months the Commission had planted 27,361 hectares, which was the largest area completed by the Commission in any one year up to that time. Of this total, 8,704 hectares were planted in England, 4,761 hectares in Wales and 13,896 hectares in Scotland, requiring over 104 million trees.

By 1959, the Commission's fortieth anniversary, the report for the year considered that substantial progress had been made in repairing the damage caused by the two world wars. But, in the main, the harm had been 'repaired' by the extensive planting of non-native conifers. Additionally, despite all the activity, 80 per cent of British timber needs were still met by imports. Indeed, in the 1960s and 1970s the organisation still had a very narrow focus, many foresters regarding themselves as 'tree farmers', with wildlife being regarded as a constraint, not a benefit. Despite this, there were a few dissenting voices. For example, W. H. Rowe, a forester from Oxford, wrote about forestry on an ecological basis in his book *Our Forests*. He stated that forests are 'a living community throbbing with life', and to preserve this community advocated the use of mixed woods and, where possible, natural regeneration to avoid monotonous forests planted in straight lines and geometric patterns. But at the same time the prime objective in Rowe's eyes was still the production of timber.

In 1954 James Macdonald, Director of Research and Education for the Commission, argued that research should not only be aimed at creating efficient forests by developing mechanical and other plantation techniques, but that a better ecological understanding of the forests was also necessary for successful forestation of bare hill land and moorland. But the tide was against ecological forestry, and

# World Wars and Conifers

short-rotation forestry based on large-scale mechanical cultivation of Sitka spruce became firmly established by the early 1960s. Frank Fraser Darling had described the upland moors and peatlands in Scotland as a 'wet desert' and was convinced that these areas had to be reclaimed for the restoration of the forests that had once thrived there, and if that could not be done through natural regeneration then it had to be done artificially. Some people were very concerned about this approach. In the 1950s, for example, Arthur Cuthbert, later the district officer in Perthshire, was employed by the Forestry Commission on a large woodland survey. During this he observed that in many areas before the planting of conifers the existing trees were ring-barked. He was appalled by this practice and included a long personal letter in the final report of his survey protesting against it, saying that he had not gone into forestry to kill trees but to plant new ones and, importantly, to care for the existing forests.

Despite official policy, there were foresters studying and protecting the wildlife of their forests. Donald MacCaskill, for instance, a keen naturalist and photographer, helped the BBC with the production of a number of wildlife films. In the case of a glen where eagles were known to be nesting, he designed the new planting so that the eagles were not disturbed. Earlier in his career, when he was ordered by his superiors to cut down the oakwoods on the banks of Loch Awe, he prevaricated and delayed because he believed that the trees should be protected. This attitude amounted to a refusal to carry out the agreed policy, but by doing so he saved the oaks. Another forester, John Davies, recalled seeing wildcats in the Central Belt of Scotland and pine martens in the Great Glen, where they had been absent for a long time. Referring to the wildcat, he wrote of 'the excitement we felt in the 1960s when we found them breeding in Carron Valley Forest, outside Falkirk. I have no doubt they will continue to move south.' Davies attributed the spread of these and other animals to the expansion of the forests since 1919, and he was convinced that the process would continue with the creation of new coniferous blocks.

Unfortunately, the annual reports of the Forestry Commission during the 1960s and 1970s do not mention wildlife. Beyond the enthusiasms of individual foresters, its protection was not part of the Commission's remit. The workers could not really protect wildlife in their daily work because it was not part of the programme and not budgeted for, so they had to do it during their own time. Fred Donald, Assistant District Officer in Kincardine and Angus, recalled that one of his foresters, Struan Stewart, was an expert on deer and would stay up all night to see them, record their numbers and study their foraging patterns.

The Commission was also silent about ancient woodlands and native broadleaved trees, which were in many cases underplanted with conifers, or removed, as late as the 1980s. As a result of a favourable tax regime and technological advances the wetland areas of the 'Flow Country' in northern Scotland, the largest expanse of blanket peat in the northern hemisphere, were also drained and planted with even-aged monocultures of non-native species,

*A Scottish wildcat in a coniferous forest. The expansion of their range in the 1960s was assumed to be due to the increase in planted areas.*

primarily Sitka spruce. In 1986 existing forest policy began to be questioned when the National Audit Office published a review examining the economic justification for investing public funds in creating new conifer forests on marginal land in the far north of Scotland. Following the 1988 budget the Commission, which had supported the tax incentives on forestry, was seriously challenged by their removal and commented in its annual report that it needed 'a period of adjustment' to the new situation.

In this decade though, mainly as a result of initiatives by George Peterken, then the forestry expert in the Nature Conservancy Council, and Oliver Rackham, the Forestry Commission at long last accepted the importance of ancient woodlands and agreed that they needed protection. The key moment was a conference at Loughborough in 1982 on 'Broadleaves in Britain', when the organisation realised that it was out of step with the rest of forestry thinking and attitudes changed, particularly about the loss of ancient woodlands. Following the event, there was a comprehensive review that culminated in the organisation committing itself to their protection. As a result, in the 1990s a completely new agenda was adopted, multipurpose forestry, which combined timber production, recreation and nature conservation.

Over the years the Commission had acquired an interest in all, or part, of many of the native pinewoods in Scotland, including high-profile sites such as Glen Affric, the Black Wood of Rannoch and Glenmore. Early, and relatively modest, conservation work on these was enhanced with the announcement of an ambitious plan to restore all of the remnants of native pine forests in its ownership and to create the conditions which would allow them to expand, largely by natural regeneration. This involved a major programme of removal of non-native species and a change in the management of deer to allow natural regeneration to flourish. Considerable progress has been made towards these targets, which should ensure that the original area of relatively healthy native pinewood of some 3,000 hectares will be allowed to expand to at least 10,000 hectares.

This landscape-scale restoration project is being achieved in partnership with a variety of organisations, including local communities, and, when linked with similar projects by bodies such as the RSPB, and some private owners, has the potential to create some truly significant areas of healthy, regenerating pinewood.

In Wales, Harold Hyde, Keeper of Botany in the National Museum of Wales, was also concerned about the expansion of coniferous forests, commenting in 1961 that there was a danger of losing 'the few remaining remnants of natural or seminatural woods which yet remain and from which we may derive information of priceless value'. Pointing to forest nature reserves such as those being established at Highmeadow and Wyndcliff in Monmouthshire, and in the Aber valley in Caernarfonshire, as examples of good practice, he expressed the hope that 'this conservative attitude may be extended to exclude clear felling of broadleaved woods wherever practicable'. Hyde's wish was granted, at least for Coedydd Aber near Bangor, which is now a National Nature Reserve, protecting the largest continuous area of old sessile oakwood along the north Wales coast. Here the Rhaeadr Fawr waterfall tumbles down from the Carneddau mountains into a deep basin in the river valley below. The humidity produced near the waterfall and along the edges of the river, especially near the gorge, creates ideal conditions for a variety of mosses, liverworts and ferns. The lichen fauna is one of the most interesting in north Wales, with over a hundred species recorded.

In south Wales Wyndcliff Wood, above the famous Horseshoe Bend on the River Wye, is home to the 'Eagles Nest', one of the best viewpoints in the area. A superb example of a Lower Wye Valley woodland, with ancient beech and yew as well as lime, ash and hazel coppice, Wyndcliff Wood also contains a number of rare whitebeams, including round-leaved whitebeam – which has a total population probably numbering no more than 500 trees. The ancient woods here form an almost unbroken chain along the steep slopes and have long been regarded as an important habitat. George

Peterken considers that they can be ranked with ancient wood-pastures such as the New Forest, Caledonian pinewoods, oceanic woodlands including the Atlantic hazel woods, and East Anglian coppices, as one of the five most important woodland groups in Britain.

The Lower Wye woods are in fact one of the best examples in Britain of what are now called 'ravine woods', containing lime and oak along with ash, wych elm and beech. Elsewhere they are found mainly in valleys on the continent, though there are also smaller examples in the White Peak in Derbyshire and a few other places. Highmeadow, the remaining woodland mentioned by Harold Hyde was less fortunate than the others. Influenced by the industrial heritage left by charcoal burning and iron-ore smelting in the nineteenth century, along with the gradual introduction of conifers from the late 1800s, it has had a more mixed history, losing some of its original character.

In the late 1980s the approach of many organisations, including the Forestry Commission, changed, from just saving the 'few remaining remnants' to reversing their fragmentation through the planting of new native forests. Natural regeneration, like that encouraged in the native pinewoods, also has a role, as we will see in the final chapter.

# CHAPTER 12

# *New Forests*

*So, I say that we had better be without gold than without forests.*

John Evelyn

With only about 13 per cent of the land area covered by forests, many of them consisting of non-native species, Britain is now one of the least forested countries in Europe, and its ecosystems are very heavily modified. Alongside Ireland, it has the lowest rate of natural regeneration, the least amount of standing and lying dead wood, and one of the highest proportions of forestry plantations. *Plant Atlas 2020*, published by the Botanical Society of Britain and Ireland in 2023, records that Sitka spruce, the predominant commercial forestry tree, has had the greatest increase in range of any of the recorded species. It has regenerated freely along tracks, in cleared areas within plantations and on adjacent land, in some cases many kilometres from the nearest seed sources. More than half of Britain's native plant species have declined, and they are now outnumbered by alien species. In contrast, on average over 44 per cent of Europe is covered by forests, many of them native.

Ireland is in an even worse situation, with only about 200 square kilometres of ancient broadleaved forests surviving, having shrunk from covering almost 100 per cent of the island to a minuscule 0.2 per cent. On the tops of the barest hills and buried in the deepest bogs are to be found the roots, stems and other remains of these lost forests, mostly of oak and pine. Flowering plants typical of forests and woodlands, such as bluebells, persist in the now open countryside as a reminder of the past. As Eoin Neeson concluded in his study of 'Woodland in history and culture', published in *Nature in Ireland*, deforestation there is a 'full circle, from a country very largely covered by natural woodland, through one virtually denuded of tree cover, to one in which virtually all woodlands are cultivated as a crop and in which forestry is tree farming'. The original forests have been more thoroughly eradicated than in any other European country, and as a result it is a landmass largely dominated by improved grassland, intensively grazed by cattle and sheep. Indeed, David Cabot has described Ireland today as 'a huge open space with vast stretches of empty land extending to the horizon'. The common perception, heavily promoted by tourist boards, that Ireland is an unspoilt 'Emerald Isle' is a fantasy.

In June 2021 the United Nations announced its 'Decade on Ecosystem Restoration', which has been described as 'a rallying call for the protection and revival of ecosystems all around the world, for the benefit of people and nature'. Restoration, the campaign says, is 'a proven measure to fight the climate crisis and enhance food security, water supply and biodiversity'. There is a never-ending call for action to restore our damaged world, reinforced in 2022 when representatives from 196 countries met in Montreal for COP15 – the grandly titled Fifteenth Conference of the Parties to the United Nations Convention on Biological Diversity. One of the main objectives of the convention is restoring the world's forests but, in many countries, it seems that the political will, and funding, is lacking.

The motivation for creating new forests had already been given new impetus in 2020 when, at its annual meeting in Davos,

Switzerland, the World Economic Forum launched One Trillion Trees, an initiative aimed at increasing the world's current estimated inventory of around three trillion trees by a third. Typically, only a minority of seedlings planted as a result of these initiatives survive, because the wrong trees are planted in the wrong places, and many are left untended, partly because ownership and management of the trees is not handed over to local communities.

Community involvement is critical, and there are encouraging signs of local people in Britain and Ireland taking action to preserve, or restore, areas of ancient woodland. In 2023, for example, the residents of Brockley in southeast London raised £100,000 to buy Gorne Wood, the closest surviving patch of ancient woodland to the City of London, to save it from developers. Squeezed between a row of back gardens and the railway line to London Bridge, the small wood is another fragment of the Great North Wood mentioned in the Preface.

The residents of Brockley, and everyone else concerned about our surviving ancient forests, should take heart from what is happening elsewhere in the world. It is a very different situation, but after the government of Nepal relinquished control of forests to the villagers who depend on them, between 1992 and 2016 the forest cover nearly doubled. 'Once communities started actively managing the forests, they grew back mainly as a result of natural regeneration,' said Jefferson Fox, principal investigator of the NASA Land Cover Land Use Change project that had been monitoring the area. Previously, the forests were heavily grazed by livestock and picked over for firewood and, as a result, had become degraded. Today, community forests occupy nearly 2.3 million hectares, about a third of Nepal's forest cover, and are managed by over 22,000 community forest groups comprising three million households.

Britain and Ireland do not have the same space, and access to land is much more difficult, with around half of England being owned by less than 1 per cent of its population, many of whom are descendants of the Norman invaders. But the message is clear.

Community involvement in forests is the way forward if we are to protect these areas and ensure not only their survival but also their expansion.

Very much larger land purchases are taking place in Scotland, with the Langholm community acquisition of 43 square kilometres to create the new Tarras Valley Nature Reserve – one of southern Scotland's largest community land buyouts. They have been joined by Oxygen Conservation, which has bought 45 square kilometres of adjoining land from the Buccleuch Estate, creating a total of almost 90 square kilometres of connected rewilding. Here and elsewhere, the pace of community involvement, and interest in forests, is expanding exponentially.

A number of these initiatives can be traced back to 1987, when the first Community Forest in Britain was established with the purchase of Wooplaw Forest in the Scottish Borders. The project originated in 1985 with Tim Stead, a wood sculptor, who had decided to use only native timber and had the idea of restoring this resource as well as using it. He produced hundreds of hand-made hardwood axe heads, which he sold to raise money to buy land for growing trees. The subsequent publicity attracted the attention of a number of people involved in the native woods movement, including Eoin Cox, Donald McPhillimy and Alan Drever, and they joined Tim to create a community woodland. In 1987 this led to the formation of Borders Community Woodland to take the project forward, and a large public meeting was organised in Melrose. Around the same time Wooplaw came on the market and within three months the project succeeded in securing sufficient funds to purchase the site. The World Wide Fund for Nature (WWF) also asked No Butts (a company formed by Eoin and Tim) to explore the potential for a large Scottish woodland millennium project, which quickly evolved into the Millennium Forest for Scotland Trust. The project ceased to exist following the winding-up of the Millennium Commission in 2006, but it is estimated that during its lifetime it restored over

22,000 hectares of forest and created 200 kilometres of new hiking trails.

If anyone can be credited with starting the movement to create new forests in England, it is two staff in the former Countryside Commission, Mike Taylor and Penny Marsden. In 1989, they were asked to draft a new woodland policy for the organisation, but when they showed it to Adrian Phillips, their director general, he apparently thought it was boring and told them to think again. As a result, Mike and Penny came up with the idea, out of the blue, of developing a 'national forest for England'. They had no idea how big it was going to be, who was going to implement it, or even the location, so they ran a competition to see what the various local authorities could come up with. Unexpectedly, a local newspaper in the Midlands, the *Leicester Mercury*, took up the challenge and created a huge groundswell of support for a new forest in the Needwood and Charnwood area, which took everyone by surprise. The proposal was to link the remnants of these two ancient forests with new planting. The area had suffered from the closure of the coal and clay industries in the 1980s and the landscape of the central area was degraded. The campaign run by the newspaper was so successful that at one point the post office in Cheltenham complained about the amount of mail they were having to deliver to John Dower House, the Countryside Commission's headquarters. It seems that, prompted by the newspaper, children from all the primary schools around Needwood and Charnwood had written letters explaining why their area should be chosen, and sackloads of mail were appearing every day.

Although there were other bids for a national forest, none had the community support of the Needwood and Charnwood bid, which completely overwhelmed the competition, so in the end it was not a difficult decision. All the major landowners were also supportive, including the Coal Authority, which still owned large areas of land in the region. Strangely, the only organisation that was initially not behind the project was the Forestry Commission, and Mike and

Penny had to make several trips to their headquarters in Edinburgh before they were convinced. As mentioned in the previous chapter, however, the Forestry Commission was looking for a new role at the time – and this eventually helped to win the argument.

The National Forest is now managed by a charity and non-profit organisation sponsored by the Department for Environment, Food and Rural Affairs. Since 1991 over nine million trees have been planted, with woodland cover in the area having increased from around 6 per cent in 1991 to 19.5 per cent in 2013. The initiative involved more than tree planting though, and today it is recognised as one of the most ambitious and imaginative regeneration projects in England. Keeping all the various politicians and landowners on board has been a challenge, but the National Forest is now an accepted part of the Midlands landscape.

One of the unsuccessful bids came from the local authorities in the Warwickshire area, who were keen to regenerate the Forest of Arden, covering an area similar to that of the original forest, but

*The Conkers Visitor Centre in the National Forest in Leicestershire attracts thousands of people each year.*

266                     *Forgotten Forests*

excluding Coventry and the eastern edge of Birmingham. Recently the proposal has been partly reinvigorated by Solihull Council, which is planning a huge programme of tree planting across the borough as part of the council's commitment to plant a quarter of a million trees within 10 years. Other parts of Arden are being reforested by the Heart of England Forest, the original vision for which came from local landowner Felix Dennis, a publisher, poet and philanthropist. He wanted to plant a 'joined-up' forest that would provide a habitat for wildlife, as well as a place for everyone to enjoy. It now covers a mosaic of habitats across 2,800 hectares, including more than 1,600 hectares of new woodland and almost 250 hectares of ancient woodland. So far, the charity has planted nearly 1.9 million trees on land which it has purchased.

Since the UK government launched its 25 Year Environment Plan in 2018, there has been an emphasis on the importance of tree planting, with an aspiration to increase woodland cover in the UK. In 2021 the government said that it would treble tree cover before the next general election in 2024, with 'mass forestry' schemes across England, the aim being to increase biodiversity, capture carbon and make landscapes more resilient to flooding and drought. Many newly planted trees, however, died in the record heatwave of 2022. Also unveiled were plans to create a new Northern Forest extending from Liverpool to Hull, following the route of the M62 motorway. Led by the Woodland Trust, in cooperation with the Community Forest Trust, the aim is to plant 50 million trees over 25 years, as a legacy for future generations. Though the new forest has received initial government support, the initiative is far from fully funded, so it remains to be seen how successful it is. In fact, only around 8 per cent of the planned trees have been planted in the promised community forests planned for the edges of various cities, and the charity set up to create a separate Great North Forest was declared bankrupt.

Despite the funding issues, with politicians always promising more than they eventually deliver, England is entering a new age of tree planting, with a level of concern not seen since the seventeenth century – although this time it is not timber for ships but recreation and tourism, economic regeneration and rural diversification that are the driving forces for woodland creation. The various projects also claim that they are making a significant contribution to climate change mitigation and adaptation, through creating a more resilient landscape, even if this is rarely quantified in any meaningful way and depends on the trees surviving beyond the first couple of years.

Other initiatives in England include Severn Treescapes: Wye to Wyre, a joint project between the three Wildlife Trusts in Gloucestershire, Herefordshire and Worcestershire which aims to improve connectivity between three of England's largest woodlands: the Wye Valley and Forest of Dean in the south and the Wyre Forest in the north. Perhaps less well known than the first two, the Wyre Forest is a remarkable survivor. The largest woodland National Nature Reserve in the country and a medieval hunting forest, this ancient lowland oakwood is now slowly being restored by Forestry England and Natural England. The 'Foresta de Wyre' is mentioned in the Domesday Book, but the area is known to have been wooded since at least 900 CE. One of the UK's largest 'wildland' partnerships is Wild Ennerdale. Based in one of the most remote valleys in the Lake District National Park, this is a joint initiative between the main landowners in the valley, Forestry England, the National Trust, United Utilities and Natural England, and it aims to let natural processes shape the landscape and ecology. As a result of this approach, on 15 November 2022 Natural England declared Wild Ennerdale as a National Nature Reserve.

The National Forest for Wales aims to establish a nationwide network of publicly accessible woodlands and forests. Described as a long-term project to match the scale and ambition of the Wales Coast Path, linking together a network of woodlands across the country, it will also focus on improving existing woodlands to meet the National Forest standard. The first fourteen sites to be announced are already part of the Welsh government estate, however, and are managed and maintained by Natural Resources Wales, so should already be in good condition. If it is not to be simply yet another rebranding exercise, the real challenge will be involving private landowners, and it remains to be seen how much of an incentive the various grant schemes will be in encouraging people to create new expanses of woodland.

In Wales, sheep farming is an industry that dominates the landscape to the detriment of everything else. In the century from 1867, sheep numbers more than doubled from around 2.5 million to over 6 million. This upward trend was interrupted only by the Second World War, when more crops were grown at the expense of grassland, and by the harsh winter of 1947, when many animals froze to death. By 2021, the total number of sheep and lambs in Wales stood at 9.46 million, around three sheep for every person in the country. This is despite the fact that even the 2021 Survey of Agriculture and Horticulture in Wales accepts that sheep provide poor returns to the farmer. The total amount of land used for agriculture now accounts for 90 per cent of the total land area of Wales. Although the area of woodland in Wales has increased, and now stands at 306,000 hectares, in this scenario there is little space for restoring forests. When Brechfa Forest was planted, admittedly with non-native species, it was interpreted as the destruction of the traditional way of life in a Welsh-speaking area. The surviving ancient woodlands of Wales therefore need to be seen in a broader ecological, historical and cultural context if they are to be successfully integrated into a new forest.

As the archaeologist Alex Brown has explained, a basic knowledge of previous forests should be considered a fundamental part of all landscape restoration projects, yet to date the issue has not really been considered. Historical sources can provide valuable insights into recent woodland ecology, but in general they lack detailed information on the composition, extent or management of woodland before the late medieval and early modern periods.

Investigations of ancient forests and woods have also been hampered by a lack of suitable pollen deposits. To date, relatively few sites have been investigated, almost all in lowland England, including Epping Forest and, more recently, within ancient and ornamental woodlands in the New Forest. A major gap exists, therefore, in our understanding of the long-term ecological history of the surviving ancient woodlands, particularly in areas with significant concentrations such as Wales. As the current structure of ancient woodlands is determined largely by past management practices, understanding the influence of people should be an important aspect of restoration strategies.

Human impacts have, for example, resulted in significant changes to the structure and composition of Wentwood in south Wales over the last 2,000 years, as described in Chapter 6. The result is an area that is now dominated by non-native trees that bear little resemblance to the woodland expected to occur naturally here, raising questions about what the aim should be in restoring the site. Should the focus be on restoring the oak- and hazel-dominated woodland of the Roman period, the oak–hazel–ash wood of the early Middle Ages, or the wood-pastures, high forest, coppice and hunting reserves of the Wentwood in which oak, hazel and birch were important components? Expansion of the existing ancient woodland, containing mainly oak, hazel, ash and birch, would only result in a habitat similar in composition to that evident in the pollen record prior to the planting of conifers in the nineteenth century. There is a debate to be had as to how far to go back in time in the restoration process, and how resilient the result would be in the face of climate change.

Only time will tell whether large-scale plantings of what will inevitably be even-aged saplings lead to the creation of real forests. The features associated with ancient forests and their ecology only appear over time and are the result of a cycle that is constantly renewing itself. One of the most important aspects of long-established forests, for instance, is the presence of large bodies of dead wood. Rotting wood liberates carbon and other stored minerals, making these available to new plants. These elements are redistributed around the dead trees by fungi and their mycelial networks. Dead wood also acts as a nursery for seedlings, especially in forests with a thick organic layer, and has been found to protect tree seeds against pathogens. The later stages of forest development have become so rare though that the majority of threatened forest-dwelling species are restricted to these old forests.

The key feature of the oaks in Sherwood Forest, for example, is that over 70 per cent of them are hollow, having, like the Major Oak, succumbed to heart-rot, and most have an average of four dead branches. Around 80 per cent of the trees have also lost their tops at some time, resulting in a 'stag-headed' appearance.

*Over 70 per cent of the oaks in Sherwood Forest have heart-rot and are hollow but provide habitats for a wide variety of insects.*

## New Forests

These features, a large girth, loss of bark on the trunks and many dead and fallen limbs, are obvious signs of decay, and a significant reduction in their crowns indicates that these trees are in the last stages of their long lives. Oak trees are often said to take 300 years to grow, 300 years to live and 300 years to die. While dying, though, they provide habitats for a wide variety of insects. Sherwood is especially notable for its rich invertebrate fauna, particularly the groups of beetles, spiders and flies which are closely associated with and dependent upon the various micro-habitats provided by old trees and dead or decaying wood. There are also many woodland fungi, including the nationally rare oak polypore. The area has been well studied since the Victorian period, with 316 species of beetles recorded to date. Among the many rarities are a small ant-like beetle found in the cavities of hollow trees, a darkling beetle, so called because it is a 'seeker of dark places', and a rare species of leaf beetle linked with ancient oaks. The largest false-scorpion in Britain, only eight millimetres long, is also a Sherwood speciality, as is a cobweb spider linked with ant nests in dead and dying trees. These species, however important they are for the forest ecosystem, are usually invisible to the average visitor.

Other ancient trees are to be found in the moist Atlantic oakwoods of western Britain and Ireland. One of these, Coed y Bleiddiau, 'Forest of the Wolves', in north Wales is a small remnant of the oakwoods that once stretched along the coastline of Europe from Scotland to Portugal. Because of the high humidity they are often described as 'temperate rainforests', and they support numerous rare ferns, mosses, liverworts, lichens and fungi. Apart from Wales, areas of temperate rainforest can be found in Ireland, Scotland and, in England, the Lake District, the Forest of Bowland, the Yorkshire Dales, the Pennines and parts of Somerset, Devon and Cornwall. These 'rainforests' are of global importance, and there are plans to extend their area, mainly by planting trees adjacent to the remaining sites.

272         *Forgotten Forests*

Welcome as these initiatives focused on planting trees are, many of them end up covering large areas with plastic tree guards, at the very time when concern about microplastics in the environment is increasing. Since the 1970s, saplings have generally been planted in translucent tubes to protect them from being eaten by browsing animals. Research analysing the life cycles of the plastic and the trees, however, has concluded that it is better to lose a certain percentage of saplings than to use plastic guards to protect them. This is because there are significant carbon emissions from the manufacture of the guards, and they are rarely collected after use. Eventually sunlight breaks them down, and small pieces of plastic pollute the environment and harm wildlife.

The National Trust, one of the biggest landowners in England, aims to plant 20 million trees by 2030 and is testing sustainable alternatives to plastic guards, including using crates, cardboard tubes and, mimicking natural processes, shrubs like gorse and hawthorn to protect saplings. The Woodland Trust has also decided to stop using single-use plastic tree guards on its land, and is funding research to find viable alternatives. Just how ingrained the use of plastic tree guards is can be seen from the cover of the long-awaited UK Forestry Standard Practice Guide *Designing and Managing Forests and Woodlands to Reduce Flood Risk*, which was published in 2022. This otherwise excellent, and much needed, document has a photograph on the front cover showing a few widely spaced trees in plastic tubes in the Upper Eden valley, near Kirkby Stephen, Cumbria. A missed opportunity to send the right message about allowing nature to take its course.

The most viable alternative is indeed not to use any tree guards at all. In fact, many forest ecologists say that creating space for nature is usually a better approach to restoring forests than planting. 'Allowing nature to choose which species predominate . . . allows for local adaptation and higher functional diversity,' says Robin Chazdon in her book *Second Growth: the Promise of Tropical Forest Regeneration in an Age of Deforestation*. Trees sown by nature are always

## New Forests

more plentiful, healthier and larger than even well-cared-for transplants. This message seems not to have been heard by Forestry and Land Scotland, which plans to plant tens of millions of new trees in the coming years, including non-native conifers such as Norway and Sitka spruce and Douglas fir, along with Scots pine, oak, alder and birch. Instead, a hydroponics unit, where plants are grown indoors in tightly controlled conditions, is being trialled. This is expected to produce saplings six times faster than it takes to grow them naturally outdoors, where it would take about eighteen months for a tree seedling to reach 40–50 millimetres in height; instead, the growing time is apparently around ninety days. But the root system of a natural seedling is more robust than that of a tree grown in a nursery, since it has not been disturbed by being transplanted. There is also some evidence that transplants are richer in nutrients, which makes them more attractive to grazing animals. The risks due to tree disease also make it less desirable to introduce potentially infected seedlings from outside the area.

Other organisations also seem to be unaware that nature will replant forests without human help. In 2022, for example, St Hilda's College in Oxford bought Radley Large Wood, an ancient woodland, assuming that it could offset its carbon emissions by planting trees in the wood. As George Monbiot commented, 'You would think that Oxford University would have more of a grasp on carbon stocks, sinks and sources. Or indeed the fact that trees naturally grow in woods.' Around 40 per cent of the wood has been affected by ash dieback, and the college aims to clear the dead trees and plant around 14,400 new trees, the species of which are not mentioned. Likewise, in Wales the National Trust is apparently undertaking 'woodland creation' by planting 375,000 trees on the edges of its existing woods to make them larger and better for wildlife. Given nearby seed sources, this is probably a waste of money and time. Wildlife would benefit more from natural regeneration with its diversity than it ever would from rows of transplanted seedlings. In some circumstances, however, such as on historic medieval parkland, the approach is justified. In Scotland, the managers of the Cadzow Oaks have used 'halo planting' to ensure that there are future generations of oak trees on the site. Acorns are collected from individual oaks and raised in nurseries in batches that can be planted out near the parent tree, but beyond the shade of its canopy. This approach mimics natural regeneration, while allowing the land to continue to be used to graze cattle.

It should be clear from the preceding chapters that a forest is more than a collection of trees, and that the ecosystem that surrounds them is as important as the trees themselves. This is especially true of mycorrhizal fungi, which have a symbiotic relationship with the roots of plants. They aid early tree establishment and growth, provide access to otherwise inaccessible soil nitrogen, and protect seedlings from pathogens in exchange for photosynthetically fixed carbon. We now know that fungi influence the growth of entire forests, and the thread-like system is so vast and interconnected that it is sometimes referred to as the 'wood-wide web'. Just as variations in the composition of the human gut microbial community are linked to human health, so the fungi regulate the health of forest trees. Nursery-grown transplants generally lack this support, which is one of the reasons why the trees keep dying. The relationship between mycorrhizal fungi and their trees is an obligate one – that is, you cannot have one without the other. A more holistic view of forest management is needed that considers the ecosystem below ground as well as that above the surface. Studies have shown that using fungi as a tool for restoration can be cost-effective and have long-term benefits.

In the Cairngorms, conservation-minded landowners such as the National Trust for Scotland at Mar Lodge, or Anders Holch Povlsen on the Glenfeshie Estate, are allowing their forests to regenerate slowly using naturally fallen seeds, a much more successful strategy than planting trees. In Scotland 1,425 hectares of new native woodland will also be created by unfenced natural regeneration over the next five years in two neighbouring glens managed by WildLand Limited in the Cairngorms National Park. The new woodland in Glen Feshie and Glen Tromie will include Scots pine, birches, willows, rowan, aspen, alder and juniper. This is more than all the new woodland created, by both planting and natural regeneration, in the whole of England in 2019. A further 2,200 hectares of native woodland is expected to establish in the glens in the following five years. Good results have also been obtained in the Scottish Highlands using deer fencing. Although the fencing is expensive, trees have reappeared far from mature seed-bearing trees in these locations, without planting, and it seems that even years of heavy browsing by deer didn't kill all the trees.

Despite these initiatives, many of Scotland's surviving pinewoods are under threat and in poor condition. A survey carried over four years between 2018 and 2021 by Fiona Holmes and James Rainey for Trees for Life has shown that nearly a quarter of the remaining pinewoods are threatened and will be lost without further action. James Rainey was quoted as saying that 'These pinewoods should be playing a key role in Scotland's fight-back against the climate and nature emergencies, but right now most are on their last legs.' It has been estimated that a total of only 17,000 hectares survives. The main barrier to their recovery is the artificially high deer population, which is seriously impacting their health. Dramatic improvements are taking place where deer populations are being effectively managed at a landscape scale. The survey also found improvements inside deer fences, but the recovery at these sites is now being reversed, as most of the deer fences have been breached.

An important finding from the survey was that twice as many tree species would regenerate successfully if the grazing pressure was removed. At Gleann Fuar in Argyll and Bute, for example, effective deer fencing has allowed the forest to recover with natur-ally generating Scots pine, birch, rowan and juniper, alongside other species. In comparison, Gleann Còsaidh, in the Highlands, is still an empty landscape with the remains of a lone tree still visible. When the area was mapped in 1872 the tree was still alive, a remnant of yet another lost forest. A local place-name, Cluain Doire Sheangan, the 'pasture wood of the ants', paints a vivid picture of what also used to be present here, with large wood ant nests below ancient trees and people visiting in summer to pasture their cattle.

Deer fencing has also been used by the Carrifran Wildwood Project in the Moffat Hills, which is being led by the Borders Forest Trust. Here the Trust has had to rely on tree planting, as there were no local seed sources and no signs of regeneration. The vision is to restore the ecology of an entire catchment to approximately the state it would have been in around 6,000 years ago, and remarkable progress is being made. A rowan in the valley, one of the few remaining trees present prior to restoration, was voted Scotland's Tree of the Year in 2020.

Again, in Scotland, the Mountain Birch Project, a project

*A lone rowan at Carrifran, now surrounded by new native woodland, was named Scotland's Tree of the Year in 2020.*

*New Forests* 277

drawing expertise from a variety of organisations including the Norwegian Institute for Nature Research, is seeking to restore the forest zone that is known elsewhere in Europe as the 'birch belt'. A habitat that has been almost completely obliterated in Scotland, it has been absent from our landscapes for so long that it has faded from memory. Mountain birch, a high-altitude form of the familiar downy birch, once grew extensively across Scotland's mountains above the 600-metre contour. Adapted to life at these high altitudes, it is now extremely rare, being restricted to a few individuals in refuges such as small islands on lochs and cliffs, places where grazing animals cannot reach. Across Scandinavia, where conditions are similar to those in Scotland, mountain birch grows at higher elevations than Scots pine, covering the hillsides and merging near the tree line with alpine willows, dwarf birch and juniper scrub. There are also distinct montane forms of juniper, rowan and bird cherry. It is also likely that grey alder used to grow at these altitudes, but it is now extinct in the wild in Britain and Ireland, although it has been planted for over two centuries, and is often used on reclamation sites because of its nitrogen-fixing capability.

Another species largely missing from Scottish woodlands is aspen. On the continent, aspen is a major component of coniferous forests, in some places covering between 15 and 20 per cent of the area. Today in Scotland though aspen exists mainly as small, isolated fragments, often consisting of a single relict tree. Only 160 hectares of aspen woodland remain, a scarce and very threatened resource, and only 25 hectares have any statutory protection. The species provides an important habitat for a number of invertebrates, many of which are only associated with aspen, such as the endangered aspen hoverfly, whose larvae require decaying wood. Aspen also provides nesting sites for several species of hole-nesting birds, including woodpeckers. It also supports many rare mosses, such as the aspen bristle moss, which was thought to be extinct until it was rediscovered in Rothiemurchus in the 1990s. Aspens like fairly wet conditions and, at some point in their history, they would have shared the landscape with beavers. The tree was their preferred food and an excellent building material. Beavers fell mature aspen, using the large limbs and trunks for dam and lodge building, while storing the smaller branches to eat during the winter. Studies in North America have shown that because of this preference beavers travel further to harvest aspen trees than other woody species. In turn, by building dams, beavers increase the availability of groundwater, improving the habitat for aspen and its many associated species.

In Northern Ireland the Woodland Trust has purchased Mourne Park, near Kilkeel in County Down, and the area is now open to the public for the first time in 500 years. The park includes 73 hectares of ancient woodland, an incredibly rare resource in the province, covering just 0.04 per cent of the area, and the Trust has plans to convert the rest of the forest, which is currently occupied by conifers, into broadleaved forest. Red squirrels and pine martens are present along with a wide variety of other species. With help from the community, the Trust is also replanting a site in the Belfast Hills, Glas-na Bradan Wood to create a new woodland.

The situation in the Republic of Ireland remains difficult. Although the Department of Agriculture, Food and the Marine has made efforts to include native trees in its plans, its priority is to cover 18 per cent of Ireland with forestry plantations by 2046, with only 30 per cent of that area consisting of broadleaved species, mostly rapidly growing willows. As I write, Coillte, the Irish state forestry company, is reported to be planning to sell 50,000 hectares of land to a British fund to develop as industrial forestry plantations that will be devoid of native species, as part of a deal to help the organisation meet its climate targets. The tide may be slowly turning, however, as Micheál Martin, Taoiseach between 2020 and 2022, has been reported as saying that 'we must purchase land for native woodlands and for simple rewilding at its most basic because the biodiversity challenge is so crucial'. Given the chance, as in other parts of these islands, trees will come back on their own. Ireland's National Forest Inventory, which was updated in February 2023, shows that between 2006 and 2022 'semi-natural' forests were responsible for one-third of new forests. These self-sown forests have appeared due to changes in land management, including the end of industrial peat extraction and a reduction in the intensity of agricultural activity in some areas. In all, some 26,760 hectares of native woodland have become established without human involvement and at no financial cost. A lesson for the future, given that the remainder of the new forests were monocultures of non-native conifers with virtually no value for wildlife or people. Natural regeneration barely figures in the draft Forest Strategy, being only mentioned in passing.

The old forests that have survived in Ireland belonged mostly to English and Anglo-Irish nobles who kept their estate grounds wooded for both beauty and hunting. Muckross House and Gardens, for example, form the gateway to the Killarney National Park in County Kerry. The park contains the largest, and most important, surviving fragments of oak forest on the whole island. Indeed, it is one of the very few places left that have been continuously covered by forests since the end of the last glaciation, some 10,000 years ago. The trees are, sadly, said to be dying because of grazing pressure, and there are extensive areas of invasive rhododendron, but, despite concerns over many years, no effective action has yet been taken to restore the area.

Among the trees in Killarney can be found Ireland's last herd of red deer, one of the few native mammals to survive deforestation. Meanwhile sika deer, which originated in Asia, are destroying many of the remaining native woodlands throughout the country – but, oddly, the Irish Deer Commission considers them as an important part of Ireland's natural heritage. Their protected status is nonsensical and should be removed as soon as possible, as they are apparently causing considerable damage. One of the sites being affected by overgrazing, from red deer, sika deer, sheep and goats, is Tomies Wood near Killarney, one of the last natural oak forests in Ireland. The tourist literature for the site does not mention the grazing pressure, which is obvious even from the publicity photographs, but does highlight the 'attractive rhododendron forest', yet another species which presents a serious threat to Killarney's oakwoods. Killarney National Park is so overgrazed that native tree species can only survive in the places that deer cannot reach, including the crooks of mature trees, birch trees growing high in the air on old dead oaks.

Elsewhere in the park, exotic species such as rhododendron also occur in Reenadinna Wood, which is said to be the largest remaining yew forest in Europe, covering an area of around 25 hectares. A complex of pure yew, mixed yew and hazel, and mixed yew and ash, it is one of only three such forests in Europe, the others being located in the Czech Republic and, as described in Chapter 8, at Kingley Vale in West Sussex. Most of the yew trees now growing

*Red deer stag with hinds during the rutting season. Killarney National Park supports what is thought to be the last herd of red deer in Ireland.*

in Reenadinna are estimated to be between 150 and 300 years old, although pollen studies show that yew has grown in this area over the past 5,000 years. It is very difficult to date yew trees as they do not grow in the same way that other trees such as oak and ash do, putting on growth rings each year. It is also thought that yew trees can stay 'dormant' for a number of years, not changing in size or shape. Enclosures were erected in 2001 around two large blocks of yew to control grazing by deer, which have done considerable damage to the site over the past few decades. As a result, the shrub layer of hazel and holly is poorly developed, but there is regeneration within the enclosures.

While the sika is classed as a protected species in Ireland, the wild boar, a native animal beneficial to forest ecosystems, is classed as invasive and generally shot on sight. In England it's a similar story, since the only wild boars in the New Forest are farmed animals kept in fenced enclosures. Pannage, the ancient practice of releasing domestic pigs into a forest to eat fallen acorns, beechmast, chestnuts and other nuts does take place here but the pigs, including Tamworth, Gloucestershire Old Spot, British Saddleback and Wessex Saddleback breeds, have a ring through the nose which stops them from rooting in the ground with their snouts, something that pigs normally do, to prevent them 'causing damage to the forest'. Once again, this highlights a complete misunderstanding of forest ecology. It would be better if they were allowed to root around, since free-roaming pigs, and indeed wild boars, break down vegetation such as brambles, demolish bracken, and turn over the soil, allowing dormant seeds to geminate. But this 'damage' seems to be regarded as unsightly, showing just how much people have become disconnected from the natural world. Wild boars have re-established themselves in the Forest of Dean, and Chantal Lyons, who has written a book about them, has often noticed oak seedlings growing there in old boar 'rootings' and wonders if jays have been involved, because the loose soil is easy to plant acorns in.

While high densities of deer can cause considerable damage to woodlands, efforts are being made to reintroduce the larger forest animals. In England, as part of the Wilder Blean Project near Canterbury, in 2022 three bison were released into a large enclosure with the hope that they will assist in the transformation of a dense pine forest into a vibrant natural area. The bison were joined by other grazing animals, including Exmoor ponies, 'Iron Age' pigs and longhorn cattle, whose natural behaviour will complement the bison in managing the landscape without the need for human intervention. All 7,000 bison currently living in Europe are, however, descended from just twelve zoo animals, and the species is classed as 'near threatened'. Another 'ecosystem engineer', the bison has been described as a keystone species that plays an important role in European landscapes, supporting a wide variety of other species through its behaviour. An important part of their diet is obtained by browsing bushes, bramble and trees and they therefore have a significant impact on the vegetation, creating a rich mosaic of habitats.

A survey commissioned in 2022 by Scottish Environment Link found that an overwhelming majority of people in Scotland want forestry policy to prioritise native woodlands. There are targets to expand the existing forests, but it remains to be seen what the final balance will be between native and non-native species. And will people be supportive of restoring the whole of the forest ecosystem, which includes the large carnivores?

The poet and environmentalist Mandy Haggith has suggested that in order to reforest Scotland brown bears are needed. As mentioned in Chapter 1, they are excellent seed dispersers, and the absence of bears leaves a gap in the forest ecosystem. The forests of every continent contain bears, ranging from the spectacled bears of South America to the moon bears and sloth bears of Asia. But bears are rarely mentioned in discussions of rewilding. George Monbiot, in his book *Feral*, dismisses them as 'difficult and dangerous', although he thinks that wolves could be successfully reintroduced. The main issue seems to be that people confuse brown bears with the American 'grizzly' bear. European brown bears are neither aggressive nor dangerous. In Sweden, which has an estimated population of 3,000 brown bears, only two people have been killed since records began in 1900. Both were hunters who had wounded the animal first. Sheep would undoubtedly be at risk from bears, but given the current levels of grazing, especially in the uplands, fewer sheep would be a good thing. Romania manages to support the largest population of bears in Europe, almost 6,000 animals, while the sheep population has been increasing. In 2020, there were approximately 10.5 million sheep in the country, but by shepherding and protecting them at night with dogs there have been few conflicts with bears. For the few losses that do occur, farmers are compensated.

The Eurasian lynx is Europe's third-largest land carnivore. Only the brown bear and wolf, with which the lynx traditionally shared our forests, are larger. For many people large carnivores are now unfamiliar and alien animals. As David Hetherington, author of

*There is an ongoing debate about reintroducing lynx to Britain. This animal was photographed in the Bavarian Forest National Park, Germany.*

*The Lynx and Us*, has pointed out, this disconnect is probably most pronounced in the case of the lynx, which has always had a much lower cultural profile than the other two species. With reintroductions and natural recolonisation resulting in the return of bears, wolves and lynx to landscapes across mainland Europe over the past few decades, it seems likely that Britain will be one of the last areas of Europe to regain its large carnivores, while Ireland is even further behind in the debate.

Unlike the position in continental Europe, lynx obviously cannot colonise Britain and Ireland themselves and must be reintroduced. Lynx bones from North Yorkshire and from Sutherland have been radiocarbon-dated to the Roman era, while another bone from North Yorkshire has been dated to the early medieval period. The species may also have survived in the Highlands until the sixteenth century. In a late-fifteenth-century poem by the Welsh poet Dafydd Nanmor the beast is described as *llew brych*, a 'speckled lion', and said, like the roebuck, to move to higher ground in summer. Unusually, this reference appears to describe the natural behaviour of both a lynx and its favoured prey, suggesting that lynx were following deer onto higher ground as they took advantage of seasonal feeding opportunities. There is another later reference to British 'lions', this time from northern Scotland. Writing in 1587, the English clergyman William Harrison describes how there used to be very many 'lions' in northern Scotland, but goes on to say they are no longer recorded, explaining that he does not know how and when they were destroyed. The latest estimates suggest that Scotland is now home to Europe's largest red deer population, dwarfing those of much bigger countries such as France, Germany, Sweden and Spain. The reintroduction of lynx to Scotland is ecologically feasible, but across Europe there is conflict between lynx and human hunters of woodland deer, while in Britain concerns are also expressed about attacks on sheep.

The debate around reintroducing large carnivores can get quite polarised, with strong opinions on both sides, but while we argue

*Pine martens are quietly reoccupying their former range, now that they are no longer persecuted by gamekeepers.*

the merits, or otherwise, of the approach the smaller animals are quietly coming back. Pine martens, for instance, were once one of our most common carnivores, thriving in the ancient forests. Throughout the nineteenth century, they were persecuted by gamekeepers and killed for their fur, while their habitat disappeared. Once present throughout Ireland, by the twentieth century the species was extinct across the majority of the island, surviving only in a few isolated and fragmented populations mainly in the west. In Britain the species was also close to extinction, but there is now a healthy population of over 4,000 individuals in Scotland and around 2,700 animals in Ireland.

Until recently pine martens had not regained their old range in England, but with the breeding success in Scotland and increased woodland cover it was felt that it was only a matter of time before the population spread over the border. In the summer of 2015, the first conclusive sighting of a pine marten in England in over a hundred years was captured on a trail camera near the Welsh border in Shropshire, and there were also well-publicised reports of animals seen in Cornwall. Work was already under way to boost the remnant population in Wales, and by 2017 a total of 51 pine martens had been released. Following feasibility studies, 35 pine martens have also been successfully reintroduced into the Forest of Dean to bolster the expanding Welsh population and establish a population in Gloucestershire. Studies in Scotland have shown that when pine martens move into an area they displace grey squirrels, and it is hoped that this will allow red squirrels to return. It has been suggested that, as red squirrels once coexisted with pine martens, they are more used to the predator. Other theories include the fact that grey squirrels are more vulnerable than red squirrels because they feed on the ground, or, because they are heavier, they are unable to seek safety in the upper branches of trees.

Another species missing from our forests and woodlands is the wildcat. Trail-camera surveys conducted from 2010 to 2013 across the species' range in Scotland estimated that there were only 115 to 314 individuals left, but the Saving Wildcats project is, at the time of writing, planning to release 22 wildcat kittens into carefully selected locations in the Cairngorms National Park. At the other end of Britain, conservationist and farmer Derek Gow has been working with the Devon Wildlife Trust and the Royal Zoological Society of Scotland, who are also involved in the Cairngorms project, to release between 40 and 60 wildcats into the countryside in Devon and Cornwall. He has described the initiative as 'just one small step in the right direction', pointing out that 'returning wildcats to our forests will help rejuvenate them'.

It must be remembered, however, that many of these species are currently restricted to a fraction of their historical range due to human impacts, making it hard to understand their real ecological preferences. The biases in the historical archives also pose a challenge, since they often only record presence rather than abundance. The records are also often derived from hunted animals, an action which might well have affected the natural distribution of the species concerned, in contrast to modern scientific surveys. Care must be taken therefore when deriving species distribution and conservation insights from historical data. Today, many species on this planet, including even large marine mammals such as sperm whales, are 'refuge species'. These are animals and plants that have been pushed out of their preferred habitat by human activity and are now confined to areas where it is harder for them to survive. Their distributions are still being shaped by the ghost of human predation over many generations.

Despite these constraints, given a chance species will often return on their own, to habitats that are sometimes less than ideal. Towards the end of the first decade of the twenty-first century, for example, BirdWatch Ireland began to receive an increasing number of phone calls and emails concerning strange black and white birds visiting bird tables in gardens. At first no one knew what they were, as they had been absent from Ireland for hundreds of years, but they turned out to be great spotted woodpeckers. These sightings, mainly along the east coast of Northern Ireland, particularly in County Down, caused great excitement amongst Irish birdwatchers. Shortly afterwards, the woodpeckers were found to be breeding in the remaining fragments of old-growth woodland in Counties Down and Wicklow. In Britain the population of great spotted wood-peckers has increased dramatically in recent years, and this may have forced young birds to make the relatively short journey west-wards across the Irish Sea in search of new territories. Great spotted woodpeckers were once widespread in Ireland, and they have a long history, as demonstrated by the femurs of two birds found during an excavation of the Edenvale cave complex near Ennis in County Clare, which were dated to the Bronze Age. They may have persisted as a breeding species until the ninth century, as references to woodpeckers can be found in the nature poems written by the early Christian monks and hermits.

Future prospects for forests in light of climate change, such as the recent and extensive fires in many parts of the world, look challenging. Climate modelling suggests that there will be substantial restructuring of the ecosystems we are familiar with today. A study published in the journal *Forestry* in 2023 warns that forests in the UK are heading for a 'catastrophic ecosystem collapse' within the next fifty years due to a variety of threats, including disease, extreme weather and wildfires, with massive numbers of trees dying. The impact of tree diseases in particular could well be severe. Ash dieback, for instance, a highly destructive disease of ash trees caused by a fungus originating from Asia, which arrived via wind-borne spores and imported plants, is now present in most parts of Britain and Ireland. Trees exude black fluid from vertical fissures on their trunks and usually die within four to six years of the first symptoms.

Despite the current emphasis on new planting to assist in mitigating climate change, the existing ancient trees in Britain and Ireland have a more important role than was previously suspected. Research in Wytham Wood, near Oxford, one of the most scientifically studied woodlands in the world, has shown that it is very difficult to replace old trees by simply planting saplings. The study, which mapped almost 1,000 trees, using lasers and 3D scanning, showed that old trees in particular were critical carbon stores and, as a result, it is now thought that forests lock away twice as much carbon as previously estimated. Before this study, the figures for Britain estimated that the total weight of carbon held in forests was 213 megatonnes, of which nearly 50 per cent was captured by broadleaved trees. We are now looking at a figure of well over 400 megatonnes.

While forests, and ancient trees generally, are now known to be substantial reservoirs of carbon, without bears, lynx, wildcats and other similar animals they can never be properly functioning ecosystems. Indeed, an important paper published in the journal *Nature Climate Change* in 2023 showed that there is now scientific evidence that protecting and restoring wild animals and their roles in the ecosystem can greatly improve natural carbon capture and storage. Concluding that, while the animals themselves only account for

0.3 per cent of the carbon currently locked away in the Earth's biomass, through their activities they can improve the situation by anywhere between 15 per cent and 250 per cent. The authors therefore highlighted the importance of reintroducing wild animals, stressing the need to restore whole ecosystems and move beyond mere tree planting. The mass planting of trees in plastic tubes will not produce sustainable forests. Reducing our carbon emissions, by drastically reducing the use of fossil fuels, is also not going to be enough, and we need to harness the power of nature to remove carbon from the atmosphere. The many projects described in this chapter show how we can reinstate forests in these islands in a more effective way. Where possible, these initiatives need to include the existing ancient trees, so that the new woodlands are as diverse as possible and there is plenty of old wood.

A study by the University of Nottingham has, in fact, highlighted that there are more ancient and veteran trees than previously recorded. To be classed as ancient, a tree must be exceptionally old for its species. For example, an oak tree is considered a 'veteran tree' when it is 150 years old, but it is not 'ancient' until it reaches 400 years. In total, there are 169,967 trees recorded in the Woodland Trust's Ancient Tree Inventory. The majority are in England, with smaller numbers in Scotland, Wales, Northern Ireland and the Republic of Ireland. Like many of the patterns in the data, this geographical distribution probably reflects the distribution of recorders as well as the impacts of history described in this book. Using the inventory and a number of different mathematical models it seems, for example, that there could be between 1.7 million and 2.1 million ancient trees in England, of which only 115,000 are currently recorded on the database. These trees, often remnants of ancient forests, have a role to play in our future that we do not yet fully understand.

# ACKNOWLEDGEMENTS

First, I have to thank Myles Archibald, Publishing Director at HarperCollins, for suggesting that I write this book and helping me shape its structure. His continued support and encouragement is much appreciated. Hazel Eriksson, Senior Editor, and Eve Hutchings, Project Editor, have also been a welcome source of advice, and efficiently guided the production process. In addition, I must record my gratitude to Hugh Brazier, who has been involved in all my books to date, including three previous books in the Collins New Naturalist series. Hugh is not one to seek praise but I have, over the years, benefited greatly from his meticulous attention to the text. It would also be remiss not to acknowledge Eoin Cox, founder of The Big Tree Society, for his wise advice on various matters to do with Scottish trees and forests and the loan of numerous books. My thanks again to Tim Rich for his ongoing botanical support.

In relation to specific information, I have profited from the advice of Mike Baillie, Professor Emeritus of Palaeoecology, and his colleague, Research Fellow David Brown, at Queen's University Belfast, on Irish oaks and dendrochronology; Chris Ellis, Head of the Cryptogamic Plants and Fungi Section at the Royal Botanic Garden Edinburgh, on nutrient flows between salmon and forests; Richard Lloyd and Mike Taylor, both formerly with the Countryside Commission, regarding the background to the creation of the National Forest in England; Rob Jarman from the University of Gloucester on the history of sweet chestnut in Britain; Bryan Kennedy for the details of land management schemes in Ireland

and the impact of sheep on habitats; Tom Nisbet, Head of Physical Environment Research in Forest Research, for his thoughts on plastic tree tubes. Jamie Woodward, Professor of Physical Geography at the University of Manchester, provided information on footprint beds; Keith Kirby, visiting researcher at the University of Oxford, kindly read an early draft of Chapter 1; George Peterken, a forest ecologist, read a draft of Chapter 11; while Scott Timpany, Environmental Geoarchaeologist at Orkney College, University of the Highlands and Islands, checked the chapter on submerged forests. Finally, Alex Purvis, Library Services Assistant in Northumberland Libraries, has been an enormous help in sourcing the many inter-library loans and other documents that were required. My apologies to anyone I may have accidentally omitted from this list.

Regarding the various visits I undertook while writing the book, I must, in particular, thank Max Barclay, Senior Curator in charge of Coleoptera at the Natural History Museum in London, for a delightful time behind the scenes studying specimens of bog oaks and great capricorn beetles. In the wider landscape, Nick Baimbridge, Head Forester on the Blenheim Estate, escorted me around High Park and the awe-inspiring medieval oaks, while his colleague Filipe Salbany ensured that I saw one of the colonies of wild bees. The book is not, however, intended as a field guide. An account of an area or site, or a photograph, should not therefore be regarded an invitation to visit.

I acknowledge the literary executor of Leonard Clark for permission to use an extract from his writings on the Forest of Dean, and Sonia Hughes, Administrator at Y Lolfa, the copyright owners, for the lines from Waldo Williams's poem *Yr hen allt*.

The illustrations that are not my own are individually credited, but I must specifically thank Carolyn White of Carlisle Library for locating the pencil sketch of the last old tree in Inglewood Forest; Averil Shepherd for the photograph of the Great Wishford Grovely ceremony; Dayna Woolbright, Newman Curator at Lynn Museum, for the photograph of Seahenge; Derek Fanning for the photograph of the Brian Boru Oak; Roger Ulrich for his copyrighted photograph of Trajan's Column; and Clare McNamara, Image Library Officer at the National Museum of Ireland, for arranging the first photographs of the Kiltubbrid Shield.

Last, and certainly not least, I am grateful for the continued support of my Welsh family: my wife Melanie, and my daughters Caitlin and Bethan. While, as described in this book, the Welsh are no longer a forest people, my family's interest in the natural environment and the history of their native land has been a continual source of inspiration.

# BIBLIOGRAPHY

The books and articles listed here are the main published sources referred to during the writing of this book. For reasons of space, I have not included details of most of the material obtained from the internet, as subjects are easily searchable. A number of publications have been referred to in the drafting of more than one chapter, and in such cases only the first instance is recorded; hence the short lists for Chapters 6 and 7.

## *Preface*

Anon. (2010) An interview with David Attenborough, Marcia McNutt and Iain Stewart. *Earthwise* 26. British Geological Survey.

Chitty, L. F. (1964) Flint dagger found at Catherton, Cleobury Mortimer, south Shropshire. Unpublished note in author's collection.

Coles, J., Heal, S. V. E. and Orme, J. (1978) The use and character of wood in prehistoric Britain and Ireland. *Proceedings of the Prehistoric Society* 44, 1–45.

Condry, W. (1974) *Woodlands.* Collins Countryside Series 3. Collins, London.

Farjon, A. (2022) *Ancient Oaks in the English Landscape*, 2nd edition. Royal Botanic Gardens, Kew.

Frieman, C. J. (2014) Double edged blades: re-visiting the British (and Irish) flint daggers. *Proceedings of the Prehistoric Society* 80, 33–65.

Grahame, K. (1908) *The Wind in the Willows.* Methuen, London.

Noble, G. (2006) *Neolithic Scotland: Timber, Stone, Earth and Fire.* Edinburgh University Press, Edinburgh.

Pauly, D. (1995) Anecdotes and the shifting baseline syndrome of fisheries. *Trends in Ecology and Evolution* 10, 430.

Penfold, H. (1905) The Capon Tree, Brampton, and its memories. *Transactions of the Cumberland & Westmorland Antiquarian & Archaeological Society* (series 2) 5, 129–144.

Proulx, A. (2022) *Fen, Bog and Swamp: a Short History of Peatland Destruction and Its Role in the Climate Crisis.* Fourth Estate, London.

# Bibliography

Shokouhi, M. (2019) Despirited forests, deforested landscapes: the historical loss of Irish woodlands. *Études Irlandaises* (11), 17–30.

Stokes, J., Miles, A. and Parker, E. (2002) *Great British Trees.* Tree Council, London.

Wolfe, L. M. (1979) *John of the Mountains: the Unpublished Journals of John Muir.* University of Wisconsin Press, Madison.

Worrell, R., Pryor, S. N., Scott, A. *et al.* (2002) *New Wildwoods in Britain: the potential for developing new landscape-scale native woodlands.* LUPG report. English Nature, Peterborough.

## Chapter 1: After the Ice

Alexander, K., Green, T., Butler, J., Allen, M. and Woods, R. (2018) Britain's natural landscapes: promoting improved understanding of the nature of the post-glacial vegetation of lowland Britain. *British Wildlife* 29, 330–338.

Atkinson, T. C., Briffa, K. R. and Coope, G. R. (1987) Seasonal temperatures in Britain during the past 22,000 years reconstructed using beetle remains. *Nature* 325, 587–592.

Bain, C. (2013) *The Ancient Pinewoods of Scotland: a Companion Guide.* Sandstone Press, Sheffield.

Bartosiewicz, L., Zapata, L. and Bonsall, C. (2010) A tale of two shell middens: the natural versus the cultural in 'Obanian' deposits at Carding Mill Bay, Oban, western Scotland. In A. M. VanDerwarker and T. M. Peres (eds.), *Integrating Zooarchaeology and Paleoethnobotany*, pp. 205–225. Springer, New York.

Bengtsson, J., Nilsson, S. G., Franc, A. and Menozzi, P. (2000) Biodiversity, disturbances, ecosystem function and management of European forests. *Forest Ecology and Management* 132, 39–50.

Bennett, K. D. (1983) Postglacial population expansion of forest trees in Norfolk, UK. *Nature* 303, 164–167.

Bennett, K. D. (1989) A provisional map of forest types for the British Isles 5000 years ago. *Journal of Quaternary Science* 4, 141–144.

Broughton, R. K., Bullock, J. M., George, C. *et al.* (2021) Long-term woodland restoration on lowland farmland through passive rewilding. *PLoS One* 16 (6), e0252466.

Brunning, R. (2006) *Wet & Wonderful: the Heritage of the Avalon Marshes.* Somerset Heritage Service, Taunton.

Buckland, P. C., Buckland, P. I. and Hughes, D. (2005) Palaeoecological evidence for the Vera hypothesis? In *Large Herbivores in the Wildwood and Modern Naturalistic Grazing Systems.* English Nature Research Report 648, pp. 62–116.

Clarke, D. L. (1976) Mesolithic Europe: the economic basis. In G. de G. Sieveking, I. H. Longworth and K. E. Wilson (eds.), *Problems in Economic and Social Archaeology*, pp. 449–481. Duckworth, London.

Cocker, M. (2007) *Crow Country.* Jonathan Cape, London.

Conneller, C. (2021) *The Mesolithic in Britain: Landscape and Society in Times of Change*. Routledge, London.

Coppins, A., Coppins, B. and Quelch, P. (2002) Atlantic hazelwoods: some observations on the ecology of this neglected habitat from a lichenological perspective. *British Wildlife* 14, 17–26.

Coppins, A. M. and Coppins, B. J. (2010) *Atlantic Hazel*. Scottish Natural Heritage, Edinburgh.

Cross, J. R. (2006) The potential natural vegetation of Ireland. *Biology and Environment: Proceedings of the Royal Irish Academy* 106B, 65–116.

EUROPARC-España (2017) *Old-Growth Forests: Characteristics and Conservation Value*. Ed. Fundación Fernando González Bernaldez, Madrid.

Fowler, J. (2002) *Landscapes and Lives: the Scottish Forest through the Ages*. Canongate Books, Edinburgh.

Froyd, C. A. and Bennett, K. D. (2006) Long-term ecology of native pinewood communities in East Glen Affric, Scotland. *Forestry* 79, 279–291.

García-Rodríguez, A., Albrecht, J., Szczutkowska, S. *et al.* (2021) The role of the brown bear *Ursus arctos* as a legitimate megafaunal seed disperser. *Scientific Reports* 11, 1282.

Gill, R. M. A. and Beardall, V. (2001) The impact of deer on woodlands: the effects of browsing and seed dispersal on vegetation structure and composition. *Forestry* 74, 209–218.

Godwin, H. (1975) History of the natural forests of Britain: establishment, dominance and destruction. *Philosophical Transactions of the Royal Society of London B* 271, 47–67.

Hannan, M. (2015) Highland cow may be descended from the ancient aurochs. *The National*, 28 October 2015.

Hemming, J. (2002) *Bos primigenius* in Britain: or, Why do fairy cows have red ears? *Folklore* 113, 71–82.

Jarman, R., Chambers, F. M. and Webb, J. (2019) Landscapes of sweet chestnut (*Castanea sativa*) in Britain: their ancient origins. *Landscape History* 40 (2), 5–40.

Jobling, J. A. (2010) *The Helm Dictionary of Scientific Bird Names*. Christopher Helm, London.

Kitchener, A. C. and Doune, J. (2012) A record of the aurochs, *Bos primigenius*, from Morayshire. *The Glasgow Naturalist* 25, 138–139.

Leroy, T., Plomion, C. and Kremer, A. (2019) Oak symbolism in the light of genomics. *New Phytologist* 226, 1012–1017.

Lonsdale, D. (2016) Powdery mildew of oak: a familiar sight with some hidden surprises. *Arb Magazine* Spring 2016, 48–53.

Manning, A. D., Burlton, B., Cavers, S. *et al.* (2023) The wild Scots Pines (*Pinus sylvestris*) of Kielderhead. *British & Irish Botany* 5, 209–220.

Mitchell, F. (1976) *The Irish Landscape*. Collins, London.

Mitchell, F. J. G. (2005) How open were European primeval forests? Hypothesis testing using palaeoecological data. *Journal of Ecology* 93, 168–177.

Mitchell, F. J. G. (2006) Where did Ireland's trees come from? *Biology and Environment: Proceedings of the Royal Irish Academy* 106B, 251–259.

Momber, G. (2011) Submerged landscape excavations in the Solent, southern Britain: climate change and cultural development. In J. Benjamin, C. Bonsall, C. Pickard and A. Fischer (eds.), *Submerged Prehistory*, pp. 85–98. Oxbow Books, Oxford.

Monbiot, G. (2013) *Feral: Rewilding the Land, Sea and Human Life*. Allen Lane, London.

Oosthoek, K. J. (2013) The nature and development of the forests since the last ice age. In *Conquering the Highlands: a History of the Afforestation of the Scottish Uplands*, pp. 11–32. ANU Press, Canberra.

Oppenheimer, S. (2006) *The Origins of the British*. Constable & Robinson, London.

Pesendorfer, M. B., Sillett, T. S., Koenig, W. D. and Morrison, S. A. (2016) Scatter-hoarding corvids as seed dispersers for oaks and pines: a review of a widely distributed mutualism and its utility to habitat restoration. *The Condor* 118, 215–237.

Rackham, O. (2006) *Woodlands*. New Naturalist 100. Collins, London.

Rackham, O. (2011) Ancient forestry practices. In V. R. Squires (ed.), *The Role of Food, Agriculture, Forestry and Fisheries in Human Nutrition*, Vol. 2, pp. 29–47. Encyclopaedia of Life Support Systems.

Rhind, P. and Jones, B. (2003) The vegetation history of Snowdonia since the late glacial period. *Field Studies* 10, 539–552.

Rotherham, I. D. (ed.) (2013) *Trees, Forested Landscapes and Grazing Animals*. Routledge, Abingdon.

Sandom, C. J., Ejrnæs, R., Hansen, M. D. and Svenning, J. C. (2014) High herbivore density associated with vegetation diversity in interglacial ecosystems. *Proceedings of the National Academy of Sciences of the USA* 18, 4162–4167.

Sherwood, H. (2023) Oldest carved piece of wood to be found in Britain dates back 6,000 years. *The Guardian*, 7 June 2023.

Simmons, I. G. (2000) *An Environmental History of Great Britain from 10,000 Years Ago to the Present*. Edinburgh University Press, Edinburgh.

Smith, G. and Walker, E. A. (2014) Snail Cave rock shelter, north Wales: a new prehistoric site. *Archaeologia Cambrensis* 163, 99–131.

Smout, T. C. (ed.) (1997) *Scottish Woodland History*. Scottish Cultural Press, Newbattle.

University of Central Lancashire (2023) Earliest human remains discovered in northern Britain. *Phys. org*, 25 January 2023.

Vera, F. W. M. (2000) *Grazing Ecology and Forest History*. CABI Publishing, Wallingford.

Whitehouse, N. J. and Smith, D. (2010) How fragmented was the British Holocene wildwood? Perspectives on the 'Vera' grazing debate from the fossil beetle record. *Quaternary Science Reviews* 29, 539–553.

Wilde, W. R. (1861–1864) On an ancient Irish wooden shield. *Proceedings of the Royal Irish Academy* 8, 487–493.

Willis, A.J. (1994) Arthur Roy Clapham. 24 May 1904-18 December 1990. *Biographical Memoirs of Fellows of the Royal Society* 39, 72–90.

Woodhead, T. W. (1931) Post-glacial succession of forests in Europe. *Science Progress in the Twentieth Century* 26, 250–261.

Wordsworth, W. (1835) *A Guide Through the District of the Lakes in the North of England: with a Description of the Scenery, &c. for the Use of Tourists and Residents.* Hudson and Nicholson, Kendal.

Worrell, R. (1996) *The Boreal Forests of Scotland.* Forestry Commission Technical Paper 14.

Wygal, B. T. and Heidenreich, S. M. (2014) Deglaciation and human colonization of northern Europe. *Journal of World Prehistory* 27, 111–144.

Yalden, D. (2013) The post-glacial history of grazing animals in Europe. In I. D. Rotherham (ed.), *Trees, Forested Landscapes and Grazing Animals*, pp. 62–69. Routledge, Abingdon.

Yalden, D. and Albarella, U. (2009) *The History of British Birds.* Oxford University Press, Oxford.

## Chapter 2: Under the Waves

Aldhouse-Green, S. H. R., Whittle, A., Allen, J. R. L. *et al.* (1992) Prehistoric footprints from the Severn Estuary at Uskmouth and Magor Pill, Gwent, Wales. *Archaeologia Cambrensis* 141, 14–55.

Anon. (1844) Caledonian Canal operations, and discoveries in Loch Oich. *Inverness Journal*, 21 June 1844.

Bailey, G., Momber, G., Bell, M. *et al.* (2020) Great Britain: the intertidal and underwater archaeology of Britain's submerged landscapes. In G. Bailey, N. Galanidou, H. Peeters, H. Jöns and M. Mennenga (eds.), *The Archaeology of Europe's Drowned Landscapes*, pp. 189–219. Springer, Cham.

Bell, A. D., Timpany, S. and Nayling, N. (2005) Mesolithic to Neolithic and medieval coastal environmental change: intertidal survey at Woolaston, Gloucestershire. *Archaeology in the Severn Estuary* 16, 67–83.

Burns, A., Woodward, J., Conneller, C. and Reimer, P. (2022) Footprint beds record Holocene decline in large mammal diversity on the Irish Sea coast of Britain. *Nature Ecology & Evolution* 6, 1553–1563.

Campsie, A. (2018) Archaeologists survey Scotland's forests under the sea. *The Scotsman*, 25 January 2018.

Charlesworth, J. K. (1963) *Historical Geology of Ireland.* Oliver & Boyd, Edinburgh.

# Bibliography

Clapham, A. J. (1999) The characterisation of two mid-Holocene submerged forests. PhD thesis, Liverpool John Moores University.

Cockburn, H. (2023) One of Britain's largest sunken forests reveals its secrets. *The Guardian*, 16 June 2023.

Cooper, W. D. (1850) *The History of Winchelsea, One of the Ancient Towns Added to the Cinque Ports.* John Russel Smith, London.

Dereham, W. (1712) Observations concerning the subterraneous trees in Dagenham, and other marshes bordering upon the River Thames, in the County of Essex. *Philosophical Transactions of the Royal Society* 27, 478–484.

Elton, C. (1938) Notes on the ecological and natural history of Pabbay, and other islands in the Sound of Harris, Outer Hebrides. *Journal of Ecology* 26, 275–297.

Fleming, K., Johnston, P., Zwartz, D. *et al.* (1998) Refining the eustatic sea-level curve since the Last Glacial Maximum using far- and intermediate-field sites. *Earth and Planetary Science Letters* 163, 327–342.

Forgrave, A. (2022) Incredible prehistoric forest re-emerges on Welsh beach. *Wales Online*, 30 October 2022.

Gerald of Wales (1191 and 1193/94) *The Journey Through Wales, and The Description of Wales.* Translations of *Itinerarium Cambriae* and *Descriptio Cambriae* by Lewis Thorpe. Penguin, Harmondsworth, 1978.

Haslett, S. K. and Willis, D. (2022) The 'lost' islands of Cardigan Bay, Wales, UK: insights into the post-glacial evolution of some Celtic coasts of northwest Europe. *Atlantic Geoscience* 58, 131–146.

Hunt, A. (1913) A supposed submerged forest in south-west Scotland. *Geological Magazine* 10, 475-475.

Ingram, J. (trans.) (1823) *The Anglo-Saxon Chronicle*, Vol. 180.

Innes, J., Roberts, D. and Chiverrell, R. C. (2006) Coastal and sea level history. In R. C. Chiverrell and G. S. P. Thomas (eds.), *A New History of the Isle of Man, Volume 1: Evolution of the Natural Landscape*, pp. 286–296. Liverpool University Press, Liverpool.

International Cryosphere Climate Initiative (2022) *State of the Cryosphere 2022: Growing Losses, Global Impacts.* ICCI.

James, R. (1880) *Poems of Richard James*, edited by A. B. Grosart. Chiswick Press, London.

Jehu, T. J. (1904) The glacial deposits of northern Pembrokeshire. *Transactions of the Royal Society of Edinburgh* 47, 53–87.

Martin, M. (1703) *A Description of the Western Islands of Scotland circa 1695, and A Late Voyage to St Kilda.* Reprinted by Birlinn, Edinburgh, 1994.

North, F. J. (1957) *Sunken Cities: Some Legends of the Coast and Lakes of Wales.* University of Wales Press, Cardiff.

O'Brien, T. (2018) Undersea hunt begins for 'lost landscapes' off Irish coast. Lost frontiers: ancient forest submerged near Bray first recorded 100 years ago. *The Irish Times*, 24 February 2018.

300                 *Forgotten Forests*

Parker, C. (2019) Perfect storm reveals east Cork's 'subaquatic wonder' on Youghal beach. *Irish Examiner*, 28 February 2019.

Pennick, N. (1987) *Lost Lands and Sunken Cities.* Fortean Tomes, London.

Plot, R. (1686) *The Natural History of Stafford-shire*. Printed at the Theater, Oxford.

Reid, C. (1913) *Submerged Forests.* Cambridge University Press, Cambridge.

Siggins, L. (2014) Storms reveal 7,500-year-old 'drowned forest' on north Galway coastline: evidence confirms Galway Bay once covered in forests and lagoons. *The Irish Times*, 7 March 2014.

Sinclair, J. (1794) *The Statistical Account of Scotland*, Vols. 10 and 13. Edinburgh

Sinel, J. (1914) The submerged forest. In *Prehistoric Times and Men of the Channel Islands*, pp. 124–131. J. T. Bigwood, Jersey.

Smith, C. (1774) *The Ancient and Present State of the County and City of Waterford.* W. Wilson, Dublin.

Smith, C. (1774) *The Ancient and Present State of the County and City of Cork: Containing a Natural, Civil, Ecclesiastical, Historical, and Topographical Description Thereof.* Guy & Company.

Stone, P., Millward, D., Young, B. *et al.* (2010) *British Regional Geology: Northern England*, 5th edition. British Geological Survey, Keyworth, Nottingham.

Timpany, S. (2005) A palaeoecological study of submerged forests in the Severn Estuary and Bristol Channel, UK. PhD thesis, University of Reading.

Travis, C. B. (1926) The peat and forest bed of the south west Lancashire coast. *Proceedings of the Liverpool Geological Society* 14, 263–277.

Urbanus, J. (2019) Submerged Scottish forest. *Archaeology (Archaeological Institute of America)*, May/June 2019.

Ury, E. (2021) Sea-level rise is creating 'ghost forests' on an American coast. *The Guardian*, 8 April 2021.

Westley, K. and Woodman, P. (2020) Ireland: submerged prehistoric sites and landscapes. In G. Bailey, N. Galanidou, H. Peeters, H. Jöns and M. Mennenga (eds.), *The Archaeology of Europe's Drowned Landscapes*, pp. 221–248. Springer, Cham.

## *Chapter 3: Axes and Agriculture*

Anon. (1942) The most fertile land in the British Isles. *Illustrated Sporting and Dramatic News*, 24 July 1942.

Asaw, D. D. and Barclay, M. V. L. (2018) *Dermestoides sanguinicollis* (Fabricius, 1787) (Cleridae: Korynetinae), a rare saproxylic beetle new to Britain. *The Coleopterist* 27, 49–53.

Bell, M. and Noble, G. (2012) Prehistoric woodland ecology. In A. M. Jones, J. Pollard, M. J. Allen and J. Gardiner (eds.), *Image, Memory and Monumentality: Archaeological Engagements with the Material World*. Prehistoric Society Research Paper 5. Oxbow Books, Oxford.

# Bibliography

Berry, J. and Parham, D. (2019) Rediscovering the Poole Logboat. *British Archaeology*, November/December 2019.

Borczyk, B., Gottfried, I., Urban, R. G. and Kania, J. (2022) Great capricorn beetle-created corridors as refuges for lizards. *Herpetozoa* 35, 59–63.

Bromwich, R. and Evans, D. S. (eds.) (1992) *Culhwch ac Olwen: an Edition and Study of the Oldest Arthurian Tale.* University of Wales Press, Cardiff.

Bulgarian Academy of Sciences and Ministry of Environment and Water of Bulgaria (2011) *Red Data Book of the Republic of Bulgaria.* electronic edition.

Cooke, R., Gearty, W., Chapman, A. S. A. *et al.* (2022) Anthropogenic disruptions to longstanding patterns of trophic-size structure in vertebrates. *Nature Ecology & Evolution* 6, 684–692.

Dempster, M. (1888) The Folk-lore of Sutherland-shire. *Folk-Lore Journal* 6, 149–189.

Donchev, A. (1968) *Time of Parting.* William Morrow, New York.

Dutton, A., Fasham, F. J., Jenkins, D. A., Caseldine, A. E. and Hamilton-Dyer, S. (1994) Prehistoric copper mining on the Great Orme, Llandudno, Gwynedd. *Proceedings of the Prehistoric Society* 60, 245–286.

Ennion, E. A. R. (1949) *Adventurers Fen.* Herbert Jenkins, London.

Fenland Black Oak CIO (undated) The Fenland Black Oak project: a table for the nation.

Garbett, G. G. (1981) The elm decline: the depletion of a resource. *New Phytologist* 88, 573–585.

Godwin, H. and Clifford, M. H. (1938). Studies in the post-glacial history of British vegetation. I. Origin and stratigraphy of fenland deposits near Woodwalton, Hunts. II. Origin and stratigraphy of deposits in southern Fenland. *Philosophical Transactions of the Royal Society B* 229, 323–406.

Heybroek, H. M. (2015) The elm, tree of milk and wine. *iForest: Biogeosciences and Forestry* 8, 181–186.

Innes, J. B., Blackford, J. J. and Rowley-Conwy, P. A. (2013) Late Mesolithic and early Neolithic forest disturbance: a high-resolution palaeoecological test of human impact hypotheses. *Quaternary Science Reviews* 77, 80–100.

Jones, M. (ed.) (1988) *Archaeology and the Flora of the British Isles: Human Influence on the Evolution of Plant Communities.* Oxford University School of Archaeology, Oxford.

Malone, C. (2001) *Neolithic Britain and Ireland.* Tempus, Stroud.

Marren, P. (1990) *Woodland Heritage: Britain's Ancient Woodland.* David & Charles, Newton Abbot.

McCarthy, M. (1999) Shifting sands reveal 'Stonehenge of the Sea'. *The Independent*, 9 January 1999.

McClatchie, M. and Potito, A. (2020) Tracing environmental, climatic and social change in Neolithic Ireland. *Proceedings of the Royal Irish Academy: Archaeology, Culture, History, Literature* 120C, 23–50.

McGrail, S. (1978) *Logboats of England and Wales, with Comparative Material from European and Other Countries*. British Archaeological Reports British Series. BAR Publishing, London.

Monbiot, G. (2013) Sheepwrecked: how Britain has been shagged by the white plague. *The Spectator*, 30 May 2013.

Mowat, R. J. C., Cowie, T., Crone, A. and Cavers, G. (2015) A medieval logboat from the River Conon: towards an understanding of riverine transport in Highland Scotland. *Proceedings of the Society of Antiquaries of Scotland* 145, 307–340.

Nelson, E. C. (1993) *The Trees of Ireland: Native and Naturalized*. Lilliput Press, Dublin.

Noble, G. (2006) Tree architecture: building monuments from the forest. *Journal of Iberian Archaeology* 8, 53–72.

Noble, G. (2017) *Woodland in the Neolithic of Northern Europe: the Forest as Ancestor*. Cambridge University Press, Cambridge.

Nordhagen, R. (1954) Ethnobotanical studies on barkbread and the employment of wych elm under natural husbandry. *Danmarks Geologiske Undersøgelse II, Række* 80: 262–308.

Ó hÓgáin, D. (1999) *The Sacred Isle: Belief and Religion in Pre-Christian Ireland*. Boydell Press, Woodbridge.

Orschiedt, J. (2020) Violence in Palaeolithic and Mesolithic hunter-gatherer communities. In G. Fagan, L. Fibiger, M. Hudson and M. Trundle (eds.), *The Cambridge World History of Violence*, pp. 58–78. Cambridge University Press, Cambridge.

Parker, A. G., Goudie, A. S., Anderson, D. E., Robinson, M. A. and Bonsall, C. (2002) A review of the mid-Holocene elm decline in the British Isles. *Progress in Physical Geography: Earth and Environment* 26, 1–45.

Pitts, M. (2001) Excavating the Sanctuary: new investigations on Overton Hill, Avebury. *Wiltshire Archaeological and Natural History Magazine* 94, 1–23.

Rackham, O. (2003) *Ancient Woodland: its History, Vegetation and Uses in England*, new edition. Castlepoint Press, Colvend.

Rejzek, M. and Barclay, M. (2017) *Pogonocherus caroli* Mulsant, 1863 (Cerambycidae: Lamiinae) new to Britain, from two localities in Scotland. *The Coleopterist* 26, 123–127.

Robinson, M. (2002) *English Heritage Reviews of Environmental Archaeology: Southern Region Insects*. Centre for Archaeology Report 39/2002. English Heritage.

Rösch, M. (2012) Forest, wood, and ancient man. *Interdisciplinaria Archaeologica: Natural Sciences in Archaeology* 3, 247–255.

Salisbury, A., Malumphy, C. and Barclay, M. (2015) Recent records of capricorn beetles *Cerambyx* spp. in England and Wales (Cerambycidae). *The Coleopterist* 24, 40–44.

Sheehy Skeffington, M. and Scott, N. (2021) Is the Strawberry Tree *Arbutus unedo* (Ericaceae), native to Ireland, or was it brought by the first copper miners? *British & Irish Botany* 3, 385–418.

# Bibliography

Sheehy Skeffington, M. and Scott, N. (2022) The Strawberry Tree and how it may have reached Ireland. *British Wildlife* 34, 85–93.

Swali, P., Schulting, R., Gilardet, A. *et al.* (2023) *Yersinia pestis* genomes reveal plague in Britain 4000 years ago. *Nature Communications* 14, 2930.

Williams, R. A. and Le Carlier de Veslud, C. (2019) Boom and bust in Bronze Age Britain: major copper production from the Great Orme mine and European trade, c. 1600-1400 BC. *Antiquity* 93, 1178–1196.

Woodcock, K. (2022) Table made from 5,000-year-old oak tree to be unveiled at Ely Cathedral in honour of The Queen. *Ely Standard*, 6 May 2022.

Yalden, D. and Albarella, U. (2009) *The History of British Birds*. Oxford University Press, Oxford.

## Chapter 4: What the Romans Did for Forests

Ackroyd, P. (2007) *Thames: Sacred River*. Chatto & Windus, London.

Bezant, J. (2016) Treescapes and landscapes: the myth of the wildwood and its place in the British past. In P. Davies (ed.), *Modern Pagan Thought and Practice*. Moon Books/John Hunt Publishing, Winchester.

British History Online *An Inventory of the Historical Monuments in Essex, Volume 1, North West* (London, 1916). www. british-history. ac. uk/rchme/essex/vol1.

Brown, A. D. (2010) Pollen analysis and planted ancient woodland restoration strategies: a case study from the Wentwood, southeast Wales, UK. *Vegetation History and Archaeobotany* 19, 79–90.

Brown, A. D. (2013) From Iron Age to Early Medieval: detecting the ecological impact of the Romans on the landscape of south-east Wales. *Britannia* 44, 250–257.

Burnham, B. C. and Davies, J. L. (2010) *Roman Frontiers in Wales and the Marches*. Royal Commission on the Ancient & Historical Monuments of Wales, Aberystwyth.

Choi, C. Q. (2019) Muddy find shows how foreign timber helped build ancient Rome. *Inside Science*, 4 December 2019.

Cleere, H. F. (1981) The iron industry of Roman Britain. PhD thesis, University College London.

Dark, P. (2000) *The Environment of Britain in the First Millennium AD*. Duckworth, London.

Deforce, K., Bastiaens, J., Crombé, P. *et al.* (2020) Dark Ages woodland recovery and the expansion of beech: a study of land use changes and related woodland dynamics during the Roman to Medieval transition period in northern Belgium. *Netherlands Journal of Geosciences* 99, e12.

Fox, A. (2019) Living trophies: trees, triumphs, and the subjugation of nature in early Imperial Rome. PhD thesis, University of Nottingham.

Fox, A. (2019) Trajanic trees: the Dacian Forest on Trajan's Column. *Papers of the British School at Rome* 87, 47–69.

Fraser Darling, F. (1947) *Natural History in the Highlands and Islands*. New Naturalist 6. Collins, London.

Fulford, M. (1990) The landscape of Roman Britain: a review. *Landscape History* 12 (1), 25–31.

Gil, L., Fuentes-Utrilla, P., Soto, Á. *et al.* (2004) English elm is a 2,000-year-old Roman clone. *Nature* 431, 1053.

Grüll, T. (2012) Ecological changes in the Roman Mediterranean. 15th Annual Mediterranean Studies Association Congress, Pula, Croatia.

Hoskins, W. G. (1954) *The Making of the English Landscape*. Hodder & Stoughton, London.

Jarman, R., Chambers, F. M. and Webb, J. (2019) Landscapes of sweet chestnut (*Castanea sativa*) in Britain: their ancient origins. *Landscape History* 40 (2), 5–40.

Johnson, A. (1983) *Roman Forts of the 1st and 2nd Centuries AD in Britain and the German Provinces*. St. Martin's Press, New York.

Jones, M. E. (1996) *The End of Roman Britain*. Cornell University Press, Ithaca, NY.

Lyte, H. C., Maxwell, S., Stenvson, W. H. and Flower, C. T. (eds.) (1912) *Calendar of Various Chancery Rolls: Supplementary Close Rolls, Welsh Rolls, Scutage Rolls*. Public Record Office, HMSO, London.

McNeill, J. R. (2002) Forests and warfare in world history. Lynn W. Day Distinguished Lectureship in Forest and Conservation History. Forest History Society meeting Durham, NC.

Milne, G. (2022) What can archaeology and woodland history tell us about growing more trees? *British Archaeology*, May/June 2022.

Nairn, D. (1890) Notes on Highland woods, ancient and modern. *Transactions of the Gaelic Society of Inverness* 17, 170–221.

Rackham, J. (ed.) (1994) *Environment and Economy in Anglo-Saxon England*. CBA Research Report 89. Council for British Archaeology, York.

Richards, J. (2022) What are British elm species? *BSBI News* 150, 22–23.

Rion, S., Smart, C., Pears, B. and Fleming, F. (2013) The fields of Britannia: continuity and discontinuity in the *pays* and regions of Roman Britain. *Landscapes* 14, 33–53.

Rogers, A. (2012) Exploring Late Iron Age settlement in Britain and the near continent. In T. Moore and X.-L. Armada (eds.), *Atlantic Europe in the First Millennium BC*, pp. 638–655. Oxford University Press, Oxford.

Tacitus (1942) *Complete Works of Tacitus*, translated by A. J. Church and W. J. Brodribb. Random House, New York.

Wilson, S. McG. (2015) *The Native Woodlands of Scotland: Ecology, Conservation and Management*. Edinburgh University Press, Edinburgh.

Witcher, R. (2013) On Rome's ecological contribution to British flora and fauna: landscape, legacy and identity. *Landscape History* 34 (2), 5–26.

Wrathmell, S. (2017) Woodland in Roman Britain. *Britannia* 48, 311–318.

# Bibliography

## Chapter 5: A Reliable Resource

Arnold, T. (ed.) (1890) *Memorials of St Edmunds Abbey Published by the Authority of the Lords Commissioners of Her Majesty's Treasury, under the Direction of the Master of the Rolls.* Printed for HM Stationery Office by Eyre and Spottiswoode, London.

Berryman, R. D. (1998) *Use of the Woodlands in the Late Anglo-Saxon Period.* British Archaeological Reports British Series 271. BAR Publishing, London.

Bintley, M. D. J. and Shapland, M. G. (eds.) (2013) *Trees and Timber in the Anglo-Saxon World.* Oxford University Press, Oxford.

Birrell, J. R. (1980) The medieval English forest. *Journal of Forest History* 24 (2), 78–85.

Bond, J. A. (2000). *Blenheim: Landscape for a Palace,* 2nd edition. Sutton Publishing, Stroud.

Carnicelli, T. A. (1969) *King Alfred's Version of St Augustine's Soliloquies.* Harvard University Press, Cambridge, MA.

Charles-Edwards, T. and Kelly, F. (1983) *Bechbretha: an Old Irish law-tract on bee-keeping.* Dublin Institute for Advanced Studies, Dublin.

Child, M. (1981) *English Church Architecture: a Visual Guide.* Batsford, London.

Falk, S. J. (2009) *Warwickshire's Wildflowers: the Wildflowers, Shrubs and Trees of Historic Warwickshire.* Brewin Books, Redditch.

Ferguson, D. (2021) 'No one knew they existed': wild heirs of lost British honeybee found at Blenheim. *The Observer,* 7 November 2021.

Flight, T. (2017) The wolf must be in the woods: the real and mythical dangers of the wilderness. *History Today* 67 (6).

Hale, S. (2016) Butchered bones, carved stones: hunting and social change in Late Saxon England. Masters thesis, Eastern Illinois University.

Hooke, D. (1989) Pre-Conquest woodland: its distribution and usage. *Agricultural History Review* 37, 113–129.

Hooke, D. (2009) *The Anglo-Saxon Landscape: the Kingdom of the Hwicce.* Manchester University Press, Manchester.

Hooke, D. (2010) *Trees in Anglo-Saxon England: Literature, Lore and Landscape.* Boydell Press, Woodbridge.

Jones, R. L. C. (2016) Responding to modern flooding: Old English place-names as a repository of traditional ecological knowledge. *Journal of Ecological Anthropology* 18 (1).

Kirby, D. P. (1974) The Old English forest. In T. Rowley (ed.), *Anglo-Saxon Settlement and Landscape,* pp. 120–130. British Archaeological Reports, Oxford.

Linnell, J. D. C. and Alleau, J. (2016) Predators that kill humans: myth, reality, context and the politics of wolf attacks on people. In F. M. Angelici, (ed.), *Problematic Wildlife,* pp. 357–371. Springer, Cham.

Littlejohns, G. (2021) Wildlife in Anglo-Saxon times. *Ða Engliscan Gesiðas (The English Companions).* www.tha-engliscan-gesithas.org.uk.

# 306 *Forgotten Forests*

Mackay, A. W. and Tallis, J. H. (1994) The recent vegetational history of the Forest of Bowland, Lancashire, UK. *New Phytologist* 128, 571–584.

Marshall, E. (2018) What is a wolf? The power of the cultural icon versus the animal. *Reforesting Scotland* 58.

Marvin, G. (2011) *Wolf.* Reaktion Books, London.

McGovern, T. H., Vesteinsson, O., Fridriksson, A. *et al.* (2007) Landscapes of settlement in northern Iceland: historical ecology of human impact and climate fluctuation on the millennial scale. *American Anthropologist* 109, 27–51.

Murphy, P. L. and Trow, S. (2005) Coastal change and the historic environment: building the evidence base. *English Heritage Conservation Bulletin* 48, 8–12.

Page, M. (2003) The extent of Whittlewood Forest and the impact of disafforestation in the later Middle Ages. *Northamptonshire Past and Present* 56, 22–34.

Rackham, O. (2022) *The Ancient Woods of South-East Wales.* Edited by Paula Keen, with contributions from David Morfitt, George Peterken and Simon Leatherdale. Little Toller, Beaminster.

Richards, J. D. and Haldenby, D. (2018) The scale and impact of Viking settlement in Northumbria. *Medieval Archaeology* 62, 322–350.

Roberts, B. K. (2015) Northumberland: reflections on prehistoric, Roman and Old English settlement. *Archaeologia Aeliana* 44, 31–74.

Swanton, M. (1997) *The Anglo-Saxon Chronicle.* Translated and edited by Michael Swanton. Dent, London.

Toulmin-Smith, L. (ed.) (1907) *The Itinerary of John Leland in or about the Years 1535–1543.* George Bell and Sons, London.

Wager, S. J. (1998) *Woods, Wolds and Groves: Woodland of Medieval Warwickshire.* John & Erica Hedges, Oxford.

Wychwood Project (2014) *Blenheim High Park Management Plan.* Self-published.

Yorke, B. (1999) *The Anglo-Saxons.* Sutton Publishing, Stroud.

## *Chapter 6: Taming the Landscape*

Baillie, M. G. L. (1979) An interim statement on dendrochronology at Belfast. *Ulster Journal of Archaeology* 42, 72–84.

Beglane, F. (2018) Forests and chases in medieval Ireland, 1169–*c.* 1399. *Journal of Historical Geography* 59, 90–99.

Bennett, M. (2001) *Campaigns of the Norman Conquest.* Osprey Publishing, Oxford.

Burke, K. (2023) Shakespeare's First Folio: State Library of NSW takes the Bard's 'radical' 400-year-old book out of the vault. *The Guardian*, 5 December 2023.

Doan, J. E. (1997) 'An Island in the Virginian Sea': Native Americans and the Irish in English discourse, 1585–1640. *New Hibernia Review / Iris Éireannach Nua* 1, 79–99.

Harris-Gavin, J. R. (2020) Ireland's forest fallacy. *Éire-Ireland* 55, 150–172.

# Bibliography

Jones, A. (1913) *Flintshire Ministers Accounts 1301–1328.* Flintshire Historical Society, Prestatyn.

Linnard, W. (1979) The history of forests and forestry in Wales up to the formation of the Forestry Commission. PhD thesis, University of Wales.

Linnard, W. (1982) *Welsh Woods and Forests: History and Utilization.* National Museum of Wales, Cardiff.

McAlister, V. (in press) *The Insular Globe: Animals and Colonizing Landscapes, Ireland c. 700–1700.*

McKeown, G. (2020) Oldest oak tree in Ireland shows signs of life. *The Irish Times*, 4 December 2020.

Miles, A. (2012) *Heritage Trees: Wales.* Graffeg Books.

Morris, S. (2022) North Wales' ancient felled Pontfadog oak returns in five cloned saplings. *The Guardian*, 6 July 2022.

Simon, B. (ed.) (2005) *A Treasured Landscape: the Heritage of Belvoir Park.* The Forest of Belfast, Belfast.

Vidal, J. (2013) The Pontfadog oak was the oldest of the old, revered, loved . . . and now mourned. *The Observer*, 28 April 2013.

## Chapter 7: The Forest Economy

Astill, G. and Grant, A. (eds.) (1988) *The Countryside of Medieval England.* Blackwell, Oxford.

Birrell, J. (1969) Peasant craftsmen in the medieval forest. *Agricultural History Review* 17, 91–107.

Geaney, M. (2016) Timber bridges in medieval Ireland. *Journal of Irish Archaeology* 25, 89–104.

Green, S. G. and Manning, S. (1889) *English Pictures Drawn with Pen and Pencil.* Religious Tract Society, London.

Hole, C. (1976) *A Dictionary of British Folk Customs.* Hutchinson, London.

Hutton, R. (2001) *The Stations of the Sun: a History of the Ritual Year in Britain.* Oxford University Press, Oxford.

Jones, R. and Page, M. (2006) *Medieval Villages: Beginnings and Ends.* Windgather Press, Oxford.

Langdon, J. and Watts, M. (2005) Tower windmills in medieval England: a case of arrested development? *Technology and Culture* 46, 697–718.

Langton, J. (2022) *Forest vert: the holly and the ivy. Landscape History* 43 (1), 5–26.

Magraw, D. and Thomure, N. (2017) Carta de Foresta: the Charter of the Forest turns 800. *Environmental Law Reporter* 47 ELR 10934.

Stone, J. B. (1906) *Sir Benjamin Stone's Pictures: Festivals, Ceremonies and Customs.* Cassell, London.

Weixel, E. M. (2009) The forest and social change in early modern English literature, 1590–1700. PhD thesis, University of Minnesota.

# 308 *Forgotten Forests*

## Chapter 8: Death, Recovery and Dissolution

Bannister, A. T. (1902) *The History of Ewias Harold, its Castle, Priory and Church, with illustrations and an appendix containing translations of many of the Mss. (Latin and Norman French) on which the history is based.* Jakeman & Carver, The Bible and Crown Press, Hereford.

Brady, L. (2021) Inglewood Forest in Three Romances from the Northern Gawain Group. *Leeds Medieval Studies* 1, 1–15.

DeLange, K. C. (1997) The effects of the Black Death on the lower gentry and offices of coroner and verderer in fourteenth century England. MA thesis, Iowa State University.

Edlin, H. L. (1960) The history of forests and land use in Wales. *Nature in Wales* 6 (2).

Gerald of Wales (1982) *Topographia Hiberniae (The History and Topography of Ireland).* Translated by J. J. O'Meara. Dolmen Press, Portlaoise.

Gwynn, A. (1935) The Black Death in Ireland. *Studies: An Irish Quarterly Review* 24 (93), 25–42.

Heldring, L., Robinson, J. A. and Vollmer, S. (2015) Monks, gents and industrialists: the long-run impact of the dissolution of the English monasteries. NBER Working Paper 21450.

Hill, K. D. (2002) Assarting and governmental development in twelfth-century England: a study of the pipe roll evidence concerning illegal land clearance, 1154–1189. PhD thesis, Iowa State University.

Hodgson, V. A. (2016) The Cistercian Abbey of Coupar Angus, c. 1164 – c. 1560. PhD thesis, University of Stirling.

Jefferson, S. (1840) *The History and Antiquities of Cumberland Vol. 1.* J. B. Nichols & Son.

Kelly, F. (1999) Trees in early Ireland: Augustine Henry Memorial Lecture. *Irish Forestry* 56, 39–57.

Kelly, M. (2004) *A History of the Black Death in Ireland.* The History Press, Cheltenham.

Laing, D. (ed.) (1872) *The Orygynale Cronykil of Scotland by Andrew of Wyntoun.* Edmonston and Douglas, Edinburgh.

Para, H. (2020) Monastic development and dissolution in Wales: continuity or change for Uchelwyr? A case study of Strata Florida's Blaenaeron Grange. PhD thesis, University of Wales Trinity Saint David.

Poyner, D. R. and Mountford, E. P. (2005) Long-term patterns of land use, evolution of the fieldscape and hedge composition in the parish of Highley. *Transactions of the Shropshire Archaeological and Historical Society* 80, 17–51.

Rigby, S. H. (2000) Gendering the Black Death: women in later medieval England. *Gender & History* 12, 745–754.

Ruhaak, R. (2019) Towards an alternative Black Death narrative for Ireland: ecological and socio-economic divides on the medieval European frontier. *Journal of the North Atlantic* 39, 1–16.

# Bibliography

Rutz, C., Loretto, M.-C., Bates, A. *et al.* (2020) COVID-19 lockdown allows researchers to quantify the effects of human activity on wildlife. *Nature Ecology & Evolution* 4, 1156–1159.

Scott, B. (2005) The dissolution of the religious houses in the Tudor Diocese of Meath. *Archivium Hibernicum* 59, 260–276.

Stokstad, E. (2020) The pandemic stilled human activity. What did this 'anthropause' mean for wildlife? *Science Insider*, 13 August 2020.

Whitehead, D. (2007) Veterans in the arboretum: planting exotics at Holme Lacy, Herefordshire, in the late nineteenth century. *Garden History* 35 (Supplement 2), 96–112.

Williams, G. (1946) *The Burning Tree: Poems from the First Thousand Years of Welsh Verse.* Faber, London.

Yeloff, D. and Van Geel, B. (2007) Abandonment of farmland and vegetation succession following the Eurasian plague pandemic of AD 1347–52. *Journal of Biogeography* 34, 575–582.

## Chapter 9: The Floating Forest

Addley, E. (2022) Oldest English shipwreck given government protection. *The Guardian*, 20 July 2022.

Albion, R. G. (1926) *Forests and Sea Power: the Timber Problem of the Royal Navy, 1652–1862.* Harvard University Press, Cambridge, MA.

Badenoch, C. O. (1994–95) Border woodlands I – Berwickshire; Border Woodlands II – Roxburghshire. *History of Berwickshire Naturalists' Club*, 115–133, 272–286.

Barkham, P. (2024) Herd of tauros to be released into Highlands to recreate aurochs effect. *The Guardian*, 10 October 2024.

Beaver, D. C. (2008) *Hunting and the Politics of Violence Before the English Civil War.* Cambridge University Press, Cambridge.

Chesterton. G. K. (1915) *Wine, Water and Song.* Methuen, London.

Crone, A. and Mills, C. M. (2012) Timber in Scottish buildings, 1450–1800: a dendrochronological perspective. *Proceedings of the Society of Antiquaries of Scotland* 142, 329–369.

Drew, C. (1841) *A Collection of Poems on the Forest of Dean and its Neighbourhood.* Chas. C. Rough.

Evelyn, J. (1776) *Silva: or a Discourse of Forest-Trees and the Propagation of Timber in His Majesties Dominions.* London.

Firth, C. H. and Rait, R. S. (eds.) (1911) *Acts and Ordinances of the Interregnum, 1642–1660.* British History Online. www.british-history.ac.uk/no-series/acts-ordinances-interregnum.

Flower, N. (1980) The management history and structure of unenclosed woods in the New Forest, Hampshire. *Journal of Biogeography* 7, 311–328.

Gilchrist, R. M. (1913) *The Dukeries.* Blackie & Son, London.

Gilpin, W. (1791) *Remarks on Forest Scenery, and Other Woodland Views (Relative Chiefly to Picturesque Beauty): Illustrated by the Scenes of New-Forest in Hampshire.* R. Blamire, London.

James, N. D. G. (1990) *A History of English Forestry.* Blackwell, Oxford.

Marsden, P. (2009) *Your Noblest Shippe: Anatomy of a Tudor Warship.* Archaeology of the Mary Rose, vol. 2. Oxbow Books, Oxford.

McCracken, E. E. (1959) The woodlands of Ireland circa 1600. *Irish Historical Studies* 11, 271–296.

Melby, P. (2012) Insatiable shipyards: the impact of the Royal Navy on the world's forests, 1200–1850. Student thesis, Western Oregon University.

Mills, C. M. and Crone, A. (2012) Dendrochronological evidence for Scotland's native timber resources over the last 1000 years. *Scottish Forestry* 66, 18–33.

Nisbet, J. (1905) *The Forester: a Practical Treatise on British Forestry and Arboriculture for Landowners, Land Agents, and Foresters*, vol. 1. Blackwood, Edinburgh.

Oster, R. M. (2015) *Great Britain in the Age of Sail: Scarce Resources, Ruthless Actions and Consequences.* Technical Report, Air Command and Staff College, Maxwell Air Force Base, AL.

Payne, C. (2022) Remarkable trees: prints and drawings in the King's Topographical Collection which depict celebrated and culturally meaningful trees. British Library, London. www. bl. uk/picturingplaces/articles/remarkable-trees.

Pollitt, R. L. (1971) Wooden Walls: English Seapower and the World's Forests. *Forest History Newsletter* 15, 6–15.

Rackham, O. (1976) *Trees and Woodland in the British Landscape: the Complete History of Britain's Trees, Woods and Hedgerows.* Dent, London.

Razgour, O., Montauban, C., Festa, F. *et al.* (2023) Applying genomic approaches to identify historic population declines in European forest bats. *Journal of Applied Ecology,* Open Access 1-13.

Smith, J. R. (2009) Shipbuilding and the English international timber trade 1300–1700: a framework for study using niche construction theory. *Nebraska Anthropologist* 49.

Standish, A. (1611) *The Commons Complaint Wherein is Contained Two Speciall Grievances.* William Stansby, London.

Standish, A. (1615) *New Directions of Experience for the increasing of Timber and Firewood.* William Stansby, London.

Strutt, F. and Cox, J. C. (1903) Duffield forest in the sixteenth century. *Journal of the Derbyshire Archaeological and Natural History Society* 25, 181–216.

Thorne, S. J. (2022) The Royal Navy's war on trees. *Legion: Canada's Military History Magazine*, 15 February 2022.

Tubbs, C. R. (1986) *The New Forest.* New Naturalist 73. Collins, London.

# Bibliography

## Chapter 10: Industry and Animals

Blake, W. (1811) *Milton: a Poem in Two Books.* W. Blake.

Clarkson, L. A. (1974) The English bark trade, 1660–1830. *Agricultural History Review* 22, 136–152.

Cooper, M. M. D., Patil, S. D., Nisbet, T. R. *et al.* (2021) Role of forested land for natural flood management in the UK: a review. *Wiley Interdisciplinary Reviews: Water* 8, e1541.

Cross, J. R. (2006) The potential natural vegetation of Ireland. *Biology and Environment: Proceedings of the Royal Irish Academy* 106B, 65–116.

Henderson, D. M. and Dickson, J. H. (eds.) (1994) *A Naturalist in the Highlands: James Robertson, His Life and Travels in Scotland, 1767–1771.* Scottish Academic Press, Edinburgh.

Jones, M. (1989) *Sheffield's Woodland Heritage.* Sheffield City Libraries, Sheffield.

Kerr, G. and Nisbet, T. R. (1996) *The Restoration of Floodplain Woodlands in Lowland Britain.* Forestry Commission Research Division R&D Technical Report W15.

Lo, M., Narulita, S. and Ickowitz, A. (2019) The relationship between forests and freshwater fish consumption in rural Nigeria. *PLoS One* 14 (6), e0218038.

Macadam, W. I. (1886) Notes on the ancient iron industry of Scotland. *Proceedings of the Society of Antiquaries of Scotland* 21, 89–131.

Macdonald, A. R. and McCallum, J. (2013) The evidence for early seventeenth-century climate from Scottish ecclesiastical records. *Environment and History* 19, 487–509.

Mason, J. F. A. and Barker, P. A. (1961) The Norman castle at Quatford. *Transactions of the Shropshire Archaeological and Historical Society* 57, 37–62.

McParlan, J. (1802) *A Statistical Survey of the County Mayo.* Dublin Society, Dublin.

Richards, E. (1970) The prospect of economic growth in Sutherland at the time of the Clearances, 1809 to 1813. *Scottish Historical Review* 49, 154–171.

Ryder, M. L. (1968) Sheep and the Clearances in the Scottish Highlands: a biologist's view. *Agricultural History Review* 16, 155–158.

Scott, H. C. M. (2018) *Fuel: an Ecocritical History.* Bloomsbury, London.

Wakana, H. (2012) History of 'uotsukirin' (fish-breeding forests) in Japan. In M. Taniguchi and T. Shiraiwa (eds.), *The Dilemma of Boundaries.* Springer, Tokyo.

## Chapter 11: World Wars and Conifers

Anderson, M. L. (ed. Taylor, C. J.) (1967) *A History of Scottish Forestry.* 2 volumes. Nelson, London.

Aston, G. (1996) *Forest Folk: True Stories of the Old Men of the Woods Spanning More Than Fifty Years.* Self-published, Cinderford.

Cabuts, P. (2010) Trees of the third war: forests, photography and Wales. Paper presented at Emerging Landscapes Conference, University of Westminster.

Chapman, A. (1924) *The Borders and Beyond.* Gurney & Jackson, London.

312 *Forgotten Forests*

Clark, L. (1965) *A Fool in the Forest.* Dobson Books, London.

Forestry Commission England (2015) *Highmeadow Forest Plan 2015–2025.* Forestry Commission.

House, E. (undated) The impact of the First World War on the woods and forests of Scotland. www.forestry-memories.org.uk/pictures/document/3760.pdf.

Hyde, H. A. (1961) *Welsh Timber Trees: Native and Introduced.* National Museum of Wales, Cardiff.

Langton, J. (2016) Land and people in late sixteenth-century Glyn Cothi and Pennant Forests. *Welsh History Review / Cylchgrawn Hanes Cymru* 28, 55–86.

O'Carroll, N. (2004) *Forestry in Ireland: a Concise History.* COFORD, Dublin.

Oosthoek, J. K. (2013) *Conquering the Highlands: a History of the Afforestation of the Scottish Uplands.* ANU Press, Canberra.

Peterken, G. (2008) *Wye Valley.* New Naturalist 105. Collins, London.

Rowe, W. H. (1947) *Our Forests.* Faber and Faber, London.

Ryle, G. B. (1947) Forestry in south Wales: a generation of destruction and conservation. *Reports and Transactions of the Cardiff Naturalists' Society* 79, 23–30.

Steven, H. M. and Carlisle, A. (1959) *The Native Pinewoods of Scotland.* Oliver & Boyd, Edinburgh.

Williams, W. (2023) *The Peacemakers.* Bilingual edition, with parallel translations by T. Conran. Y Lolfa, Aberystwyth.

## Chapter 12: New Forests

Anthony, M. A., Crowther, T. W., van der Linde, S. *et al.* (2022) Forest tree growth is linked to mycorrhizal fungal composition and function across Europe. *ISME Journal* 16, 1327–1336.

Bennett, S., Bouwes, N. and Rogers, P. C. (2019) Beaver and aspen: synergy among keystone species. Western Aspen Alliance. Utah State University. WAA Brief no. 6.

Brown, A. D. (2010) Pollen analysis and planted ancient woodland restoration strategies: a case study from the Wentwood, southeast Wales, UK. *Vegetation History and Archaeobotany* 19, 79–90.

Calders, K., Verbeeck, H., Burt, A. *et al.* (2022) Laser scanning reveals potential underestimation of biomass carbon in temperate forest. *Ecological Solutions and Evidence* 3, e12197.

Carrell, S. (2022) 'A growing machine': Scotland looks to vertical farming to boost tree stocks. *The Guardian*, 1 October 2022.

Carrington, D. and Davis, N. (2022) Wild bison return to UK for first time in thousands of years. *The Guardian*, 18 July 2022.

Chazdon, R. L. (2014) *Second Growth: the Promise of Tropical Forest Regeneration in an Age of Deforestation.* University of Chicago Press, Chicago, IL.

# Bibliography 313

Cosgrove, P. and Amphlett, A. (eds.) (2002) *The Biodiversity and Management of Aspen Woodlands: Proceedings of a one-day conference held in Kingussie, Scotland, on 25th May 2001.* Cairngorms National Park Authority, Grantown on Spey.

Cross, J. and Lynn, D. (2013) Results of a monitoring survey of yew woodland. Irish Wildlife Manuals 72. National Parks and Wildlife Service, Dublin.

D'Arcy, G. (1999) *Ireland's Lost Birds.* Four Courts Press, Dublin.

Daltun, E. (2022) *An Irish Atlantic Rainforest: a Personal Journey into the Magic of Rewilding.* Hachette, Dublin.

Department of Agriculture, Food and the Marine (2023) *Ireland's National Forest Inventory 2022: Main Findings.* Government of Ireland, Dublin.

EUROPARC-España (2017) Old-growth forests: characteristics and conservation value. Fundación Fernando González Bernaldez, Madrid.

Gayle, D. (2023) Brockley residents raise £100,000 to save patch of ancient London woodland. *The Guardian*, 28 January 2023.

Gill, V. (2022) UK's old trees critical to climate change fight. *BBC News*, 20 December 2022.

Haggith, M. (2015) Prepare for bears! *Reforesting Scotland* 51, 42.

Haria, A. H. and Price, D. J. (2000) Evaporation from Scots pine (*Pinus sylvestris*) following natural re-colonisation of the Cairngorm mountains, Scotland. *Hydrology and Earth System Sciences* 4, 451–461.

Hetherington, D. and Geslin, L. (2018) *The Lynx and Us.* Scotland: the Big Picture, Kingussie.

Horton, H. (2022) Tales of killer wild boar in UK are hogwash, say environmentalists. *The Guardian*, 30 December 2022.

Horton, H. and Barkham, P. (2022) Study suggests existence of up to 2.1m ancient and veteran trees in England. *The Guardian*, 30 June 2022.

Letessier, T. B., Mannocci, L., Goodwin, B. *et al.* (2023) Contrasting ecological information content in whaling archives with modern cetacean surveys for conservation planning and identification of historical distribution changes. *Conservation Biology* 37, e14043.

Lyons, C. (2024) *Groundbreakers: the Return of Britain's Wild Boar.* Bloomsbury, London.

Morris, M. G. and Perring, F. H. (1974) *The British Oak: its History and Natural History.* The Botanical Society of the British Isles, Durham.

Neeson, E. (1997) Woodland in history and culture. In J. W. Foster and H. C. G. Chesney (eds.), *Nature in Ireland: a Scientific and Cultural History*, pp. 133–156. Lilliput Press, Dublin.

Nisbet, T. (2022) *Designing and Managing Forests and Woodlands to Reduce Flood Risk: UK Forestry Standard Practice Guide.* Forestry Publishing Group, Roslin.

Nolan, V., Reader, T., Gilbert, F. and Atkinson, N. (2020) The Ancient Tree Inventory: a summary of the results of a 15-year citizen science project recording ancient, veteran and notable trees across the UK. *Biodiversity and Conservation* 29, 3103–3129.

O'Mahony, D., Turner, P. and O'Reilly, C. (2012) Pine marten (*Martes martes*) distribution and abundance in Ireland: a cross-jurisdictional analysis using non-invasive genetic survey techniques. *Mammalian Biology – Zeitschrift für Säugetierkunde* 77, 351–357.

Pearce, F. (2021) *A Trillion Trees: How We Can Reforest Our World*. Granta Books, London.

Pearce, F. (2022) Phantom forests: why ambitious tree planting projects are failing. *Yale Environment 360*, 6 October 2022.

Peterken, G. F. and Hughes, F. M. R. (1995) Restoration of floodplain forests in Britain. *Forestry* 68, 187–202.

Policelli, N., Horton, T. R., Hudon, A. T., Patterson, T. R. and Bhatnagar, J. M. (2020) Back to roots: the role of ectomycorrhizal fungi in boreal and temperate forest restoration. *Frontiers in Forests and Global Change* 3.

Rainey, J. and Holmes, F. (2023) *Caledonian Pinewoods: Findings from the Caledonian Pinewood Recovery Project*. Trees for Life, Forres.

Schmitz, O. J., Sylvén, M., Atwood, T. B. *et al.* (2023) Trophic rewilding can expand natural climate solutions. *Nature Climate Change* 13, 324–333.

Sheail, J. (1997) The new National Forest: from idea to achievement. *Town Planning Review* 68, 305–323.

Shrubsole, G. (2022) *The Lost Rainforests of Britain*. William Collins, London.

Statistics for Wales (2021) June 2021 survey of agriculture and horticulture: results for Wales. Welsh Government, Cardiff.

Stroh, P. A., Walker, K. J., Humphrey, T. A., Pescott, O. L. and Burkmar, R. J. (2023) *Plant Atlas 2020: Mapping Changes in the Distribution of the British and Irish Flora*. BSBI and Princeton University Press, Oxford.

Tew, E. R., Ambrose-Oji, B., Beatty, M. *et al.* (2023) A horizon scan of issues affecting UK forest management within 50 years. *Forestry* 2023, cpad047.

Van Den Hoek, J., Smith, A. C., Hurni, K., Saksena, S. and Fox, J. (2021) Shedding new light on mountainous forest growth: a cross-scale evaluation of the effects of topographic illumination correction on 25 years of forest cover change across Nepal. *Remote Sensing* 13, 2131.

Weston, P. (2021) Trees should be planted without plastic guards, says UK study. *The Guardian*, 24 August 2021.

# ILLUSTRATION CREDITS

All illustrations are copyright © Jonathan Mullard or believed to be out of copyright, except as indicated below.

The publisher would like to thank those listed below for providing illustrations, and for permission to reproduce copyright material in this book. Whilst every effort has been made to trace and acknowledge all copyright holders, we apologise for errors or omissions, and invite readers to inform us so that corrections can be made in any future editions.

Page 15: John Richards
Page 17: Katherine Grundy, Creative Commons, CC BY-SA 3.0
Page 20: National Museum of Ireland
Page 22: Emily Richens
Page 27: Luc Viator, Creative Commons, CC BY-SA 3.0
Page 31: Amgueddfa Cymru – Museum Wales
Page 37: Jon Moses
Page 41: Alastair Rae, Creative Commons, CC BY-SA 3.0
Page 47: David Evans
Page 49: Matthew J. Thomas
Page 52: Scott Timpany
Page 54: Joe O'Shaughnessy
Page 62: M. S. Bretherton, Alamy Stock Photo
Page 63: Hans M. Heybroek
Page 72: Norfolk Museums Service
Page 76: Max Barclay, Natural History Museum
Page 78: Max Barclay, Natural History Museum
Page 80: Fenland Black Oak CIO, James Harris Photography,
Page 82: Howard Crowdy
Page 87: Lord Harris, Creative Commons, CC BY-SA 3.0
Page 90: Jacek Karczmarz, Creative Commons, CC BY-SA 3.0

316            *Forgotten Forests*

Page 94: Roger Ulrich

Page 99: David Dixon, Creative Commons, CC BY-SA 2.0

Page 106: Stephen Dorey – Gloucestershire, Alamy Stock Photo

Page 115: Acabashi, Creative Commons, CC BY-SA 4.0

Page 127: Sheila Wiggins, Creative Commons, CC BY-SA 4.0

Page 133: Birmingham Museums Trust

Page 143: Rory Francis, Creative Commons, CC BY-SA 2.0

Page 148: Andy Dingley, Creative Commons, CC BY-SA 3.0

Page 155: Carol Di Rienzo Cornwell, Alamy Stock Photo

Page 156: Forest Service Northern Ireland

Page 157: Derek Fanning

Page 165: British Library

Page 168: Averil Shepherd

Page 188: Carlisle Library, © cumbriaimagebank

Page 191: Eamon Curry, Creative Commons, CC BY 2.0

Page 197: Geni, Creative Commons, CC BY-SA 4.0

Page 199: Coralie Mills

Page 207: Ballista, Creative Commons, CC BY-SA 3.0

Page 209: British Library

Page 222: Cathy Fitzgerald

Page 239: Richard Sutcliffe, Creative Commons, CC BY-SA 2.0

Page 246: DGB, Alamy Stock Photo

Page 248: Joan Gravell, Alamy Stock Photo

Page 256: Clement Philippe, Arterra Picture Library, Alamy Stock Photo

Page 265: The National Forest

Page 276: Aiden MacCormick, Creative Commons, CC BY-SA 4.0

Page 280: Justus Cuveland, imageBROKER.com GmbH & Co. KG, Alamy Stock Photo

Page 283: Wildlife GmbH, Alamy Stock Photo

Page 285: Wildlife GmbH, Alamy Stock Photo

# INDEX

Page references in *italics* indicate images.

Abbey Dore 187, 193
Abbots Bromley Horn Dance 169–70, *169*, 173
Abernethy Forest/Abernethy National Nature Reserve 5, 238–41, *239*, 245
afforestation 151, 196, 246–8, 150
aging, trees and 88–9, 123–4, 154, 155, 188, *188*, 205, 206
alder 19, 20, *20*, 21, 23, 26, 56, 73, 87, 91, 105, 198, 230, 231, 233, 273, 275, 277
Alfred, King 114–15, 116–17, 119, 125, 135
Amroth 47–8, *47*, 56
Anglesey 31, 75, 96, 97
Anglo-Saxons 50, 105, 109, 112, 113–38, *115*, *118*, *127*, *128*, *130*, *133*, 226
Anglo-Saxon Chronicle 50, 105, 122, 125, 131–2, 135
anthropause 182–3
Antonine Wall 101, 104
Arden, Forest of 132–4, *133*, 265–6
Arles Museum of Antiquity 101, *102*
Arthur, King 45, 86, 98, 190
ash 19, 24, 26, 62, 109, 119, 126, 128, 150, 155, 161, 175, 181, 211, 220, 231, 233, 258–9, 269, 280–1; ash dieback 273, 288
aspen 23, 24, 52, 220, 240, 275, 277–8
Aughty, Forest of 5, 157, 221
auroch 34–7, *36*, 39, 41, 56–8, 85

Baillie, Mike 161, 183, 204, 291
Baimbridge, Nick *128*, 130, 292

Ballachuan hazelwood 17, *17*, 18
Ballochbuie Forest 240
Balnagown Wood 239–40
barbastelle bat 213
Barclay, Max 77, 79, 292
bark 16, 64, 73, 82–3, 91, 116, 150, 168, 173, 204, 227–9, 271
Barnsdale Forest 189
Barnsley 189
Barri, Gerald de (Gerald of Wales/ Giraldus Cambrensis) 45–6, 56, 139, 146, 157, 158, 181, 187; *Descriptio Cambriae* 140; *Itinerarium Cambriae* 46, 140
beams 87, 96, 115, 117, 148, 149, 162, 175, 176, 198, 218
bears 23, 29, 41, 57, 65, 236, 282–4, 288
Beast of the Charred Forests 84
Beaumaris 149
Beaver, Daniel 201
beavers 23, 34, 39, 41, 58, 78–9, 278
Bede, Venerable 114, 137
beech 16, 21, 26, 28, 49, 92, 110, 111, 124, 148–9, 167, 171, 172, 174, 211, 213, 224, 247, 251, 258, 259, 281
bees 129–31, 150, 151, 189, 292
beetles 37–8, 42, 64, 66–7, *76*, 77, 78, *78*, 79, 129, 175, 271, 292
Beinn Eighe 24, *25*
Belvoir Park 155, *156*; Belvoir Oak 155
Berneray 51–2
Bernicia 110, 134
Białowieża Forest World Heritage Site 90–1, *90*

biodiversity 79, 182, 261, 266, 279
birch 17–20, 23–4, 26, 51–3, 56, 110,
    135, 156, 161, 177, 198, 205,
    220–1, 230, 233, 237, 240–1, 252,
    269, 273, 275–7, 280
bird cherry 277, 231
Birklands 203–6
Birnham Wood 5; Birnham Oak 5
Bisham Woods 111
bison 34, 39, 90, 282
Black Death 179–85, *180*, *184*, 194
black poplar 233–4
blackthorn 16, 27, 198, 231
Black Wood of Rannoch 245, *246*, 251,
    257
Blair, William 193
Blake, William: *Milton* 219, 224
Blenheim Estate 127–30, *128*, 292; bees
    at 129–30, *130*
Blennerhasset, Thomas: *A Direction for the*
    *Plantation in Ulster* 159
Board of Agriculture for Scotland 243
Bodfari, Forest of 5, 146
bogs 17, 22, 62, 79, 84, 85, 86, 159, 261;
    bog oaks 76–83, *76*, *80*, *82*, 89,
    91, 292
Bond, James: *Blenheim: Landscape for a*
    *Palace* 127, 128
Borders Community Woodland 263
Borders Forest Trust 276
boreal forest 22–3, *25*
box tree 16, 119
Boxford 31–2, *31*, 119
Boyle, Earl of Cork, Sir Richard 159–60
Boyne, River 69, 166
bramble 27, 34, 111, 281, 282
Brechfa Forest 248–50, *248*, 268
Brecknock Forest 146
Breen Forest 155–6
Breos, William de 167
*Bretha Comaithchesa* 'judgments of neigh-
    bourhood' 181–2
Brian Boru Oak 156–7, *157*, 292–3
Brig o' Waithe 52
Broadleaves in Britain conference (1982)
    257
Brodsworth Community Woodland
    189–90
Bromley Hurst, Needwood Forest 173

Bronze Age 4, *4*, 29, 55, 56, 71–5, 77,
    82–7, 108, 287; Early 4, *4*, 72, 83,
    85; Late 77, 87
Brown, Alex 268–9
Brown, David 82–3, 291
Brunel, Isambard Kingdom 216
Brunswick Dock 48
Buccleuch Estate 263
Burley Old Inclosure 248
Burren, County Clare 14, 18
Burwell Fen Farm 81
button jelly lichen 23–4

Cabot, David 155, 261
*Cad Goddeu* ('Battle of the Trees') 98
Cadzow Oaks, Clyde Valley Woodlands
    National Nature Reserve 199, *199*,
    274
Caesar, Julius 99; *Commentaries* 92–3; *De*
    *Bello Gallico* 92
Cagnacci, Francesca 183
Cahermurphy oakwoods 221
Cairngorms 229, 274; National Park 237,
    239, 274–5, 286
Caledonia 23–4, 51, 97–8, 100, 239,
    251, 259
*Caledonia Silva* 97
Callants 2
Camden, William 46–7, 48, 203
Canadian Forestry Corps 244–5, 246,
    251
Candos, Robert de 107
Cannock Chase 171
Cantiaci (or Cantii) 105–6
Cantre'r Gwaelod, or the Lowland
    Hundred 45
Capon Tree 1–3, *2*, 210, *210*
carbon dioxide 59, 266, 270, 272, 273,
    274, 288–9
Cardigan 97, 144
Cardigan Bay 45, 55
Carmarthen 144, 146, 248–9
carpenters 145, 162, 167, 172, 175
Carrifran Wildwood Project 276, *276*
Carron Valley Forest 255
Carsie Mains 69–70
Cat Coit Celidon, battle of 98
cathedrals 45, *80*, 81, 84, 91, *168*, 169,
    175–6, 198, 218

Catherton dagger 4, *4*
cattle 16, 35–7, *36*, 63, 65, 66, 85, 86, 103, 122, 124, 150, 153, 157–8, 165, 166, 182, 200, 208, 228, 230, 231–2, 238, 261, 274, 276, 282
Census of Woodlands (1924) 246–7
Ceremony of Quit Rents 209
Chapman, Abel 250
charcoal 32–3, 56, 106, 145, 146, 173, 219–22, 224, 226, 237, 252, 259
Charles II, King 126
Charleville Forest 154–5, *155*
charters 107, 130–1, 137–8, 164–5, *165*, 167
Cheddar Man 32
Chepstow Castle 148, *148*, 149, 151
Chesterton, G. K.: 'The song of the oak' 218
Chestnuts Wood 253
Chillingham Castle, Northumberland 36, *36*
Chirk Castle 141
Cilcochwyn Farm 143
Cistercians 186, 188, 192–3
Clark, Leonard 253, 292
Claycastle beach 54
clearance, forest 35, 60, 61, 63, 66, 67, 70, 84–7, 91, 95, 104, 120, 132, 135, 144–7, 181, 182, 186–7, 192, 213
Clidro, Robin 222, 224
climate change 7, 13, 14, 17, 20, 30, 38, 43, 51, 59, 64, 71, 77, 83–6, 100, 109, 111, 229, 261, 267, 269, 275, 278, 287–8
closed canopy 8, 33, 34, 40, 125–6
Cluain Doire Sheangan 276
Clyde Valley Woodlands National Nature Reserve 26, 199, *199*
Cnut, King 115–16, 136
coal 166–7, 219, 226, 242–3, 252, 264
Coed Marchan 222, 223
Coed Mwstwr 222
Coed y Bleiddiau 271
Coedydd Aber 258
Coedysbys 140–1
Coille na Glas-Leitire 24–5
Coillte 278
Coit Mawr 113
Coles, John 4

colliers 219, 224, 225
Collingwood Oaks 217–18, *217*
Collins New Naturalist series 98, 213
Columella: *De Re Rustica* 108
Committee for Compounding with Delinquents 202
commons 165, 195, 200–1
community forests 262–3, 266
Condry, William 5
conifer 6, 21, 23, 126, 152, 162, 204, 215, 247–51, *248*, 253–9, *256*, 269, 273, 277, 278, 279
Conon logboat 89
Conwy valley 149, 185
Cooper, William Durrant 49
Copford church, Essex 116
Copper Alley 134
Copper, Herefordshire 124
copper mining 74, 75, 212
coppice 7–8, 18, 75, *106*, 124, 126, 153, 198, 220, 221, 223, 253, 258, 259, 269
Copster, Lancashire 124
Corpus Christi Great Horn 35
Countryside Commission 264, 291
Cowbeach, Sussex 124
Cox, Eoin 263, 291
crag-and-tail features 11–12
Cranberry Rough nature reserve 19
Cratloe Woods 162
craw-sown 28
creel houses 176–7
Crittenden, Peter 237
Crogen, Battle of 141, 142, *142*
Cromwell, Oliver 160
Crooked Family 3
cross-beams (cross-tree) 175
crucks 175, 177
Curley Oak 151–2, *152*
Cwm Idwal 11, *12*

Dagenham Idol 83
*dairthech*, or wooden church 116
Dale Abbey 190–1
Darby, Abraham 226
Dark Ages 122
Darling, Frank Fraser 98, 253, 255
Darnaway Castle 89, 176
Darwin, Charles 11, 12

320        *Forgotten Forests*

David I, King 176
Davies, John 255
dead trees 70, 120, 270, 273
dead wood 66, 168, 213, 260, 270
death-watch beetle 67
decay/decomposition 18, 71–3, *72*, 120,
     128, 149, 194, 201, 205, 207, 211,
     215, 230, 271, 277
deer 16, 27, 29, 35, 85, 123, 128–9, *128*,
     138, 166, 168, *170*, 171, 183,
     196–7, 202, 211, 223, 237, 238,
     241, 256, 257, 275, 278; fallow deer
     39, 129, 163; red deer *22*, 23, 34,
     39, 40, 41, 57, 58, 85, 154, 237,
     279–80, *280*, 284; reindeer 23, 39,
     40, 169; roe deer 28, 34, 39, 41, 58,
     222, 229–30; sika 154, 279, 280–2
deforestation 6, 68, 85, 94–7, 104, 123,
     133–6, 143–5, 153, 160–1, 178,
     181, 182, 200, *205*, 208, 214, 223,
     234, 261, 272–3, 279
dendrochronology 8, 56, 61–2, *82*, 155,
     183, 291
Dereham, Vicar of Upminster, Reverend
     William 48
Devon Wildlife Trust 286
Dinefwr, castle at 146
Diodorus 94–5
disease, tree 64, 73, 77, 108, 126,
     129–30, 273, 288
dissolution of the monasteries 185, 193
Doan, James 159
dockyards 198, 213–14, 216–17
Doggerland 44, 55
*dolabella* (short-handled hatchet) 102–3
Domesday Book 69, 126, 137, 140, 171,
     267
domestic animals 65, 85–6, 124, 229–30
Dornoch Cathedral 84, 176
dottards 198
Douglas fir 273
Douglas, David 238
Drever, Alan 263
Drew, Catherine 208
drought 28, 51, 266
drowned landscape 45, *47*
drumlins 12
Drumshambo ironworks 221–2
Duffield Frith 5, 198

Dulwich Upper Wood 9
Dunboy, siege of (1602) 158, 159
Dunne, Lady *188*, 189
Dutch elm disease 64, 108
Dyfflynarskiri 153
Dyffryn Ceiriog 141, 144
Dymsdale Forest 49, *49*

East Glen Affric 22
Ecclesall Woods 225–6, *225*
economy, forest 164–78
ecosystem: ecosystem engineers 78–9,
     282; forest 19, 35, 229–30, 231,
     233, 234, 271, 274, 281, 282; term
     19
edge habitats 85
Edward I, King 97, 145, 147, 150, 173
Edward III, King 179
Edward, the Black Prince 150
Egbert, King 113, 141; stone of 113
Egypt 59, 75, 77, 94
elephants 16, 33, 43, 91, 172
Elgin 35, 89
Elizabeth I, Queen 158, 193, 198, 201
Elizabeth II, Queen 81
elk 34, 39, 40, 41, 85
elm 19, 20, 21, 24, 26, 61, 63–6, *63*,
     101, 103, 150, 175, 192, 220, 231,
     259; Dutch elm disease 64, 108
Elton, Charles 52–3
Ely Cathedral *80*, 81, 91, 176
English Civil War (1642–51) 201
Epping Forest 5, 269
Ethandune, Battle of (878) 125
EU Birds and Habitats Directives 90
Evelyn, John 107, 208, 260
Ewloe 141, 150–1
Exeter Cathedral 45
extinction 16, 25, 36, 37, 41, 42–3, 55,
     66, 77, 85, 91, 160, 234, 277, 285

Falkirk Tryst 228
Farjon, Aljos: *Ancient Oaks in the English
     Landscape* 7, 129
Farquharson, James 239
Fawcett, Derek 32
Fen Clay marine transgression 76
Fenland Black Oak Project 81–2
*Fiannaíocht*, Fenian cycle of legends 75

# Index

fines 131, 201, 202

fire 6, 32–3, 39, 51, 61, 67, 75, 80, 84, 144, 151, 200, 225, 240, 251–2, 287–8

firewood 30, 74, 88, 96, 129, 150, 166–8, 194, 198, 200, 222, 262

First World War (1914–18) 241, 242–7, *246*, 251, 252

Flag Fen 29

flint dagger 3–4, *4*

Flintshire 150, 167–8

Flodden, Battle of (1513) 196

flooding 55, 76, 83, 89, 119, 266, 272

floodplains 80, 87, 186, 233–4

Flow Country 256–7

forage 63, 64, 124, 129

forest: courts 151, 165, 199; floor 42, 48, 54, 76, 120; law 136, 164, 201–2; nursery 193;
passes 144; term 7, 136, 166; year 254. *See also individual type and name of forest*

Forest Eyarth 223

Forest Fair 127–8

Forest Morfe 224

Forest of Bodfari 5, 146

Forest of Dean 105, *106*, 107, 145, 172, 173, *174*, 201, 208–11, 252–3, 267, 281, 286, 292

Forest of Selkirk 181

Forest Strategy 279

forester *128*, 130, 150, 151, 167, 168, 180, 218, 239, 241, 252, 254, 255, 256, 292

Forestry Act (1919) 247

Forestry Commission 7, 171, 243, 247, 250, 252, 254, 255, 256, 257, 259, 264–5

Formby Point 57–8

Fosse Way 132–3

Fowler, John 176

Fox, Jefferson 262

Fozy Moss 101–2

Fraser, Simon 243

fuel 67–8, 96, 100, 101, 105, 132, 167, 171, 174, 178, 221, 226, 228, 243, 289

fungi 18, 40, 52, 64, 125, 129, 204, 251, 270, 271, 274, 291

gardened forests 6

Garranon Wood 162

Gelling, Margaret 119

ghost forests 59

Gibbon, Edward 95

Gilchrist, Robert Murray 206

Gildas 111

Gillingham Forest 126, 127, *127*

Gilpin, William 212

glaciers/glacial periods 9, 11–12, *12*, 14, 15–16, 23, 30, 32, 39, 40, 43, 54, 58–9, 84, 172, 229

Glas-na Bradan Wood 278

glassmaking 173

Gleann Còsaidh 275–6

Gleann Fuar 275

Glen Affric 22, 23, 257

Glen Feshie 275

Glen Finglas 238

Glen Strathfarrar pinewoods 22, *22*, 23

Glen Tanar Estate 251

Glen Tromie 275

Glencree 162, 167

Glenmore 245, 257

Glentrool Forest 193

Gloucester Castle 173

glue crust fungus *17*, 18

Glyderau mountains 11, *12*

Glyn Cothi Forest 249

Glyndŵr, Owain 177, 185

Godwinson, Harold 138, 139

Goldcliff East 58

Goldcliff Priory 107

Gorne Wood 262

Gougane Barra 160

Gough Map 45

Gow, Derek 286

Grahame, Kenneth 8, 111

Grantown-on-Spey 238, 239

grassland 8, 38, 66, 261, 268

grazing 16, 23, 33–5, 37, 39–43, *39*, 61, *65*, 85–6, 100, 122, 124, 150, 152, 166, 167, 170, 172, 204, 221, 229–30, 232, 240, 250, 273, 275, 277, 279–83

great capricorn beetles 76, *76*

Great Forest of Aughty 5, 156–7, 221

Great Glen 50–1, 251, 255

Great Heathen Army 125

Great North Wood 8, 262
Great Orme 74, 183
Great Storm (1703) 211
Great Wishford 168–9, *168*, 201–2
Greensted-juxta-Ongar 114, 115, *115*
grey squirrels 250, 286
Grovely Forest 168–9
Grwyne Fawr valley 141
'Gwenallt' (David James Jones) 248
Gwenddoleu ap Ceidio 98
Gwent Is-coed 104–5
Gwent Uwch-coed 104–5
Gwilym, Dafydd ap 147
Gwynedd, Owain 141
Gwynnon, King of Kaerrihog 45

Hadrian's Wall 101, 102, *103*, 104, 111
*haga* 137–8
Haggith, Mandy 282
Hampton Roads, Battle of (1862) 216
Harold I, King 136, 138
Harris, Isle of 53, 84
Harrison, William 284
Harrying of the North 139–40
Hasholme logboat 88–9
Hassell, John 211–12, *212*
Hastings, Battle of (1066) 138, 139
Hatfield Forest 192; Hatfield Broad Oak 192
Hawarden, wood of 141
hawthorn 27, 128, 190, 192, 198, 272
Hay, Earl of Kinnoull, Sir George 220
hazel 16–21, *17*, 26, 29–30, 40, 42, 46–9,
        51, 52, 55, 61, 79, 87, 103, 105,
        110, 128, 155, 156, 181, 190, 192,
        198, 220–3, 230, 231, 240, 258,
        259, 269, 280, 281; hazel gloves
        17–18, *17*; hazel nuts 29, 30, 48–9,
        222–4
hazel hen 42
Heaning Wood 14, 32
Heart of England Forest 266
heart-rot 270, *270*
hemi-boreal 23
Henry I, King 128–9, 170
Henry II, King 46, 141–2
Henry III, King 144, 164, 192
Henry IV, King 177
Henry V, King 177

Henry VII, King 195, 196
Henry VIII, King 185, 189, 197
Henshaw, Frederick Henry 133, *133*
herbivores 15–16, 40, 43, 91
Hermit's Wood 191, *191*
Hetherington, David 283–4
high forest 34, 77, 111, 125, 269
High Park 128–30, *128*, 292
High Wood 125, 172
Highland Forest of Ferter 193, 232
Highlands, Scottish 13, 14, 18, 22, 24, 25,
        26, 84, 98, 99, 109, 176, 177, 221,
        228, 230, 231, 239, 275–6, 284;
        Clearances 232–3
Highmeadow 258, 259
Historic England 32, 107
holly 16, 24, 110, 156, 181–2, 198, 220,
        231, 281
Holme-next-the-Sea 71, *72*
honeybees 129–31, *130*; honey 129–31,
        150, 151
Honorius, emperor 111–12
hornbeam 8, 16, 110, 126
hunting 7, 31, 32, 35, 57, 58, 65, 101,
        126, 127, 129, 136, 137, 150, 151,
        154, 157, 159, 163, 164, 166, 168,
        170, 190, 196, 197, 201, 230, 267,
        269, 279
Hwicce, kingdom of the 126, 131
Hyde, Harold 258, 259

ice age 12, 14, 40, 58, 229
Iceland 135–6, 153
Imperial Estate 105
Industrial Revolution 178, 215
Inglewood Forest 188–90, *188*, 292
insects 7, 66–7, 76–9, 213, 251, *270*, 271
interglacial periods 12, 15–16, 43, 172
iron 76, 86, 88, 102, 105–6, 116, 208,
        215–16, 218, 219, 220, 221, 222,
        224–7, 259
Iron Age 4, 20, 21, 69, 86, 88, 96, 102,
        105, 132, 282; Late Iron Age 88, 96

Jack O' Kent's Oak 37, *37*, 38
Jacobite Rising (1715) 177, 221
James I, King 158, 201
James II and IV, King 196, 238
James VI, King 5

# Index

James, Richard: *Iter Lancastrense* 44
jay (*Garrulus glandarius*) 28, *28*
Jed Forest 1–3, *2*, 210
Jehu, Thomas 46–7
Jethart Callants 2, 3
John, King 164, 167
Jones, Michael 104
Jones, Richard 119, 120
Jubilee Oak table 91
juniper 17, 20, 21, 275, 277
Jupiter Feretrius 93

Kelly, Maria 181
Kenfig Castle 149
Kentchurch Court 37–9, *37*
Kerry cow 35, 36, *36*
Ketthlieconhan 147
Kichizaburo, Endo 235
Kielder Forest 25–6, 250
Kielderhead Pines 25–6, 250
Killarney National Park 154, 279, 280, *280*
Kiltubbrid Shield *20*, 21
King Alfred's church, Athelney 114–15
King Oak 154, *155*
King of the Wood 3
King's Mark 211
Kingley Vale 184, *184*, 280
Knepp Wildland Project 43
Knockanore Bog Oak 82–3, *82*
Knovill, Bogo de 144–5

Ladzka Forest 90
Lake District 73, 85, 123, 135, 228, 267, 271
Leland, John 125, 171, 189
Lewis, Isle of 53, 84
lichens 18, *22*, 23–4, 52, 125–6, 129, 213, 251, 258, 271
light forest 23
lignotuber 75
lime 19, 21, 48–9, 62, 79, 85, 150, 173, 191–2, 233, 258, 259
Lindisfarne 114, 134–5
Linnard, William 140, 226–7
liverworts 18, 258, 271
Loch Arkaig 251–2
Loch Awe 24, 255
Loch Lomond 22, 97, 176, 238

Loch Maree 24–5, *25*, 220
Loch Ness 22, *22*, 37
Lochiel Estates 240–1
logboats 51, *87*, 88–9, 91
lost forest 45, 48, 51–3, 261, 276
Louis XII, King 196
Louis XIV, King 234
Lovat, Lord 243
Low, Hamish 81–2
Lower Wye woods 258–9
lynx 23, 42–3, 58, 65, 283–4, *283*, 288
Lyonesse 45
Lyons, Chantal 281

MacCaskill, Donald 255
Macdonald, James 254–5
Mackenzie, Laird of Kintail, Kenneth 220
Mackenzie, Sir George 229
Maerdy wind farm 30–1, 32
Magna Carta 164
Major Oak 204–6, *205*, 270
Malcolm III, King 163
Malvern, Forest of 138
maple wood-boring beetle 66–7
Maredudd, Rhys ap 146
Marsden, Penny 264
Marshall, William 213
Martin, Martin 53
Martin, Micheál 278–9
Mary Queen of Scots 238
*Mary Rose* 196–8, *197*
mass forestry schemes 266
McAlister, Victoria 153
McBride, Rob 142
McCarthy, Michael 71–2
McEwen, John 243
McKnight, Ali 237
McParlan, James 221
McPhillimy, Donald 263
Melby, Patrick 214
Menevensis, Asserius; *The Life of King Alfred* 113, 119, 124
Menzies, Archibald 177
Mercia 134, 135
Mesolithic 14, 29–33, *31*, 38, 41, 42, 43, 55, 56, 57–8, 60, 67, 73, 85, 87, 223; Late Mesolithic 30, 31, 56, 57, 87

324          *Forgotten Forests*

Meydenbach, Jacob 234, 235, *235*
Middle Ages 18, 36, 129, 132, 133, 229, 269
Midland Revolt (1607) 200
migration 20–1, 26, 27, 30, 39, 40, 60–1, 76, 247
Millennium Plinth 180, *180*
Mitchell, Frank 11
Mitchell, Fraser 39–40
Moccas Park 38–9
Monbiot, George 16, 273; *Feral* 282
*Monitor*, USS 216
Monks Wood 27, 28, 34
Monmouth Rebellion (1685) 126
Monson, Admiral William 214–15
Morfe Forest 3, 224
Morison, Ivan 70–1
mountain avens (*Dryas octopetala*) 14, *15*
Mountain Birch Project 276–7
Muckross House and Gardens 154, 279
multipurpose forestry 257
Murphy, Tom Joe 82, *82*

Nanmor, Dafydd 284
NASA Land project 262
National Botanic Garden of Wales 143
National Forest 264–8, *265*, 291
National Monuments Service Ritual Site/Holy Tree 157
National Museum of Antiquities of Scotland 89
National Museum of Wales 47, 57, 258
National Nature Reserves 11, 23, 24, *25*, 26, 27, 62, *62*, 156, *184*, 199, *199*, 258, 267
National Parks 32, 85, 141, 154, 237, 238, 239, 267, 275, 279, 280, *280*, *283*, 286
National Trust 81, 267, 272, 273
National Trust for Scotland 177, 274
Natural History Museum, London 77
Natural Resources Wales 152, 268
Navan Fort 69, 71
Needwood Forest 170, *170*, 171, 173, 264
Nelson, Charles 75
Nelson, Horatio 206, 207, 211–12, 217, 218
Neolithic 4, 31, 32, 42, 56, 58, 59, 60–1,

*62*, 63, 64, *65*, 66–9, *70*, 71, 73–4, 76, 152
Nepal 262
Nethybridge 239–40, 245
New Forest 5, 78, 131–2, 210, 211–13, *212*, 233, 238, 247, 248, 252, 259, 269, 281
Nicholson, Max 82
Nile, Battle of the (1798) 212
nitrogen 236–7, 274, 277
No Butts 263
Noah's trees 46
Noble, Gordon 4, 60, 61, 67
non-native species 133–4, 182, 248, 254, 256–7, 260, 268, 269, 273, 279, 282
Nore, River 155, 234
Norman period 107, 115, 127, 136, 138, 139–41, 145, 152–3, 157, 162, 163, 182, 223–4, 262
North, Frederick 47
Northern Forest 266
Northern Gawain Group 190
Norway spruce 23
Norwegian Institute for Nature Research 277
Norwich Castle Museum 71
Norwood 9

oak 1, 5, 7, 8, 16, 90, 91, 93, 96, 100, 101, *102*, 103, 105, 109, 110, 114, 116, 119, 122, 124–31, *127*, *128*, *130*, 134, 135, 168, 187, 220, 221, 224, 227, 228, 230, 231, 233, 237, 251, 252, 253, 255, 256, 259, 261, 267; acorn 3, 27–8, *27*, 30, 35, 49, 124, 155, 157, 167, 171, 201, 205, 209, 211, 217, 218, 221, 222, 274, 281; Atlantic oakwoods 271–2; bog oaks 76–83, *76*, *80*, *82*, 89, 91, 292; clearance/felling of 85, 141–57, *155*, 161, 171–6, 183–4, 188, 189, 190, 192, 196–200, *199*, 203–6, *205*, 208–10, *209*, 211–18, *212*, *217*, 253, 255; heart-rot 270–1; logboats and 88–9; 'modern oaks' in Ireland 161–2; Oak Apple Day *168*, 169; Oak at the Gate of the Dead 141–3, *142*;

# Index

Oak Bush 3; Oak Project 70–1; origin and spread of in Britain 19, 20, 21, 23, 24, 26–8, 30–2, *31, 37*, 38, 40, 41, 46–9, 51–2, *52*, 53, 56, 61, 62, 66, 68, 69, 70; pedunculate oak 19, 90, 125–6, *142*, 154, 155, 204; restoring 267, 269, 274; sessile oak 19, 188, 222, *222*, 258; shipbuilding and 196–200, *199*, 203–6, *205*, 208–10, *209*, 211–18, *212, 217*; submerged 71–3, *72*, 77; veteran and ancient 289. *See also individual oak name*
oceanic woodlands 23, 259
old-growth forests 66, 89–90, 224, 238, 248, 287
Old Scottish Shortwool 232
Old Wood of Caledon 98
Ongar Great Park 138
ore production 74, 151, 220, 221, 226, 259
Orkney 51–2, *52*, 71, 292
outlaw 120, 121, 132, 189
over-mature trees 66
Oxford University 18, 52–3, 273
Oxygen Conservation 263

pannage 151, 281
parkland 38, 125–6, 198, 274
pastoralism 66, 153
pasture woodland 8, *37*, 38–9, 110, 120, 124, 151–2, *152*, 172, *174*, 192, 238, 259, 269
peat 22, 31, 47, 48, 53, 56, 57, 61, 62, 73, 76, 79, 83–5, 229, 256, 279
Pegges of Beauchief 223
Pennines 14, 123, 271
Pennington, Winifred 135
Perigal the Younger, Arthur 1
Peterken, George 257–9
Pett Level, Rye Bay 49, *49*
Pett, Peter 202
Pevensey, fortress at 132
Phillips, Adrian 264
Picket and Clanger Wood 126
pigs 65, 124, 166, 167, 171, 182, 222, 281, 282
Pilgrimage of Grace 185
pinewoods/Scots pine 5, 20–6, *78*, 79, 83–4, 98, 177, 220, 230, 233, 238–41, *239*, 245, 250–2, 257–9, 261, 273, 275, 277, 282
pine marten 41, 252, 255, 278, 284–6, *285*
pioneer woodland 110
pitwood 252
place-names 118–20, 124, 160
plague 73–4, 179–85, *180, 184*, 194
plantations 8, 215, 238–40, 247, 249, 250–1, 254, 260, 278
Plantation of Ulster 158–9
planting trees 26, 161, 201, 204, 207–9, 217–19, *217*, 221, 228, 236, 238–40, *239*, 247–59, *248, 256*, 260–79, 288–9
plastic tree guards 27, 272
Pliny the Elder 94, 234; *Natural History* 96–7
plough 4, *4*, 77, 81, 86, 122, 135, 166, 186
poaching 127, 201–2, 238
pollarding 124, 154, 172, 198, 211
pollen 16–21, 34, 40, 56, 60, 61, 63–7, 77, 79, 105, 108, 109, 185, 269, 281
Pompeii 100
Pontfadog 141–3, *143*
Poole logboat 87–9, *87*
Post Track 61
pottery 20, 31, 32, 92, 109, 132
Povlsen, Anders Holch 274
predators 42, 43, 65, 121, 230, 286
primary forest 66, 90
ProSilva Ireland 222, *222*
Pryor, Francis 29–30
Ptolemy, Claudius 97; *Geographia* 97

Quarry Wood 111
Quatford 223–4; Quatford Witches 224
Queen Mab 25
Queen Oak 128, *128*

Rackham, Oliver 8, 15, 33, 79, 257; *Trees and Woodland in the British Landscape* 22, 109, 214, 215; *Woodlands* 43
radiocarbon dating 20, 31, 32, 53, 55, 76, 83, 88, 284
Radley Large Wood 273
Raheen Forest 221, 222, *222*

ravine woods 259
recolonisation 20, 283–4
red squirrel 28,250, 252, 278, 286
refuge species 287
regeneration, forest 28, 34, 61, 67, 70, 86, 104, 105, 109, 122, 123, 135–7, 184, 214, 221, 229, 234, 237, 240, 254, 255, 257–9, 260–7, 272–6, 279, 281
reintroduction, species 23,281–6, *283*, 289
restoration projects 152, 233–4, 255–8, 261–4, 268–9, 274, 276
rewilding 5, 36–7, 263, 278–9, 282
rhododendron 75, 279, 280
Rhuddlan 5, 140, 145, 150–1, 154
Rhydderch Hael 98
Richard de Clare, Earl of Hereford 141
Richard, King 187
Robertson of Struan 245
Robertson, James 240–1
Robin Hood's Larder 205–6
Rodings, The 103–4
Roger Earl of Hereford 107
Rollo 138
Roman Empire 30, 63, 77, 91, 92–112, *94*, *99*, *102*, *103*, *106*, 113, 122, 123–4, 127, 132–3, 135, 137, 141, 190, 269, 283, 284
Romania 95, 283
root systems 47, 273
Rothiemurchus forests 240, 245, 251, 277–8
rotting wood 38, 79, 89, 175, 206–7, 270–1; heart–rot 270, *270*
rowan 23, 26, 52, 231, 252, 275, 276, *276*, 277
Rowe, W. H.: *Our Forests* 254
Royal Botanic Gardens at Kew 7
Royal Botanical Gardens, Edinburgh *235*, 237
Royal Forest of Treville 187
Royal Navy 3, 200, 209–18, *209*, 242
Royal Scottish Forestry Society 243
Royal Society 48, 107, 208
Royal Society of Arts 247
Royal Zoological Society 286
RSPB 52, 239, 258
Russia 6, 23, 32; wildfires (2019) 6

sacred trees 69, 93, 118
Salbany, Filipe 129–30, 292
salmon 234–7, 291
saplings 28, 111, 137, 143, 204, 239, 248, 249, 269, 272, 273, 288
scientific forestry 244
scimitar cat 16
Scotland. *See individual place name*
Scots pine 5, 20–5, 83, 84, 177, 238, 239, *239*, 240, 245, 251, 273, 275, 277
Scottish Environment Link 282
Scottish Highland cow 35, *36*
Scudamore, Viscount John 193
sea: inland forests and 235–6; levels 13, 19, 40, 44, 49, *49*, 51, 53, 54, 57, 58–9, 76, 83
Seafield Estate 238–9
Seahenge 71–3, *72*
Second World War (1939–45) 80, 248, 250, 253, 268
secondary growth 66, 110–11, 127, 135
seed: dispersal 26–9, 232, 274–5, 281–2; seedlings 34, 40, 129, 186, 229, 230–1, 232, 245, 262, 270, 273–4, 281; self-seeding 110; self-sown forests 279
Selwood Forest 113, 124–7, *127*, 132, 180, 182
semi-natural forests 107, 125, 128, 149, 240, 279
Seneca 94
Severn, River 56, 58, 87, 125, 171, 192, 224, 267
Severn Treescapes: Wye to Wyre 267
Shakespeare, William: *As You Like It* 134, 159–60; *Henry V* 223; *Macbeth* 5
Shapland, Michael 114
Shapwick Heath National Nature Reserve 62, *62*
sheep 50, 63, 65, 66, 85, 86, 120, 121, 122, 166, 206, 228, 230, 231–3, 237, 250, 261, 268, 280, 283, 284, 291–2
Sherborne, Bishop of 119, 124
Sherwood Forest 5, 126, 189, 203–4, 205, *205*, 206, 270–1, *270*
shifting baseline syndrome 9
Shigir Idol 32

shipbuilding 101, *102*, 175, 194, 195–218, *197*, *199*, *205*, *207*, *209*, *210*, *212*, *217*, 219, 220, 243, 267; shipwright 196, 202; shipyards 203, 207, 210, 214
Shokouhi, Marjan 5–6
short-rotation forestry 255
Silton Oak or Stumpy Silton 126, 127, *127*
Silva Magna, the great Wood 113
Sinclair, Sir John 25, 53, 231
Sinel, Joseph 48–9
Sitka spruce 250, 251, 255, 257, 260, 273
Skeffington, Micheline Sheehy 74
soil 19, 21, 29, 34, 46, 48, 64, 66, 85, 86, 104, 105, 107, 111, 122, 124, 132, 135, 136, 181, 200, 204, 224, 226, 240, 249, 274, 281
Solent, Battle of (15450 196
Speech Court of the Forest of Wentwood 151
Speech House, Forest of Dean 174
Spey 233, 239
Speyside 5, 238, 245, 251
Spiddal 54, *54*
St Botolph's church, Hadstock 115–16
St Hilda's College, Oxford 273
St Michael's Mount 50
St Ouen's Bay 48–9
Staffordshire Hoard 114
Stamford Bridge, battle of (1066) 138
Standish, Arthur 200
Star Carr 32, 33
Statute of Woods (1543) 194
Stokstad, Erik 182–3
Stonehenge 65, *65*, 66, 68, 71–2
storms 39, 46, 50, 53, 54, *54*, 56, 81, 82, 83, 91, 142–3, *143*, 206, 211
Strabo 95
Strangford Lough 53
Strata Florida Abbey 97
Strathnaver 232–3
strawberry tree 74–6
Struidh Wood, Isle of Eigg 18
Stuart, Countess of Seafield, Caroline 241
submerged forests 38, 44–59, *47*, 77
Suffolk Way 103–4

surnames 172–3
Survey of Agriculture and Horticulture, Wales (2021) 268
Sutcliff, Rosemary 110
Sutherland 26, 84, 230, 232–3, 284
Sutherland, John 243
Sweden 41, 200, 231, 283, 284
sweet chestnut 75, 106–7, *106*, 253
Sweet, Ray 61, *61*
Sweet Track 61–2, *62*, 83
Swift, Jonathan 215
Świsłocka Forest 90
Sydlings Copse 137
Szereszewska Forest 90

Table for the Nation 80–2, *80*
Tacitus 93, 96–7, 99
Tait, James 252
tanbark 227–8, *227*, 237, 252
tanning 150, 227–8
Tansley, Sir Arthur 18–19, 33, 43
Tarbat, Easter Ross 233
Tarras Valley Nature Reserve 263
Taylor, Mike 264, 291
temperate rainforests 271
Tertullian 93
Tetsuo, Inukai 236
Tewthi, Kingdom of 45
Thames, River 8, 13, 48, 83, 111, 125
Thomas of Merdene 175
Thomas the Roper 173
Thompson, Shaun 56
Timpany, Scott 56
Tír Tairngire 75
Tolkien, J. R. R. 98
Tomies Wood 280
Trajan's column 94–5, *94*, 100
tree, word 118
Tree of the Year, Scotland 276, *276*
tree rings 8, 83, 89, 148, 184, 198
Trees for Life 36–7, 275
Treville Forest 187–8, 191
Trim, forest of 166
Trossachs National Park 238
Troutbeck, Lake District 228
Tsar Oak 90–1
Tubbs, Colin 213
Tudors 19, 77, 153, 158, 160–1, 184, 196, 197, 198

UK Forestry Standard Practice Guide *Designing and Managing Forests and Woodlands to Reduce Flood Risk* 272
UK government, 25 Year Environment Plan 266
underwood 18, 129, 146, 151, 198
United Nations 261
*uotsukirin* (fish-breeding forests) 234–6
upstream forests 234–5
Ural Mountains, Russia 6, 32, 42
Usk 104–5, 233

Vale of Clwyd 5, 146
Vera, Frans 33–4, 39, 40, 43
Verderer's Court 174
veteran tree 155, 289
*Victory*, HMS 206–8, *207*
Vikings 116, 134–5, 138–9, 153
Vychan, Llywelyn 167–8

*Warrior*, HMS 216
Water and Forest decree (1669) 234
Watkins, William 217
Weald 105, 106, 120, 126, 131–2, 172, 186
Wentwood 104–5, 151–2, *152*, 269
Wessex 66, 125, 135, 163, 281
Wester Ross 24, 229
Westminster Abbey 116
Westminster Hall 176
Wheeler, James 209, *209*
Whitecoal 226–7
Whitehouse, Nicki 37, 38
Whitesands Bay 46–7, 56, 57
Whittlewood Forest 109, 137
Wicklow Mountains 154, 167
Wilberforce Oak 126
wild boar 34, 39, 41, 57, 58, 123, 281, 284
wildcat 161, 255, *256*, 286–7, 288
Wild Ennerdale 267
Wilder Blean Project 282
wildfires 6, 33, 251, 288
wild service tree 192
wild wood 8, 24, 37, 66, 110, 111, 190
William I, King 136, 138, 163, 164
William II, King 140–1

Williams, Waldo: *Yr hen allt* 242, 247, 292
Windsor Great Park 67, 143
Wiseman's Bridge 56
Witcher, Robert 108
wolves 41–3, 58, 65, 120–1, 159–61, 230, 271, 282–4
Women's Land Army 244–5
wood, definition of 7–8
Wood Age 4
Wood, Andrew 195
wood collier 219, 225, *225*
wood–gathering rights 167–9
Woodhenge 68
woodkerne 158–9
woodland, definition of 8
Woodland Trust 111, 152, 165, 238, 266, 272, 278; Ancient Tree Inventory 289
woodmen 145, 146
wood-pasture 8, *37*, 38–9, 110, 120, 124, 151–2, *152*, 172, *174*, 192, 238, 259, 269
woodpecker 41, *41*, 42, 287
Woodstock 127, *127*, 128
woodturning 32, 167
Wooplaw Forest 263
Wordsworth, William 34
World Economic Forum 262
Wreay Woods 189
Wroxeter (*Viroconium*) *99*, 100
wych elm 108, 259
Wychwood Forest (*Hwicciwudu*) 126–8, 131, 132, 172
Wye Valley 104, 258, 267
Wyndcliff Wood 258
Wyndham's Oak 126–7, *127*
Wyre Forest 192, 267

Yalden, Derek 41–2
Yardley, George 225, *225*
yew 16, 21, 69, 76, 79, 83, 184, *184*, 231, 258, 280–1
Yorke, Barbara 124–5
Yorkshire Sculpture Park 70–1, *70*
Young, Arthur 161, 215–16
Younger Dryas 14–15, *15*